DATE DUE

JUL 31 2008	
FEB 2 6 2014	

BRODART, CO.   Cat. No. 23-221-003

Being Right Is Not Enough

WHAT PROGRESSIVES MUST LEARN FROM CONSERVATIVE SUCCESS

Paul Waldman

WILEY

John Wiley & Sons, Inc.

Published by John Wiley & Sons, Inc., Hoboken, New Jersey
Published simultaneously in Canada

Design and composition by Navta Associates, Inc.

For general information about our other products and services, please contact our Customer Care Department within the United States at (800) 762-2974, outside the United States at (317) 572-3993 or fax (317) 572-4002.

Wiley also publishes its books in a variety of electronic formats. Some content that appears in print may not be available in electronic books. For more information about Wiley products, visit our web site at www.wiley.com.

Library of Congress Cataloging-in-Publication Data:

Waldman, Paul
   Being right is not enough : what progressives must learn from conservative success / Paul Waldman.
       p. cm
   Includes bibliographical references and index.
   ISBN-13 0-978-78960-4 (cloth)
   ISBN-10 0-471-78960-7 (cloth)
   1. Democratic Party (U.S.) 2. United States—Politics and government—2001–
3. Progressivism (United States politics) I. Title.
   JK2316.W35 2006
   320.51'30973—dc22

                                                                          2005032309

Printed in the United States of America

10 9 8 7 6 5 4 3 2 1

To my mother, who taught me the value
of righteous indignation

CONTENTS

1

RETURNING FIRE

M any liberals are congenitally gloomy folk, and a look at the contemporary American political scene gives them plenty of cause to despair. In 2004, rank-and-file Democrats became more energized and motivated than they had been in decades, as liberal books shot up the best-seller list, millions of new voters were registered in an unprecedented mobilization effort, membership in left-wing organizations surged, and by some estimates more than 10 million people contributed money to a Democratic candidate or a liberal group.[1] Yet a president who had lied to the public to justify an unpopular war, who had the worst jobs record since the Depression, who had done nothing to address the most pressing domestic issues of the day, and who had dangerously low approval ratings still managed to beat their candidate by a not insubstantial margin. Republicans control all three branches of the federal government, not to mention a majority of governorships and state legislatures. The federal courts are stacked with conservative ideologues, an imbalance that will only grow worse through George W. Bush's second term. The Senate and the Electoral College give inordinate power to small numbers of voters in conservative states, allowing

1

them to finagle victories even when in the minority. The national debate seems easily shifted from the real problems Americans face to distractions like gay marriage, partial-birth abortion, or flag burning, sure to arouse enough anger and suspicion to return Republicans to office. The party that labors on behalf of the wealthy and the powerful adopts a populist pose, while liberals are scorned as the "elite."

Talk to a liberal about this state of affairs, and in short order the discussion will become a head-shaking litany of frustrated questions. How do they get away with it? Why are so many people fooled? For God's sake, the liberal will cry, we're so right and they're so wrong—how has it come to this?

This book is not about why progressives are right and conservatives are wrong. I may feel that way—and I have no doubt that most who will read this book agree—but that argument is a sermon the choir has heard before. Instead, this book is meant as a guide for progressives, a plan for the convinced to spread their convictions. The success conservatives have enjoyed is a product of neither an inherently conservative populace nor an inherently ignorant one. It is the result of patient planning, clever strategizing, and tireless work by conservatives, and consistent bumbling and wasted energy by liberals. The time has come to level the playing field.

It was only four decades ago that liberal assumptions and goals set the bounds of reasonable debate, while conservatism lay disgraced and discredited. On Wednesday, November 4, 1964, conservatives woke up to a nightmare. Their candidate for president, Barry Goldwater, had been obliterated, losing by over twenty-two points and winning only six states. Relentless attacks from the incumbent and Goldwater's own shocking statements had convinced the American public that the Republican candidate, and by extension the people he represented, were dangerous radicals who if given power would drag the country toward nuclear Armageddon.

In Congress, things were just as bad for the right. Before the election, Democrats held a comfortable 83-seat advantage in the House; afterward, it had grown to a yawning 155 seats. Senate Republicans found themselves in an equally deep hole, numbering only 32 to the 68 Democrats, which left more than 2 Democrats for every Republican in both houses, just as only one-third of the nation's governors belonged to the GOP. The very idea of conservatism as a viable ideology with an appeal to the American electorate was considered almost ridiculous.

Thirty-six years later, it was the Democrats who were surveying the wreckage of their once-dominant party. Bill Clinton beat back his tormenters and had a number of notable policy achievements, but his presidency left his party in drastically worse shape than it had been before. When he entered the White House in 1993, Democrats controlled both houses of Congress, a majority of governorships, and a majority of state legislatures. When he left, all those prizes belonged to the GOP, as they do today.

Just before George W. Bush's inauguration in 2001, the descendant of the uncompromising conservative activists who drove Barry Goldwater's campaign stood up to address the crowd at a Republican celebration. Grover Norquist, the head of Americans for Tax Reform, should have been happy—after all, his party had just won the White House, banishing Al Gore, the heir to the Clinton presidency that Norquist had opposed with such vigor. Yet the man many people call the most important Republican activist in Washington didn't sound happy at all. Norquist told the crowd that the fight wasn't over because the enemy was still kicking. "The Democrats are the Lefties, the takers, the coercive utopians," Norquist thundered. "They are not stupid, they are evil. Evil!"[2]

More than anything else, the reversal of the years between 1964 and today happened because the faith of the men and women who rallied to Goldwater's cause remained firm.[3] Those conservative activists did not wonder whether they should "move to the center" or seek to win the hearts of those most opposed to their goals. They did not slink off the political battlefield or tell themselves that if they could not turn everything around in two or four years, then all was lost. They got to work and built a movement. And out of the ashes of defeat, that movement grew slowly and steadily until it became the dominant force in American politics, vanquishing so many liberals in its wake that some began to wonder whether the Democratic Party had a future at all.

THE MESSAGE IS THE MESSAGE

Ask an ordinary person what conservatives stand for, and he'll be able to come up with a few powerful, easily understood ideas: low taxes, small government, strong defense, and traditional values. These are the Four Pillars of Conservatism. Ask him what liberals stand for, and chances are he'll give you *the conservative caricature of liberals*: high taxes, big government, military weakness, and moral relativism.

This is no accident. Some on the left are convinced that conservative ideas are inherently more simplistic than liberal ideas, and thus conservatives have a natural advantage in a public debate dominated by media forums that favor brevity, certainty, and appeals to emotion. Because conservative ideas fit so neatly on a bumper sticker, many liberals believe, conservatives trounce liberals, though liberals are in fact correct on the merits.

Nonsense. In their full form, conservative ideas are just as complex as liberal ones. Conservative academics and think-tank denizens spend untold hours crafting analyses and arguments to support their goals. This doesn't mean they're right, but there are plenty of very smart conservatives who have thought long and hard about what they want to achieve and why. The difference is this: there are lots of other smart conservatives who have thought long and hard about how to reduce those complex ideas to simple expressions of values and beliefs. It is in this area that liberals have failed.

The American electorate includes some people who study position papers, use multiple news sources, and have a comprehensive understanding of what the parties and the candidates believe. This group, however, is a small one; far more numerous are those whose attention is only occasionally grabbed by politics. Because they have neither the time nor the inclination to assess each issue in endless detail, reaching them requires ideas that can be expressed in simple terms. This is not to say ideas must be dumbed down; there is an enormous difference between the simple and the simplistic, and some of the most powerful political statements in history were expressed simply. "Ask not what your country can do for you, ask what you can do for your country" is a simple idea, simply expressed.

The problem isn't liberal ideas; the problem is liberals. The old saying that a liberal is someone who won't take his own side in an argument contains some truth; liberals are prone to carefully consider all sides, provide evidence for their claims, and hold out the possibility that someone who disagrees might have a point. Yet that doesn't mean they don't believe what they say or are incapable of advocating it aggressively. Liberals engage conservatives in vigorous debate every day; most of them just haven't gotten the hang of how to do it right.

Conservatives have also understood that it isn't enough to describe in simple terms each of the dozens of issue positions that comprise an ideology. A series of simple arguments unconnected to one another doesn't add up to anything. What conservatives have created is a thematically unified *master narrative*, a notion we will return to at length later on. When conservatives advocate in favor of or in opposition to a piece of legislation, a candidate, or a social condition, the arguments they make are directly related in both their substance and their expression to a small number of core conservative principles.

As a consequence, every specific debate reinforces those principles, creating a coherent image of conservatism. When conservatives tell you we need tax cuts so pointy-headed bureaucrats in Washington won't waste your money, it reinforces the idea that government is a hindrance and a burden to ordinary people. When they argue against gun control by saying people should be able to protect their families with assault rifles, it reinforces the image of conservatives as self-reliant and responsible. When they oppose environmental regulations by extolling the entrepreneurial spirit of small businesspeople, it reinforces the notion that conservatives are friends of Main Street. In each case, one can draw a direct line from the core principle to the specific issue argument; each debate thus enhances and burnishes the image of conservatives and conservatism.

If progressives are to succeed in recasting their public image, they need to create their own master narrative, to see every debate as an opportunity to shape the images of both progressives and conservatives. They must also realize that in politics, ideas are unable to stand on their own merits and that compelling communication of those ideas is the sine qua non of success. Communicating effectively and persuasively with the public isn't a messy adjunct to politics, something leaders have to engage in against their wishes so they can go about the real business of governing. It is the very essence of politics, the process that builds and maintains the connections between citizens and their government. A movement that doesn't know how to communicate its ideas and its identity to the public is doomed to failure.

Again and again, liberals and Democrats have come before the American public wielding a sensible, pragmatic ten-point plan in the naive belief that the public will examine it and be persuaded. Conservatives and Republicans, on the other hand, have understood that persuasion and the political success that follows it do not flow from the quality of your ten-point plan. Progressives have been consumed with what Aristotle in his *Rhetoric* referred to as *logos*, argument based on logic, facts, and reason. Conservatives have focused on the two other kinds of persuasive rhetoric he delineated: *pathos*, the appeal to emotion, and *ethos*, the appeal based on the character of the speaker.* It is the latter on which conservatives have built decades of success. As Aristotle wrote, "It is not true, as some writers assume in their treatises on rhetoric, that the personal goodness revealed by the speaker contributes nothing to his power of persuasion; on the contrary, his character may almost be called the most effective means of persuasion he possesses."

If you don't establish trust through *ethos*, none of your arguments will be persuasive. Progressives need to understand that it isn't about your ten-point plan, it's about *you*—who you are, what your values are, and why people should trust you. Two thousand three hundred years after Aristotle made the point, it's time progressives learned this lesson.

---

*In February 2004, the pseudonymous blogger Publius of the blog Legal Fiction (lawandpolitics.blogspot.com) pointed out that though John Edwards and John Kerry were making essentially the same argument on the economy, Kerry was arguing solely through *logos* while Edwards offered a much more effective combination of *pathos* and *ethos*. Unfortunately, the Kerry campaign did not seem to take notice.

LIBERAL OR PROGRESSIVE?

Throughout this book, I use the term *progressive* to describe the ideology of the left in the present and the future, and *liberal* usually to describe the ideology of the past. In the details of policy, there is little difference between the "progressivism" and the "liberalism" of which I speak. I make the distinction to denote a new chapter in the identity and the political fortunes of the American left. The question of what to call ourselves has been the subject of some private debate recently among writers, activists, and political professionals, and I come down on the *progressive* side for two reasons. The first is that *liberal* has taken a beating over the last couple of decades, to the point where the connotations it brings up in many Americans' minds are negative ones: weakness, indulgence of criminal behavior, sexual permissiveness, and a general mushy-headed naïveté, to name a few. The truth of these stereotypes is of no particular importance; the relevant fact is that they exist.

The alternatives, then, are to fight those stereotypes or to propagate a different term whose connotations can be built from the ground up. The demonization of *liberal*, of course, did not happen by accident. Not too long ago, even Republicans thought a liberal was a good thing to be. In 1952, Dwight Eisenhower argued that for his campaign "to be fully effective, we need in Washington liberal and experienced members of Congress."[4] Or consider this stirring tribute to liberalism: "Let me give you a definition of the word 'liberal' . . . Franklin D. Roosevelt once said. . . . It is a wonderful definition, and I agree with him. 'A liberal is a man who wants to build bridges over the chasms that separate humanity from a better life.'" The speaker was none other than Richard Nixon.[5] But twenty years after Nixon made that statement during his first run at the White House, Ronald Reagan began an assault on liberalism, mocking it as an ideology both dangerous to law-abiding citizens and worthy of the distinctive Reagan ridicule, simultaneously friendly and contemptuous.

It was not until 1988, however, that *liberal* was finally turned into an epithet, and like most such conservative achievements, it could be accomplished only through the bumbling of Democrats. Referring invariably to Michael Dukakis as "the liberal governor of

Massachusetts," George Bush defined all that was frightening or unmanly about his opponent as the product of liberalism. "My opponent's views on defense are the standard litany of the liberal left," said Bush on the stump in San Diego. "The way he feels, I don't know if he could be comfortable in a great Navy town like this. I wouldn't be surprised if he thinks a naval exercise is something you find in the Jane Fonda Workout Book."[6] Har, har. Reagan chimed in, taunting Dukakis as "Liberal, liberal, liberal." Dukakis mustered only weak responses—"This election isn't about ideology, it's about competence"[7]—that did nothing but validate Bush's attacks. It wasn't until just days before the election, in a desperate last attempt to change the terms of debate, that Dukakis embraced "the liberal tradition of great presidents like Franklin Roosevelt and Harry Truman and John Kennedy."[8] By then, though, the damage had been done.

The final nail in the "liberal" coffin was pounded home by Bill Clinton. When running for president, the only time Clinton ever spoke the word *liberal* was when he proclaimed that his policies and ideas were "neither conservative nor liberal." Yet he all but declared defeat when he began to use the term this way:

> Bush is trying one more time to sucker the conservative mainstream folks of Ohio by pretending to be anti-tax, when he signed the second biggest tax increase in history, antigovernment when the conservative Heritage Foundation says he raised regulations by more than any president in twenty years, and paint me as some wild-eyed liberal when my state ranks first in the country in job growth, has the second lowest taxes in the country, the lowest state and local government spending in the country and we created manufacturing jobs while he lost 1.4 million manufacturing jobs in the United States.[9]

Here Clinton has accepted that conservatives are "mainstream folks," while liberals are incompetent, profligate tax-raisers—his proof that he isn't liberal is job growth, low taxes, and low government spending. Like much of what Clinton did, this formulation had positive short-term effects on his electoral fortunes and negative long-term effects on his party and those who support it. Ever since,

Democrats have fled from the idea of liberalism as though it were a noxious cologne whose scent would offend the nose of any who came near its wearer.

Nonetheless, the most acute "liberal" problem isn't so much with the public as it is with the chattering class. Pundits of all political stripes consider being a "liberal" or hailing from a liberal place to be a liability for a candidate in a way that being a "conservative" or hailing from a conservative place is not. (Given how often the question "Can John Kerry win, given that he's a Massachusetts liberal?" was asked, you'd think his home state was some sort of Sodom on the Bay, where children are forced to participate in animal sacrifice and the state government is run by a cabal of anarcho-syndicalists.) As we shall see, this conclusion can't be based in the matrix of issue positions that make up contemporary American conservatism and liberalism, since on most issues the liberal position is the more popular one. The majority of Americans favor legal abortion, gun control, a higher minimum wage, generous Social Security and Medicare benefits, universal health care, and strong environmental protections, to name a few.

Yet while the public is hardly conservative on these issues, there is a small but particularly noisy group whose visceral hatred of both liberals and liberalism convinces journalists and pundits alike that liberals are held in near-universal contempt. As political scientists Henry Brady and Paul Sniderman put it in a 1985 study of ideology, "liberals do not like conservatives; however, they do not dislike them nearly as much as conservatives dislike liberals."[10] For the staunchest of conservatives, anything that gets one's blood boiling can and will be described as "liberal." For instance, conservatives often articulated their venomous hatred of Bill and Hillary Clinton as an objection to their alleged liberalism. The idea that the Clintons are, in Newt Gingrich's evocative phrase, "counter-culture McGovernicks" is a rather tenuous proposition when one considers their support of the death penalty, missile defense, NAFTA, and restrictive welfare reform. And in recent decades, conservatives have grown to dislike liberals more and more with each passing year.[11] Sean Hannity once described an illicit marijuana facility as a "secret liberal lab."[12]

Given the talk-show dominance of conservative voices, it's no accident that the notion that liberalism is a repugnant malady on a par with leprosy is bandied about on a daily basis. While it's not surprising to hear it coming from conservative blowhards, the idea gets repeated by ostensibly neutral observers as well. In the media echo chamber, statements by ideologues ("John Kerry can't get elected because he's a Massachusetts liberal") get recycled as questions by journalists ("Can John Kerry get elected, given that he's a Massachusetts liberal?"). The result is that conservatives have succeeded in pushing the punditocracy—left, right, and center—to view being identified as a "liberal" as at best problematic and at worst vaguely shameful. As a consequence, politicians on the left will be forever forced to answer questions about whether they are "too liberal."

This state of affairs may be unjust and unfair, but there it is. The left is thus faced with the Herculean task of rehabilitating the term, one that would take a great deal of time and energy. The alternative is to focus not on changing impressions of what a liberal is but on forming impressions of what a progressive is.

This brings us to the second reason why *progressive* is a preferable appellation. Because the term holds no particular set of associations for the vast majority of Americans, the left has the opportunity to convince Americans that "progressive" is a good thing to be, particularly since the root of the term—progress—is something to which the left can legitimately stake a claim.

The idea of progress is embraced by all but the most curmudgeonly among us. Not only is the person who desires progress admirable in the abstract, he or she is admirable in a particularly *American* way, always looking to build, to improve, to advance. One critical element of the progressive project is not only building the articulation of ideology from basic principles, but also tying those principles to the fundamental traits, beliefs, and ideas that lie at the heart of the American creed.

Progressive also defines its opposite in an advantageous way, something of which *liberal* is no longer capable. At this stage of American life, the idea that liberals advocate liberty has become muddled to the point where it is no longer a meaningful part of the image of liberalism. Conservatives successfully combined attention to the excesses of "political correctness" (overblown, but not without some truth) with their own relentless focus on individual rights to make conservatism, in its public image if nothing else, as much the ideology of liberty as liberalism. And though we use the word *liberal* in nonpolitical contexts to mean free, expansive, and open, its colloquial usage also invokes some of the less popular elements of the liberal stereotype, including permissiveness and moral relativism.

Just as we have the opportunity to build an image of progressivism, we have an opportunity to build an image of its opposite as the opposition to progress. This highlights the least popular portions of conservative ideology and the conservative coalition: the know-nothing school board member wanting to banish science from the classroom, the intolerant anti-immigrant activist, the puritanical scold telling other people what to do in their own bedrooms.

One defining feature of conservatism throughout history has been an aversion to change, the desire to keep things as they are. The progressive, in contrast, is an advocate of progress—not simply change for its own sake, but advancement and improvement. This means scientific discovery, invention, improvements in the efficiency of government, and greater education, all linked to the American optimism that foreign visitors so often admire.

By defining progressivism as a distinct new movement, we also have the opportunity to hold up a rising generation of leaders who relish both policy and politics, who can walk into a room and leave an hour later with a pile of contributions, a long list of volunteers, and a group of voters won over for good. This is no small point, particularly for the electoral fortunes of the Democratic Party. As Slate's David Plotz pointed out during the 2000 Democratic convention, the current generation of Democratic leaders doesn't seem particularly interested in or good at the political part of politics:

The Democratic Party is suffering from a pleasure deficit. Since 1992, the Democrats have been dominated by a politician who adores politics, and the party has thrived because of it. On Monday night Democrats said farewell to President Clinton and handed the party off to Gore, Lieberman, Hillary Clinton, Tom Daschle, and Dick Gephardt. The Democratic leaders showcased in Los Angeles may well be the most earnest, most public-policy-oriented, most intelligent group of politicians ever to head a major party. They are intellectually impressive, and they have the best intentions. But they don't really like their jobs. They are skeptical of politicking, or bad at it, or both. Gore, ever obedient, has learned to pretend to love campaigning, but it will never be a natural act for him. Say this for George W. Bush: He loves to shake hands.[13]

The same is true of John Kerry: he might have turned out to be a great president, but he will never be a great politician. And think of the group he beat out for the 2004 nomination: Dean, Gephardt, Edwards, Clark, Kucinich, Graham, Sharpton, and Moseley Braun. With one or two exceptions, not exactly a collection of natural politicians.

In its 2005 Political Typology study, the Pew Research Center found that, to oversimplify its categorizations a bit, the most conservative Republicans were those most pleased with the Republican Party, but the most liberal Democrats were the least pleased with the Democratic Party. Among the pro-business group referred to by Pew as "Enterprisers," 60 percent said the GOP did a good or excellent job of "standing up for its traditional positions on such things as reducing the size of government, cutting taxes and promoting conservative social values," a view shared by 63 percent of "Social Conservatives." None of the Democratic groups were that enthusiastic about their party, and only 23 percent of the group Pew called "Liberals" felt the Democratic Party stood up for its traditional positions.[14]

There could be more than one explanation for this finding—party stalwarts like winning, for instance. But the more compelling explanation is that both the conservatives and the liberals are right: the Republican Party *has* been standing up for its traditional positions, while the Democratic Party hasn't. Democrats look at their party and see a collection of timid, ineffectual policy wonks who seem to have forgotten what made them Democrats in the first place and who get outfoxed and outfought by their opponents time and time again. At the 2004 Take Back America conference, a gathering of liberal activists, Jim Hightower said to great applause, "There are those who say that John Kerry is not liberal enough. I don't care if John Kerry is a sack of cement, we're going to carry him to victory." If progressives create a real movement, future Democratic candidates may look to them less like sacks of cement and more like leaders.

BUILDING A MOVEMENT

In August 1971, Lewis Powell, who would be nominated to the Supreme Court by Richard Nixon just months later, wrote a memo to the U.S. Chamber of Commerce that provided an action plan for the men who would fund the conservative movement in the coming decades. Powell argued that capitalism was under assault not only from "the Communists, New Leftists and other revolutionaries who would destroy the entire system," but also from "perfectly respectable elements of society: from the college campus, the pulpit, the media, the intellectual and literary journals, the arts and sciences, and from politicians." Powell told the chamber and those it represented that if they wanted to save capitalism, they had to spend every dollar they could to "conduct guerrilla warfare" against these seemingly mainstream voices, who were no less a threat to business interests than were bomb-wielding radicals.

In what could stand as a motto for the conservative movement he helped spawn, Powell wrote, "Strength lies in organization, in careful long-range planning and implementation, in consistency of action over an indefinite period of years, in the scale of financing available only through joint effort, and in the political power available only through united action and national organizations." Among Powell's recommendations were that business interests should create their own cadre of scholars to compete with liberal academicians and demand equal time for them; put pressure on universities to hire faculty committed to free enterprise; monitor television news for hostility to the free enterprise system and pressure news organizations when they found it; support conservative scholars in their efforts to publish magazine articles and books; and maintain a network of lawyers to push for business interests in the courts.

Making the audacious claim that "few elements of American society today have as little influence in government as the American businessman, the corporation, or even the millions of corporate stockholders," Powell told the chamber, "Business must learn the lesson, long ago learned by labor and other self-interest groups. This is the lesson that political power is necessary; that such power must be assiduously cultivated; and that when necessary, it must be used aggressively and with determination—without embarrassment and without the reluctance which has been so characteristic of American business." Powell told the executives that doing so would require a substantial investment, more than they had ever put toward politics before. Soon after reading the Powell memo, the beer magnate Joseph Coors put up $250,000 for what would become the Heritage Foundation, the right's premier think tank.

The degree to which Powell's memo was actually read at the time is a matter of some debate,[15] but whether it was actually utilized as a blueprint, much of what it recommended has come to pass. Though its analysis of the forces arrayed against American capital may have been a touch histrionic, it was correct in one sense: there certainly were prominent elements on the left that at the time were pressing for radical transformations in America's economic system. Three decades later, those radicals have faded from memory; today, no one who is permitted a voice in public debate advocates nationalization of major industries or 90 percent marginal tax rates. Yet the moderation of the goals of the left has not moderated the vigor with which it is fought by the right; quite the contrary. Today, modest steps such as a proposal to increase the minimum wage by a dollar or an attempt to tax investment income at a rate comparable to wage income will be met with a response whose fury Powell could scarcely have dreamed of.

Liberals often lament the fact that conservatives have so much more money at their disposal, that corporate fat cats and wealthy conservatives are ready sources of the funding needed by interest groups and candidates to wage political battle. While this may be true to a great degree, what has made the difference is not the amount of conservative money, but how it has been used.

Much of the funding for the conservative movement came from a small group of foundations, particularly the Adolph Coors Foundation, the Lynde and Harry Bradley Foundation, the Koch

Family Foundations, the John M. Olin Foundation, the Smith Richardson Foundation, and the Scaife Foundations. The last, controlled by the reclusive billionaire Richard Mellon Scaife, has pumped more than half a billion dollars into conservative causes in the last four decades.[16]

What distinguishes these foundations from their liberal counterparts is not their wealth; indeed, they are dwarfed in size by foundations such as MacArthur, Ford, and Pew, whose giving has a more liberal bent. The difference is that those liberal foundations usually fund single-issue endeavors to study and address social problems, from environmental degradation to homelessness to education in poor communities. Though the ends these foundations seek may be progressive in broad terms, unlike the conservative foundations they are not in the business of politics and they certainly don't fight conservatism in the way the conservative foundations fight liberalism. They don't direct their money toward anything remotely political or to multi-issue organizations advocating the progressive cause. The conservative foundations, on the other hand, fund think tanks like the Heritage Foundation and the American Enterprise Institute, conservative magazines, and all manner of efforts to strangle liberalism. "Conservative funders pay meticulous attention to the entire 'knowledge production' process," wrote Karen Paget. "They think of it in terms of 'a conveyer belt' that stretches from academic research to marketing and mobilization."[17] And the effects go beyond ideas. Richard Mellon Scaife can without too much exaggeration be said to have brought about the impeachment of a president: he paid for the "Arkansas Project" at the *American Spectator* magazine to dig up dirt on Bill Clinton's private life; one of the project's results was an article mentioning a woman named "Paula" who met Clinton in a Little Rock hotel room; based on the article, Paula Jones filed a lawsuit against Clinton; it was in that lawsuit that Clinton was forced to answer questions about one Monica Lewinsky. According to the National Committee for Responsive Philanthropy, conservative foundations spent a billion dollars pushing conservative causes in the 1990s alone.

With their help, the network of advocacy organizations Lewis Powell proposed has become remarkable in its wealth and influence. In 2002, the Heritage Foundation received over $52 million in grants and donations and had assets worth over $100 million. Its staff numbers over 200, class warriors all. The Hoover Institution is even larger, with a staff of 250. Heritage maintains not one but two television studios, making it easy and cheap for any program to book a Heritage staffer or fellow as a guest. The results are impressive: according to Fairness and Accuracy in Reporting, when representatives of think tanks were quoted in major news outlets in 2003, 47 percent came from conservative organizations, 39 percent came from centrist organizations, and only 13 percent came from progressive organizations. Heritage Foundation representatives were quoted more than three thousand times in major news outlets that year.[18]

Michael Schuman, who spent years raising money from liberal foundations, explained why conservative money yields so much more benefit than liberal money:

> Multi-issue institutions on the right also enable their public scholars to present a coherent, compelling story about the supposed horribles of Big Government, which much of the American public has now accepted. . . . Progressive funders, perhaps driven by the New Left's historic distrust of leadership and hierarchy, are inclined to avoid general-support funding. The natural result is a proliferation of short-term projects attached to flimsy institutions. And inherent in institutional weakness is poor press work, poorly marketed publications, poor management and poorly paid core staff with low morale and high turnover. . . . If a conservative genius wanted to disarm the left, he might have come up with the following plan: Dis progressive multi-issue groups like the Midwest Academy and Pacifica Radio and dispense money primarily to single-issue groups. Give each one just enough money to survive, but not enough to succeed. Spread your resources over thousands of projects, not key institutions, so that everyone is pitted against everyone else. Make sure the best thinkers and organizers are preoccupied with fundraising for their next paycheck rather than fighting for real change. Promote organizing around obsolete political ideas rather than develop new ideas. And *voilà*! You wind up with a left pretty much as marginalized as it is today.[19]

These liberal foundations and the groups they fund are engaged in a series of small battles: for or against this piece of legislation, that candidate, this judicial nominee, addressing that problem or this issue. What conservatives and those who fund them did was something fundamentally different: they built a *movement*. They were in it for the long haul.

This is one of the key lessons progressives must take from conservatives' success. They need to focus not on the next election or the next piece of legislation but on a political war that is waged over decades. They need to begin thinking of themselves as part of a progressive movement, a unified effort with a single overarching goal: moving public policy, and thus the country, in a more progressive direction. Anyone familiar with liberal advocacy knows that a movement perspective and long-term vision are seldom to be found among those who spend their days working for environmental protection, economic justice, improved health coverage, or any of a hundred other issues.

A perfect microcosm of the difference between the conservative and the liberal approaches can be seen in campus politics, where earnest but outgunned liberals face off against a cadre of conservatives who are better organized, better funded, and more serious about the fight. While campus liberals may outnumber campus conservatives, the conservatives regularly run circles around the liberals when it comes to gaining publicity and pushing their issues. The reason is that there are a multitude of liberal movements on campuses, one for each issue, each led by students with a year or two of organizing under their belts. There is, however, a single conservative movement with a single goal: fighting liberalism. This movement is able to call upon an extraordinary network of well-heeled national organizations created to train and promote the next generation of conservative activists. Want to start a conservative newspaper on your campus? A conservative organization will give you a tutorial in how to do it—and give you the startup money. Want to annoy the liberals at your school? A conservative group will send Ann Coulter to give a speech and pay her fee. Have an interest in Washington politics? Another group will bring you to the capital and set you up with an internship, then help you get a job when you graduate. Groups like the Leadership Institute and the Young America's Foundation are extraordinarily effective at providing young conservatives with the training, the contacts, and the assistance they need to beat liberals and prepare for a lifetime of activism. Until a short time ago, there was no group doing anything remotely similar for young liberals.[20]

The situation in national politics is much the same: an organized and coordinated right battles a disorganized left, with predictable results. Progressives do not lack for policy experts or committed activists. What they need is an infrastructure whose purpose is not fighting conservatives on this or that issue but battling *conservatism itself*.

Yet the perception that the left is a cacophonous jumble of narrowly focused interests, none willing to yield their short-term feelings to long-term goals, while the right is a smoothly operating monolith with a single set of goals whose members are forever united in their quest for power, is only half right. The right certainly bickers in public less than the left, but not because it has fewer competing interests. The goals of the right's factions are often at odds, and there are plenty of factions: the religious conservatives, the corporate conservatives, the gun-rights conservatives, the antitax conservatives, the libertarian conservatives. They are distinguished from the left by their ability to work out compromises behind closed doors, their stubborn resistance to undermining their own goals, and their fundamentally different relationship to the idea of power.

Conservatives understand power: they know what it is, they know what it can do, and they know they want to get it and keep it. While they may fight among themselves, when election day approaches, conservatives get off their butts and get to work. They care less about the symbolic—did the candidate give a major speech on our issue and make it one of the central pillars of his campaign?—than they do about whether at the end of the day, the people in power are friendly or unfriendly. As Trent Lott used to say, it's better to have 80 percent of something than 100 percent of nothing.

Too many liberals don't agree. They look at power with ambivalence, in no small part because so many of them come from outsider movements. The great liberal victories of the past—the civil rights movement, the feminist movement, the environmental movement—happened because ordinary people came together to push change from the outside, convincing government to heed their demands. As a consequence, they see government power not as something they want to grasp but as something they have to fight, something that can be influenced but not wielded. Indeed, in many liberal organizations, the idea of going to work for the government is viewed as selling out; people who leave the "good fight" to take a position in the executive or legislative branches are viewed with undisguised contempt.* This is not a sentiment you find among conservatives.

Evidence of the cohesion of the conservative movement can be found every Wednesday morning in the offices of Americans for Tax Reform, the group run by Grover Norquist. Though largely unknown outside Washington, Norquist is one of the most important figures on the right, an activist who has the ability to bring together the entire conservative coalition in one room once a week to plot strategy and coordinate the conservative message. At Norquist's Wednesday meetings one will find think-tank scholars, lobbyists, Capitol Hill staffers, administration officials, and representatives of the conservative media.

What progressives should learn from Norquist isn't just the power of organization and coordination, as important as they are. More vital is the warrior spirit that animates Norquist and his allies. They may sometimes believe that some Republican politician is or isn't their friend, but they never forget for an instant who their enemy is. The best way to describe it might be to quote the 1984 film that made the career of California's current governor. In a key scene, a soldier sent back from the future explains to the heroine the nature of her cyborg pursuer: "It can't be bargained with. It can't be reasoned with. It doesn't feel pity or remorse or fear. And it absolutely will not stop—ever—until you are dead." That is today's conservative movement. "Rather than negotiate with the teachers unions and the trial lawyers and the various leftist interest groups," Norquist once said, "we intend to break them."[21]

---

*I don't mean to say that this view is universal among those who work for liberal groups—far from it. But it is widespread enough to be unmistakable.

This seriousness of purpose is wedded to an adherence to principle and an extraordinary degree of patience. To take just one example, forty years ago the idea that Social Security might be privatized was considered not merely controversial but utterly insane, the kind of proposal that marked its advocates as crackpots. But conservatives were patient; they painstakingly built support for the idea, to the point where privatization has nearly become gospel in the Republican Party. Indeed, there is not a single prominent national Republican elected official who does not advocate some form of Social Security privatization. Though President Bush's 2005 attempt to sell privatization to the American public was a complete failure, the idea will be back.

Conservatives understood that if they believed in an unpopular idea, the answer was not to discard it but to work on making it popular, even if the effort took decades. This is a perspective that progressives must adopt: no goal should ever be rejected for the sole reason that at this particular moment, Democratic politicians with national ambitions find it too risky to espouse. If something like single-payer health care is a worthy goal, then progressives should expend the effort to convince Americans to agree, no matter how long it takes. Doing so not only stands a chance of eventually yielding results, it also establishes in the public mind the idea that your movement consists of people who have firm, principled beliefs.

Doing so also takes a measure of courage, something that is in distressingly short supply in today's Democratic Party. Progressives can't rely on Democratic politicians whose narrow focus on the next election leads them to be gripped by fear. Columnist E. J. Dionne described them this way:

> Instead of framing new choices, Democrats run away from their old commitments. Instead of reaching for greatness, they argue that they are not as bad as everyone thinks they are. The party that once galvanized a nation by declaring that there is nothing to fear but fear itself has become afraid—afraid of being too liberal, afraid of being weak on defense, afraid of being culturally permissive, afraid of being seen as apologizing for big government. Democrats are obsessed with telling people who they are not. As a result, no one knows who they are.[22]

Democrats have trapped themselves in an endless loop of fear: every lost election convinces them that the public doesn't really like them; driven by fear of further losses, they believe that only by stepping carefully and taking no risks might they succeed. So they apologize for their beliefs, internalize their opponents' criticisms, and lose again and again.

THE COMING CONSERVATIVE CRACKUP

Despite all the power they hold, their copious political skills, and their seemingly limitless financial resources, conservatives are in trouble. Their coalition is displaying tiny but unmistakable fissures; with the proper application of pressure from the left, these fissures can develop into full-blown cracks that could break the right to pieces. Though George W. Bush is worshipped as a conservative hero (with more than a few on the right believing that God Himself installed him in the Oval Office), Bush, more than anyone else, is responsible for this crackup.

Much like his predecessor, Bush made a series of moves that were pragmatic in the short term in expanding his appeal, but problematic in the long term for the party and the ideology he represents. Bill Clinton declared, "The era of big government is over," but George W. Bush brought big government back. In his first term, he brought about the largest budget deficits in American history by increasing spending while cutting taxes. He signed a Medicare prescription drug bill costing, depending on which numbers you believe, as much as a trillion dollars (though he didn't get much political benefit out of it, since senior citizens quickly realized the coverage was spotty and the bill's primary purpose seemed to be securing the profits of the pharmaceutical industry). He brought government invasion of personal privacy to new heights with the Patriot Act. He set in motion a foreign policy based on perpetual war, with a steady stream of foreign entanglements and American deaths—something inimical to the partly outdated but still extant Republican tradition of quasi-isolationism.

In short, much like Bill Clinton, George W. Bush has held his coalition together with his personality and a shared antipathy toward those who opposed him, but he will leave that coalition in grave danger. One can argue that Bushism is a distinct ideology, but even if that's the case, that ideology offers little to unify the disparate parts of the Republican coalition.

This doesn't mean it's doomed to failure, however. Ronald Reagan remains a demigod to Republicans, though his record makes the loyalty he commanded from all parts of the Republican coalition somewhat surprising. Antitax Republicans forgave him for raising taxes, religious Republicans didn't mind that he almost never went to church, family-values Republicans overlooked his divorce and his estrangement from his own children, small-government Republicans forgave the fact that government grew bigger on his watch, and fiscal conservative Republicans put out of their minds that he increased the budget deficit more than his thirty-nine predecessors combined.

The key factor in Reagan's popularity among Republicans (aside from charisma) is the fact that he was a winner. Had he lost his bid for reelection in 1984, he would have been placed alongside George H. W. Bush and Gerald Ford—well-meaning men for whom Republicans have affection but not objects of worship. Ultimately, Bush's status as a Republican icon will be determined by the outcome of his second term.

Each day of that term will see an intensifying struggle over the future of the GOP, a struggle whose outcome can benefit progressives. The prevailing interpretation of the 2004 election is that Bush won reelection because Christian conservatives came out in huge numbers to voice their opposition to gay marriage. This group—the most radical within the Republican coalition—will demand and receive great attention and concessions not just from the Bush administration but from any Republican with national ambitions. Although a raft of moderate Republicans began positioning themselves to run for president in 2008 while the 2004 election was still going on, their chances are wildly overestimated. Rudy Giuliani, for example, may be a popular figure, but he has about as much chance of winning the Republican nomination as RuPaul. There may come a day when a pro-choice, pro–gay rights candidate can become the GOP standard-bearer, but that day is decades off. That fact also makes the potential candidacy of New York governor

George Pataki an exercise in futility. Candidates like Nebraska senator Chuck Hagel—pro-life but moderate on other issues—may have a shot, but it's a long one.[23]

In short, the years between the 2004 and 2008 elections will see an internecine war within the Republican Party. No matter the outcome, this war will produce division, resentment, hurt feelings, and a large group of Republicans less than enthusiastic about working to advance the fortunes of those who relegated them to a secondary role. The question is whether progressives will be able to capitalize.

The first step toward doing so is to begin working to isolate Republicans and conservatives, shrinking their appeal by forcing them to be identified with the most unappealing elements of their coalition. The various Democratic committees have always spent a lot of time yelling about the dangers of the most extreme Republicans, people like Jesse Helms, Newt Gingrich, and Tom DeLay. It's all well and good to use them for fund-raising purposes, but progressives need to understand that the extremists are their friends and the moderates are their enemies. They shouldn't waste too much energy trying to run the likes of DeLay out of Washington; instead, it is moderate Republicans like Lincoln Chaffee, Arlen Specter, and Olympia Snowe who need to be targeted for defeat. If Democrats knew what was good for them, they'd go after the moderates with everything they've got.

The reason is that the few Northeastern moderate Republicans still in office serve to soften the sharp edges of the Republican Party, letting people believe that it is a "big tent" in which diverse views are represented. Of course, it isn't—the moderates are few and largely powerless. If they can be purged from the GOP, the party's image can be aligned with its true nature: a radical conservative group of Southerners whose goals and values are alien to those of the rest of America. As we will see in the next chapter, there is little the Democrats can do about the near-total Republican domination of the South; the answer is to use it against Republicans elsewhere.

Isolating the GOP both ideologically and geographically would make it less and less palatable to the rest of America, thus making it far more difficult for Republicans to win the White House or hold significant numbers of seats outside their strongholds. The Republican Party is a juggler, keeping all its balls in the air—the social conservatives, the libertarians, the business interests, the military hawks—only by catching and releasing each one in an instant. Force it to grab and hold one ball and the rest will tumble to the floor.

Consider the two senators from Pennsylvania, a majority Democratic state. The pro-choice Arlen Specter is one of the most moderate Republican senators, who often votes with Democrats and infuriates Republicans. Rick Santorum is one of the most conservative senators, consistently receiving perfect ratings from right-wing interest groups. He also appears to have a weird obsession with homosexuality and other kinds of sex he considers deviant; when discussing his opposition to a Supreme Court decision striking down sodomy laws, Santorum told a reporter that if we prohibit the police from arresting two men for having sex in their own home, we would be lending our implicit support to "man on dog" sex as well.[24] Santorum blamed the Catholic Church's pedophilia scandal on liberalism, and in arguing later against gay marriage, he asked, "Will heterosexuals continue to, you know, copulate, to have sex? Sure, but will they build families?"[25]

So, which of these two senators is more of a threat to the Democratic Party? Specter, without a doubt, because he makes Republicans seem moderate and thoughtful. Santorum may be a right-wing nut, but his outbursts on the love that dare not bark its name are pure gold for Democrats, because they make Republicans seem sex-obsessed, puritanical, and more than a little odd. This isn't to say that Democrats shouldn't try to defeat Santorum when he comes up for reelection, but given the choice, more energy should be put into beating Specter. There are reports that Santorum is preparing a campaign to become the leader of Republicans in the Senate when Bill Frist retires in 2006; his ascension would be a gift.

Christopher Shays, a moderate Republican congressman from Connecticut, understands the problem well. "The more the Republican Party becomes the party of the South, the Southwest, and the West," he said, "the less relevant the Republican Party will be in New England. The more Jesse Helms, Strom Thurmond, Trent

Lott, Dick Armey, and Tom DeLay are viewed as representing the Party, the harder it is for me to win elections."[26] And the harder it will be for Republicans to win the White House.

Much of the work to isolate Republicans has already been done by the Republicans themselves; all that's missing is for Americans to understand just what the national Republican Party has become. The major shift occurred in the early to mid-1990s with the ascension of the party's most conservative Southerners. The moderate Robert Michel of Illinois was replaced as Republican House leader by the fire-breathing Newt Gingrich of Georgia, who proclaimed that the battle between liberals and conservatives "has to be fought with the scale and duration and savagery that is only true of civil wars."[27] Next in line to Gingrich were Dick Armey and Tom DeLay, both of Texas. In the Senate, Bob Dole of Kansas stepped down as majority leader to be replaced by Trent Lott of Mississippi. Soon the GOP leadership in both houses consisted almost entirely of Southerners. Many have noted the increased polarization in Congress in recent years, much of which is the product of gerrymandering (representatives of safe districts have less of a need to appeal to the middle than to their base, resulting in more extreme ideologues). The other key reason, however, is that moderate Southern Democrats were replaced by extremely conservative Southern Republicans, many of whom became their party's leaders. As Jacob Hacker and Paul Pierson put it, "Republicans are galloping right while Democrats are trotting left. There is indeed a widening gap in the political middle. But it is largely the result of the transformation of the Republican Party."[28] Though George H. W. Bush was nominally from Texas, in truth his son was the first Southerner nominated for president by the GOP since the party's founding. By now, though, it has become difficult to imagine the party nominating someone who *doesn't* hail from the old Confederacy.

And the Southern brand of conservatism that dominates the GOP holds opportunities for progressives. In a country that grows more diverse by the year, Republicans have become more and more the party of whites (and white men in particular). In a country marked by religious pluralism and tolerance, Republicans have become increasingly the party of Southern evangelical Protestants. In a country where concern about wage stagnation and corporate malfeasance has grown, the Republicans have put in their lot with the low-wage, low-benefit, zero-corporate accountability cultures of Wal-Mart and Enron.[29] As author Michael Lind put it, "the Texas conservatism of George W. Bush combines seventeenth-century religion, eighteenth-century economics, and nineteenth-century imperialism."[30]

The more Southern the GOP becomes, the more these characteristics will come to the fore. So progressives should use the Republican extremists as examples but should go after the Republican moderates during elections. This would certainly go against the traditional way of thinking; in either party, people's natural impulse will be to focus their attention and efforts on the figures who infuriate them the most. This is short-term thinking, however, the kind that leaves a party in the same place it started at the end of the day. Each election has consequences for the next congressional session, but it also has consequences for the next decade and the next half-century.

When the various factions of the conservative coalition begin to fight for supremacy, one group will have an advantage: the Radical Religious Right. They have the most foot soldiers and the most passion; though it has escaped the notice of most Americans, Christian conservatives have worked methodically to take over state Republican parties. A 2002 report in *Campaigns and Elections* magazine found Christian conservatives exercising a "strong" influence in eighteen state GOPs and "moderate" influence in twenty-six more.[31] Many of these state parties have platforms that amount to little more than a repeal of modernity itself.

The most critical characteristic of the Radical Religious Right is its combination of an extremist agenda with an unwillingness to compromise. The corporate conservatives might prefer to pay no taxes at all, but they'll take substantial cuts if they can get them. Yet the Christian conservatives believe that their policy positions are quite literally handed down from God. Consequently, on issues that matter to them, they are unwilling to settle for half a loaf. Consider what happened to George W. Bush in 2004 on the issue of a constitutional amendment to ban gay marriage. Concerned about looking intolerant, Bush talked vaguely about amending the

Constitution without actually coming out in favor of the amendment, but his religious right supporters told him in no uncertain terms that he had to proclaim himself foursquare in support of the amendment, or he could not count on their support. With obvious reluctance, Bush gave in and supported the amendment (once he gave them what they wanted, Bush ceased speaking about the amendment, instead talking about "standing for marriage and family" for the rest of the campaign).

We will discuss the issue of gay marriage in more detail later; whatever role it played in Bush's victory in 2004, contrary to popular belief, it will be a key issue in building a lasting progressive majority. The important point here is that a party that must satisfy the fundamentalist Christians who are its base is one that on any number of issues risks alienating the rest of the country. So Republican politicians wishing to assemble elective majorities will be faced with a Hobson's choice: repudiate the views of the Radical Religious Right—and watch them walk away, taking their votes and organizational power with them—or embrace extreme views, thus alienating moderate voters. It hasn't happened so far only because Democrats have had neither the understanding nor the courage to make those issues work for them.

The good news is that the 2004 election effectively set the stage for progressives to isolate conservatives. Within days, a conventional wisdom emerged: George W. Bush won because his hard-core supporters turned out to vote in favor of state initiatives banning gay marriage. While greatly exaggerated (in no state did a gay marriage initiative actually make a difference in the outcome), this interpretation of the election plants the seeds for progressives to pull tolerant moderate voters away from the GOP.

GETTING TOUGH

There is one final thing progressives will need if they are to win the war of ideas: toughness. Democrats often complain that Republicans are more willing to play dirty than they are, and this is certainly true (witness the biennial efforts by Republicans to keep African Americans from voting). But it isn't because Democrats have an excess of ethics; it's because all too often they don't have the stomach for the fight. The consequence is not only electoral defeats but an image of hesitation, uncertainty, and outright wimpiness. As Jon Stewart put it after some members of Congress said they might not have voted to authorize the Iraq war if they had known the faulty nature of America's intelligence, "Democrats: always standing up for what they later realize they should have believed in."

While their leaders were hedging, rank-and-file progressives were rising up. The 2004 campaign saw a vigor and an energy on the left that surprised no one so much as progressives themselves. While George W. Bush raised an astonishing $286 million dollars for his reelection—more than doubling the record he'd set four years earlier—John Kerry nearly matched him with contributions from more than a million Americans. Membership in the progressive group MoveOn.org swelled to more than 3 million. New progressive think tanks and voter mobilization organization groups sprang up. Michael Moore's searing critique of the Bush administration, *Fahrenheit 9/11*, became the highest-grossing documentary of all time. Books by progressive authors dominated the best-seller lists for months.

The reason for all of this activity was simple: George W. Bush. From what many believe to be his theft of the presidency in 2000, to his slandering of Democratic senators as unpatriotic in the 2002 elections, to his deceptions on Iraq, Bush became the target of more progressive ire than any president in history. The key question for progressives then becomes this: can the energy that went toward defeating Bush be harnessed to create and sustain a real progressive movement?

It can, if progressives make the decision to get in it for the long haul. It's time to end the age of the wimpy liberal and inaugurate the age of the progressive warrior. There are plenty of models to look to: history is full of tough progressives who even when they worked for peace, justice, and other ideas that some on the right deride as fuzzy-headed, did so with strength, passion, and courage. Martin Luther King was a tough progressive. Mother Jones was a tough progressive. So were Robert Kennedy and Paul Wellstone.

Their heirs need to be ready to stand and fight. In the coming chapters, I lay out what I hope will be a plan to do just that.

2

BEYOND RED AND BLUE

*Why the United States Is Ready for an
Age of Progressive Dominance*

Popular wisdom has it that the United States is a conservative country, and one getting more conservative all the time. When Republicans succeed at the polls, as they did in 2002 and 2004, we are told that the country has shifted to the right, become more conservative, begun pining for traditional values. Though Democratic victories such as those in 1992, 1996, and 1998 are never greeted with the suggestion that the country has "moved left," pundits see in GOP wins a dramatic alteration in the political landscape, an unmistakable tectonic shift.[1]

Those interested in politics tend to think of public opinion as having a single linear dimension running from the left to the right, along which individuals and the nation as a whole move. But the vast majority of Americans don't think of themselves this way and barely know where to place themselves along this line.[2] Political ideology is largely foreign to the American electorate; most people have opinions that don't fit neatly into boxes marked "conservative" or "liberal." They hear these terms used by political elites and associate them with political figures or abstract ideas but seldom link them to specific issues and policy divisions.

So when we attempt to ascertain just how conservative or progressive America really is, we need to move beyond the ideological labels and investigate in greater detail the complexity of American opinion and voting patterns. When we examine the demographic, geographic, and opinion landscape, we see a picture that shows tremendous potential for progressive victories in the coming years.

Few clichés have been as overused as that of red-and-blue America, the idea that we live in two separate countries with different values, beliefs, and agendas. While this account is simplistic and at times obscures more than it illuminates—after all, 44 percent of those who cast ballots in 2004 were either Kerry voters in states Bush won or Bush voters in states Kerry won—there are some important differences between areas where Republicans dominate and areas where Democrats dominate. In addition, the current alignment is hardly a new phenomenon; the electoral map of 2004 is virtually identical to a map of slave states and free states, with the West Coast and the North, running from Minnesota to Maine, as the states where slavery was abolished.

In much of the media discussion about these differences, there is an implicit moral judgment: that red states are where the real Americans with real American values reside, where virtue bubbles up from the very ground on which the heartland folk tread. Unsurprisingly, people who live in blue states take umbrage at this suggestion, and within weeks of the 2004 election, some began collecting data showing that many blue states were particularly rich in the virtues often ascribed to the heartland, with lower rates of divorce, teen pregnancy, crime, and sexually transmitted disease, among other things.[3]

Many of these problems can be attributed to differences in overall income levels; of the top ten states in per capita income, seven were states won by Kerry, while of the bottom ten, all but one were won by Bush.[4] And despite the popular image that conservatives are self-reliant while liberals are dependent on government handouts, in truth it is the red states that suckle on the federal teat, funded by the taxes of the blue states.[5] But just as there are all kinds of voters in all kinds of places, there are all kinds of people, too. You'll find Christians and secular humanists, environmentalists and polluters, vegans and carnivores, puritans and swingers, Yankee fans and Red Sox fans in every state in the union.

The story the press wrote about the 2004 election said that it was a disaster for Democrats, as heartland Americans concerned about moral values soundly rejected the cosmopolitan elites of the Democratic Party. "It is impossible to read President Bush's reelection with larger Republican majorities in both houses of Congress," intoned the *New York Times*, "as anything other than the clearest confirmation yet that this is a center-right country—divided yes, but with an undisputed majority united behind his leadership."[6] Like much contemporary conventional wisdom, however, this story turns out to be a myth. Though Republicans gained four seats in the Senate, they were able to do so only because five Southern Democrats retired; outside the South, Democrats picked up two Republican seats. In the House of Representatives, Republicans had a net gain of three seats, but only because of the unprecedented redistricting in Texas, in which House Majority Leader Tom DeLay engineered a purge of Democrats by redrawing district lines. The Texas redistricting netted Republicans six new seats, but outside of Texas, Democrats won five Republican seats to the two Democratic seats taken by Republicans.

In state legislative battles in 2004, Democrats outperformed Republicans: before the election, Republicans controlled the legislatures in twenty-one states, with Democrats holding seventeen and eleven states with split control (the last, Nebraska, has a nominally nonpartisan, unicameral legislature). After the election, Republicans controlled twenty, Democrats controlled nineteen, and ten were split. The most dramatic gains happened in two Western states: Colorado, where both houses of the state legislature went from Republican to Democratic control and the Salazar brothers, Ken and John, took a Senate seat and a House seat away from the GOP; and Montana, where Democrats took both houses of the legislature and Democrat Brian Schweitzer was elected governor. As the Republican leader in the Colorado House said after the election, "Our party has basically made the party platform guns, God and gays, and that wasn't a winning message this election cycle when we should have been talking about jobs, the economy and health care."[7] In addition to tipping chambers in their direction, Democrats had a net gain of legislative seats nationwide, leaving them with a tiny majority of 3,658 seats around the country to the Republicans' 3,656.

All this indicates that Democrats are hardly in the dire shape one would conclude by listening to the string of postelection eulogies delivered in the national media. Nonetheless, they do face some structural challenges. The Senate in particular is skewed to favor Republicans, since they are stronger in smaller, rural states, while Democrats dominate in larger states with urban populations. Though the GOP enjoys a 55–45 majority in the Senate, those forty-five Democrats represent more voters, and received more combined votes in their last elections, than the fifty-five Republicans. Republicans enjoy a similar if somewhat smaller advantage in the House due to their far more effective exploitation of partisan redistricting. There are thirty-one states where Republicans enjoy a greater congressional representation than would be predicted by their presidential votes, compared to only nineteen where Democrats have such an advantage. For instance, at one end of the scale is Massachusetts, where Kerry and Gore averaged 64 percent of the vote, yet all ten of the state's representatives are Democrats, meaning they have in essence obtained 3.6 "surplus" congressional seats. At the other end of the scale is Florida, where Bush averaged 51 percent of the vote in the last two elections, yet 18 of the 25 seats belong to Republicans, giving the GOP a surplus of 5.2 seats. Overall, by this (admittedly crude) measure, redistricting has given the Republicans a surplus of just under fourteen seats; if fourteen seats in the House turned from Republican to Democrat, the GOP would control the House by exactly one seat.[8]

In addition, there remain some obstacles in the way of Democrats reaching the big prize: the presidency, and all the executive branch power that goes along with it. The following list shows the starting point from which the parties will compete in the next few presidential campaigns, averaging the margins of victory in each state in the 2000 and 2004 elections:

Average Margin of Victory	Democrat	Republican
Safe (10+ point margin)	California	Alabama
	Connecticut	Alaska
	Delaware	Georgia
	Washington, D.C.	Idaho
	Hawaii	Indiana
	Illinois	Kansas
	Maryland	Kentucky
	Massachusetts	Louisiana
	New Jersey	Mississippi
	New York	Montana
	Rhode Island	Nebraska
	Vermont	North Carolina
		North Dakota
		Oklahoma
		South Carolina
		South Dakota
		Texas
		Utah
		Wyoming
	168 EVs	**157 EVs**
Hard Lean	Maine	Arizona
(5–10 point margin)	Washington	Arkansas
		Colorado
		Missouri
		Tennessee
		Virginia
		West Virginia
	15 EVs	**65 EVs**
Soft Lean	Michigan	Florida
(1–5 point margin)	Minnesota	Nevada
	Oregon	Ohio
	Pennsylvania	
	55 EVs	**52 EVs**
True Swing	Iowa	
(< 1 point margin)	New Hampshire	
	New Mexico	
	Wisconsin	
	52 EVs	

We see that the Republicans start with an advantage—not an overwhelming advantage, but an advantage nonetheless. It should be noted, however, that different states have different characteristics that may see them shifting from one category to another in the future. For instance, John Kerry improved on Al Gore's margins in both of the Democratic "hard lean" states—from 5.6 to 7.2 points in Washington, and from 5.1 to 8 points in Maine—despite doing worse nationally than Gore had. This would suggest that these states are moving toward the "safe Democratic" category. On the other hand, Bush improved from 2000 to 2004 in all the Republican "hard lean" states, as one would expect, given his national improvement, with one exception: Colorado, where he declined from an 8.4-point margin in 2000 to a 4.7-point margin in 2004.

WAY DOWN IN DIXIE

In the last four presidential elections, the Republican nominee has won a total of one state in the Northeast and on the West Coast, when in 2000, George W. Bush won New Hampshire by 7,211 votes, thanks mostly to the 22,198 votes Ralph Nader garnered. Yet this run of failure has not led anyone to cry that the GOP is no longer a national party or resulted in a series of think-tank conferences on why Republicans can't win in these two regions that include more than a third of the American population. No, it is the Democrats' problems in the South that bring about the endless hand-wringing, the complaints that they are "out of touch" with "regular Americans," that they must only nominate presidential candidates who hail from the place where they get the fewest votes, that they must change their beliefs to accord more with those of the people who hold them in the least esteem.

Democrats need to wake up to this reality: neither of the two major parties is a national party. The Republicans have their regional base, and the Democrats have theirs. There will always be some Republican elected officials in the Democratic strongholds and vice versa. When it comes to the presidency, though, Democrats need to stop worrying about the South and just let it go. When they do so, they'll find new opportunities opening up to build and expand a majority in the rest of the country.

Although Bill Clinton won five Southern states in both 1992 and 1996, his margins of victory in those states were far smaller than in the rest of the country. In other words, even a moderate Southern Democrat can win in the South only when he is cruising to a blowout victory. In 2004, George W. Bush won nearly 85 percent of counties in the South and 92 percent of majority-white counties.[9] Bush won the votes of 85 percent of whites in Mississippi, 78 percent of whites in South Carolina, 76 percent of whites in Georgia, and 75 percent of whites in Louisiana.[10] It is only because blacks in those states vote overwhelmingly Democratic that the final vote tallies look like anything other than complete routs. This is not to say that Democrats cannot continue to win office in the South, but those who do will tend to be socially conservative enough that they will be unable to appeal to Democrats in other regions. The obvious conclusion is that simply putting a Southerner on the ticket will not do the Democrats much good in a close election. The South has become so socially conservative that no Democratic presidential candidate who can gain the support of Democrats in the rest of the country has much of a chance to win there in a close election, no matter how thick his drawl.

The classic Samurai treatise *Hagakure*, written in the early eighteenth century, explained that the Samurai considered himself to be already dead. This belief freed him from the fear of death and made him a more effective warrior. Democrats need to free themselves from their fear of losing the South. Instead of trying to engineer a more convincing grovel, they should approach Southerners as if they aren't going to vote for them anyway.

Fear of losing the South has led Democrats to look apologetic and weak, so that their attempts to win votes in the South not only fail there but hurt them everywhere else in the country. When Democrats cross the Mason-Dixon Line and say, "I love NASCAR and hunting, see, I'm one of you," they look ridiculous. Southerners can smell that kind of pandering a mile away, and it only makes Democrats look unprincipled to the rest of the country. What they need to do is make their case to Southerners in a way that demonstrates to everyone their strengths and their values. They have to say, "I know you haven't voted for a Democrat for president in a while. And if you don't want to vote for a Democrat because our party supported civil rights for African Americans and supports civil rights for gay Americans, then that's too bad. I believe everyone should be treated equally, and if that means I don't get your vote, well, I wouldn't want it any other way. But let me tell you some reasons you should vote for me." They won't lose a single vote they were going to get otherwise, and it will gain them votes elsewhere.

This might seem to contradict the widely praised "50 state strategy" that Howard Dean is implementing for the Democratic Party to make it competitive in every corner of the country, but in fact it does not. Dean's focus is on building the long-neglected state parties, as it should be. What Democrats have been doing is the worst of both worlds: ignoring red states for four years, then making a pathetic attempt to pander to Southern voters when a presidential election rolls around. What I advocate is exactly the opposite: support the state parties during the off years, build the farm team of activists and candidates in the South, but don't send your Northeast Brahmin to Georgia to eat grits and talk about his love for country music in October of the presidential year. It makes him look like an idiot, and it doesn't win you any votes. Democrats' focus in the South should be on nonpresidential elections.

Let us imagine two nearly identical voters—we'll call the first Bob and the second Jim. Though their fathers worked in factories where they were represented by unions and thus had good wages and benefits, those jobs left their towns years ago. Now they work for less money in jobs that seem less secure. They struggle to make ends meet and worry about losing their health insurance. Both love their country but don't feel like the American Dream has worked out as well for them as it has for some other people. Both think it's okay to have a hunting rifle but aren't sure somebody should be able to go down to the local gun shop and buy an AK-47. Neither describes himself as an environmentalist, but both think government should make sure our water and air are clean.

Bob and Jim would both appear to be persuadable, potentially voting for candidates from either party, but what if we add these pieces of information: Bob lives in Ohio; he's a Catholic but isn't sure the Church has caught up to the modern world. Jim, on the other hand, lives in Mississippi. He's a Southern Baptist who goes to church two or three times a week and thinks every word of the Bible is literally true. He and his wife home-school their kids so they'll get a proper Christian education.

Knowing this, we can say with a fair degree of certainty that Jim is not going to be voting for any Democrats for president any time soon. And it turns out that one of the clearest red/blue divides is how many evangelical or born-again voters there are in a particular state.* While there are certainly progressive evangelicals who vote Democratic, as a group they are not only overwhelmingly Republican but are also the least likely to be swayed by arguments about traditional progressive issues like economics, health care, and education. The list on page 38, using data collected in 2000 by the National Annenberg Election Survey, shows the number of respondents claiming to be evangelical or born again in every state. The states won by Bush in 2004 are in bold type.

There are a number of striking patterns in this list. Of the top ten states, seven were members of the Confederacy, one (Oklahoma) was a slave-owning territory that did not achieve statehood until 1907, and another (Kentucky) was a slave state that proclaimed its neutrality (the exception is West Virginia, which seceded from Virginia in order to stay with the Union). The other Confederate states rank 11th, 12th, 17th, and 19th. There are a few anomalies here, such as Utah, which has few evangelicals because most of the state is Mormon. But the overall pattern couldn't be clearer: the Republican strongholds in the former Confederate states are heavily evangelical, the Democratic strongholds have relatively few evangelicals, and the swing states are in between. Bush won every state that had an evangelical population higher than the national average.

When we examine the country region by region, we see that the South is far different from the rest of the country. In fact, the South stands apart from the rest of America on so many elements of demography, culture, voting behavior, and opinion that for years political

---

*These terms are often used interchangeably and have overlapping meanings. I use the term *evangelical* to mean adherents of Protestant sects that put an emphasis on evangelizing and stress the experience of being born again.

scientists have regularly included a "South/non-South" variable in their analyses to make sure they aren't overlooking something important. I have divided the country into nine politically cohesive regions, with the most conservative (including Alabama, Arkansas, Georgia, Louisiana, Mississippi, South Carolina, Oklahoma, and Texas) being referred to as the Deep South. Oklahoma and Texas are not usually considered part of the Deep South, but politically they are closer to the other states in this group than they are to any of the other groups.

State	Percentage Evangelical/ Born Again	State	Percentage Evangelical/ Born Again
Mississippi	73	Pennsylvania	32
Alabama	68	Nebraska	32
Arkansas	64	Illinois	32
Tennessee	63	Washington	32
Oklahoma	61	Maryland	31
South Carolina	61	Delaware	31
Kentucky	59	Wyoming	31
North Carolina	57	Arizona	30
Georgia	57	Colorado	30
West Virginia	56	Nevada	29
Louisiana	53	Idaho	29
Texas	51	Wisconsin	29
Missouri	47	Minnesota	29
Indiana	46	California	28
South Dakota	44	Washington, D.C.	28
Kansas	44	Maine	26
Virginia	41	New York	19
Ohio	39	New Jersey	18
Florida	39	Rhode Island	16
North Dakota	39	Utah	15
Oregon	35	Connecticut	14
Michigan	35	New Hampshire	14
Iowa	35	Massachusetts	12
New Mexico	34	Vermont	12
Montana	33	*Entire US*	*38*

The rest of the groups are, with a couple of minor exceptions, geographically contiguous (see chart below). Not-So-Deep South consists of Tennessee, Kentucky, Florida, Virginia, West Virginia, and North Carolina; Lower Midwest includes Indiana, Kansas, Missouri, and Nebraska; Midwest Swing includes Illinois, Iowa, Michigan, Minnesota, Ohio, and Wisconsin; Southwest includes Arizona, Colorado, Nevada, and New Mexico; West Coast includes California, Oregon, and Washington; Mountain Plains includes Idaho, Montana, North Dakota, South Dakota, Utah, and Wyoming; Mid-Atlantic includes Washington, D.C., Delaware, Maryland, New Jersey, New York, and Pennsylvania; and New England includes Connecticut, Maine, Massachusetts, New Hampshire, Rhode Island, and Vermont.

According to the General Social Survey, over half of those who are born-again believe that "the Bible is the actual word of God and is to be taken literally, word for word," compared to fewer than one in five other Americans. Like evangelicalism itself, this belief is far more

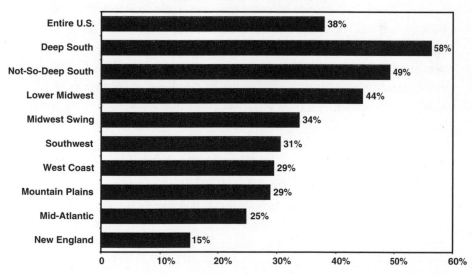

Percentage Evangelical/Born Again

Region	Percentage
Entire U.S.	38%
Deep South	58%
Not-So-Deep South	49%
Lower Midwest	44%
Midwest Swing	34%
Southwest	31%
West Coast	29%
Mountain Plains	29%
Mid-Atlantic	25%
New England	15%

Source: 2000 National Annenberg Election Survey

prevalent in the South than in the rest of the country.[12] The prevalence of fundamentalist beliefs and the South's racial history make for a mix that, to put it diplomatically, makes lots of Americans in the rest of the country uncomfortable. One study of race and religion found that evangelicals are more likely to hold negative racial attitudes than are members of other religious denominations—but only in the South, not in the rest of the country. Southern evangelicals don't differ from other evangelicals on other issues, just race.[13]

Even in 2006, the importance of racial resentment to the Republican hold on the South cannot be discounted. The movement of the South toward the Republican Party began as an unadulterated appeal to Southern white racists, who were told that if you hated the Civil Rights Act, if you hated affirmative action, if you hated the idea of government enforcing equal treatment for all citizens, there was a home for you in the GOP. As the segregationist Alabama governor George Wallace (a Democrat who became an independent) said, "I tried to talk about good roads and good schools and all these things that have been part of my career, and nobody listened. And then I began talking about niggers, and they stomped the floor."[14]

The message from Southern politicians like Wallace and national politicians like Richard Nixon and Ronald Reagan (who in 1980 traveled to Philadelphia, Mississippi, the site of the murder of civil rights workers James Chaney, Michael Schwerner, and Andrew Goodman, to announce his candidacy for the presidency with a speech on "states' rights") was this: Your anger should not be directed at those who hold power. It should be aimed not up but down, at blacks who want to change your "way of life," who want to get on the government dole, who don't know their place. Again and again, Republican politicians have gone back to the well of Southern racism to pull up a bucket full of votes, whether it was Reagan attacking "welfare queens," George H. W. Bush spreading fear of black men raping white women with the "Willie" Horton story (Horton's name was William; no one called him "Willie" until the Bush campaign got hold of him), or George W. Bush visiting Bob Jones University (where interracial dating was banned) and refusing repeated entreaties to say—wink, wink—what his position on the Confederate flag was. It is possible that Bush will be the last Republican presidential candidate to successfully exploit racial animus to gain the votes of working-class Southern whites—but I wouldn't bet on it.*

Needless to say, this record and the Republicans' persistent exploitation of racism to win votes (not to mention their reliable efforts to prevent African Americans from exercising the franchise) are things most Republicans would rather not talk about. On the national level, Republicans work hard to portray their party as a "big tent" where all are welcome. Indeed, it was conservatives, not progressives, who went after then Senate majority leader Trent Lott for saying of Strom Thurmond's segregationist 1948 presidential bid, "I want to say this about my state: when Strom Thurmond ran for president we voted for him. We're proud of it. And if the rest of the country had followed our lead we wouldn't have had all these problems over all these years, either." Down in Mississippi, they know exactly what "all these problems" means.

Conservatives understood that Lott represented the GOP's ugly side, the crazy uncle living in the attic, which is why he was forced out of his leadership post in short order. No one would allege that all or even most white Southerners are racist. But the fact is that there are enough racists that the Republican Party still believes it needs their votes. Progressives need to emphasize that the Republican Party has come to embody all that the rest of America doesn't like about the South: lingering racism, the grip of fundamentalist religion, an aversion to science and rationality

---

*We should acknowledge that these appeals had resonance outside the South—indeed, the phenomenon of "Reagan Democrats," white working-class Democrats who defected to Reagan, was driven largely by Reagan's successful exploitation of racial resentment. As pollster Stanley Greenberg wrote in 1985 summarizing his study of Macomb County, Michigan, "These white Democratic defectors express a profound distaste for blacks, a sentiment that pervades almost everything they think about government and politics. . . . Blacks constitute the explanation for their vulnerability and for almost everything that has gone wrong in their lives; not being black is what constitutes being middle class; not living with blacks is what makes a neighborhood a decent place to live. These sentiments have important implications for Democrats, as virtually all progressive symbols and themes have been redefined in racial and pejorative terms." Quoted in Thomas Edsall and Mary Edsall, *Chain Reaction: The Impact of Race, Rights, and Taxes on American Politics*. New York: W. W. Norton, 1991, p. 182.

itself, economic and social policies inimical to opportunity, and the hypocrisy of communities pledging their piety, yet rampant with crime, drug abuse, teen pregnancy, and divorce. The GOP has already become a Southern party; all that's left is to make Americans understand what they are.

LOOKING HEAVENWARD

Although progressives know where they stand on the South's racial history, when it comes to handling the issue of religion, they are conflicted and uncertain. On one hand, many of them, both the secular and the religious, are angry at the efforts of the Radical Religious Right to force the government to promote their particular brand of Christianity. On the other hand, they are inclined to be respectful of everyone's beliefs and are constantly being told that they have to do more to win the affections of the majority of Americans who are religious. But if progressives are to keep religion from being used as a bludgeon against them, they have to be willing to step aggressively into the debate about the proper role of religion in the country's political life.

The critic Susan Sontag once noted that in American public life, what is valued is "more the idea of religion than religion itself." The United States, she said, "is a generically religious society. That is, in the United States it's not important which religion you adhere to, as long as you have one. To have a ruling religion, even a theocracy, that would be just Christian (or a particular Christian denomination) would be impossible. Religion in America must be a matter of choice."[15] It is here that progressives have the opportunity to voice their concern about the increasingly strong role the Radical Religious Right plays in the Republican Party. The goals of Pat Robertson, James Dobson, Bob Jones, and the rest are not religious, they are sectarian. They seek not simply to bring the government closer to God but to bring it closer to a particular strain of Christianity.

As so often happens, media analyses on the role of religion in politics have oversimplified and overgeneralized, grouping together diverse populations who are better understood as separate entities with different voting preferences. John Green, a political science professor at the University of Akron who has studied religion and politics extensively, used survey data to divide Americans into eighteen religious groups, including three different types of evangelicals.[16] Among these groups, we see particular Republican strength among Traditionalist Evangelicals (12.6 percent of the population), Traditionalist Mainline Protestants (4.3 percent), and Traditionalist Catholics (4.4 percent). Despite estimates of the "born-again" that range as high as 40 percent of the public, it is the first group—only one in eight Americans, and 70 percent Republican—that is the true "religious right," those with orthodox and uncompromising religious beliefs. Equal in size is the group of evangelicals (those to whom Green refers as Centrist and Modernist Evangelicals) who are more open in both their religious beliefs and their susceptibility to political persuasion from progressives. Looking at similar surveys going back a decade, Green found that evangelical Protestants have been steadily moving toward the GOP, while mainline Protestants and Latino Catholics have shifted toward the Democratic Party. In 2004, "Mainline Protestants, once a strong Republican constituency, divided their votes evenly between Kerry and Bush, producing the highest level of support for a Democratic presidential candidate in recent times."[17]

Green and Steven Waldman, the editor of Beliefnet.com (and no relation to the author), used the same data to group Americans into what they called the "Twelve Tribes of American Politics." If we look at the data on these groups, we see that the hard-core of the Republican coalition—groups that Green and Waldman refer to as the Religious Right and Heartland Culture Warriors—are only about a quarter of the population.[18] While few members of these two groups will ever vote Democratic, everyone else is up for grabs. Their analysis shows that the conception of conservatives as religious and progressives as secular is far too simplistic. In fact, America's extraordinary religious diversity—a product of the separation of church and state—results in an electorate that cannot easily be divided into the religious and the nonreligious. Though it may be true that people who attend church most frequently tend to vote Republican and those who never attend vote more for Democrats, between these two poles is a variety of people with a variety of beliefs, all of whom could potentially swing toward either party at a given moment.

There is no doubt that religion has moved to the forefront of American politics, but progressives should not be intimidated by the right into fearing vigorous debate on this subject. In fact, the very enthusiasm that leaders of the Radical Religious Right have for entering the political fray threatens to alienate them from so many Americans. Three-quarters of all respondents in Green's survey believed that "Organized religious groups should stand up for their beliefs in politics." At the same time, however, half the respondents agreed with the statement "Organized religious groups of all kinds should stay out of politics." Among some groups, there was strong agreement with both statements; for instance, 63 percent of Mainline Protestants believed religious groups should stand up for their beliefs, while 61 percent said they should stay out of politics. This tells us that how religious involvement in politics is framed makes a difference in how it is perceived. When religious groups and figures appear to be taking positions based on conscience, they will have support, but when they appear partisan, disapproval of their actions will be widespread.

The message for progressives is that if you want to subvert the (already tenuous) moral authority of people like Jerry Falwell, the way to do so is to show that they are not only extremists but are also little more than partisans whose true interest is in advancing the fortunes of the Republican Party. Criticism of religious conservatives for ignoring Jesus's teachings on the poor, for instance, should be offered as evidence for the accusation of partisanship. When James Dobson issues a letter warning Democratic senators from conservative states that they "will be in the 'bulls-eye' the next time they seek re-election,"[19] as he did in January 2005, progressives should be pleased.

Much note has been made of the "church attendance gap," the fact that people who go to religious services once a week or more vote mostly for Republicans, while people who seldom or never attend services vote just as strongly for Democrats. Coming alongside the mistaken notion that the 2004 election was decided on "moral values," the nearly unanimous conclusion was that Democrats had better get religion, and fast. They were told to start being more vocal about their beliefs, to grovel before evangelical voters, and some pundits even suggested that Democrats alter fundamental policy positions on abortion and gay rights.

No one suggested that the church attendance gap might be a "problem" not for Democrats but for Republicans, despite the fact that the groups of frequent attendees and infrequent attendees, according to surveys, are roughly equal in size. According to an August 2005 Pew Research Center poll on religion and politics, 41 percent of Americans say they attend religious services once a week or more, while 46 percent say they attend a few times a year or less. In addition, evidence indicates that polls significantly overstate the frequency of church attendance. Researchers call this the "social desirability bias"—just as 70 percent of Americans will claim they voted in an election in which the actual number was closer to 50 percent, many people say they attend services more often than they actually do. The same social pressures that make one more likely to engage in a behavior also make one more likely to feel ashamed about not having engaged in it. Studies indicate that the overstatement of church attendance may be as high as 50 percent, with only half as many people showing up in the pews each weekend as the polls would suggest.[20] And by any measure, attendance at religious services has been steadily declining since the 1960s.[21]

Nonetheless, there is an assumption that frequent church attendees are "good" voters, the kind every candidate wants to win over and must pander to, while those who don't attend are bad voters—you'll take them if you have to, but you'd rather have the other kind. If we rank the states by the proportion of adults who say they attend religious services once a week or more, we see a list almost identical to the list on the proportion of evangelicals—Bush won every one of the top twenty states, from Mississippi (56 percent claiming weekly or more frequent attendance) to Virginia (42 percent).

A DIFFERENT COUNTRY

Although the evidence suggests that America is a progressive country in a variety of ways—and that Americans are getting government policy far less progressive than they would wish—it would be foolish to ignore the fact that there are some conservative strands running through American opinion, particularly when compared to the European countries whose economic development is similar to ours. One international, multiyear study, the World Values Survey, has shown that as economic development advances, countries tend to move away from traditionalism, in both religion and social opinions. They also become less focused on immediate material needs and more interested in quality-of-life issues. "The historically unprecedented wealth of advanced industrial societies, coupled with the rise of the welfare state," wrote researchers Ronald Inglehart and Wayne Baker, "mean that an increasing share of the population grows up taking survival for granted. Their value priorities shift from an overwhelming emphasis on economic and physical security toward an increasing emphasis on subjective well-being and quality of life."[22]

In this, America looks much like Europe, but it is on religion where Americans differ. When it comes to religious observance and the number of people holding absolutist views about personal morality, America most closely resembles developing countries in Latin America. Compared to Western Europe and Scandinavia, only the Irish attend religious services more than Americans do.[23] There are a number of explanations for this fact, the most compelling being that the combination of a fairly strict separation of church and state and the unusual religious diversity fed by successive waves of immigration have produced a religious culture that is both entrepreneurial and highly competitive.

One can look at Americans' religious observance from a number of angles, but the real religion gap in American society is not between the religious and the nonreligious, or between one denomination and another. "There's a fault line running through American religions," says Richard Land, a director of the Southern Baptist convention. "And that fault line is running not between denominations but through them."[24] The most important gap in American religion today is between traditionalists and modernists. Recent years have seen an emerging political and cultural alliance between conservative Protestants and conservative Catholics, something that would have been unthinkable for virtually all of American history to this point. While this alliance is a powerful one, it helps to create an important fault line. It is with the modernists—open to change, tolerant of dissent, committed to equality, at home in an evolving world—that progressives cast their lot. Progressives need to define this gap in no uncertain terms, so that on one side stand seculars, religious progressives, and religious moderates, and on the other stand the religious conservatives.

Conservatives' embrace—totally willing or otherwise—of the Radical Religious Right is politically treacherous for two reasons. First, this group's views on matters not just of theology but, more important, of social relations are widely viewed as harsh and out-dated. The idea that women should be subservient to men, that children's will must be broken with regular beatings, and that gays should be condemned for who they are, have all been rejected by most Americans. Second, what makes members of the Radical Religious Right different from other religious people is their insistence that all of us live according to *their* beliefs. This runs up against the individualism that is such a core element of American identity. As Alan Wolfe concluded after interviewing hundreds of Americans for his book *One Nation, After All*, "Clearly, most middle-class Americans take their religion seriously. But very few of them take it so seriously that they believe that religion should be the sole, or even the most important, guide for establishing rules about how *other* people should live."[25]

The views of religious fundamentalists are often expressed, furthermore, in ways that most people find troubling, if not repellent. Fundamentalists' worldviews tend to make them intolerant almost by definition, since those who make different choices are not merely wrong but in the grip of evil itself.[26] For them, evil is not an abstract idea or a way of thinking about injustice or danger but a daily presence in all of our lives. Fundamentalists are therefore prone to making statements that more tolerant people view as bordering on the hateful. In a country where tolerance and diversity are core values, this places fundamentalists clearly outside the mainstream.

Though many liberals no doubt believe that fundamentalists comprise a significant portion of the American public, in fact they are a small minority. The Barna Group, which conducts extensive research on religion and American life,[27] reports that only 5 percent of Americans have what they call a "Biblical worldview," those they describe as believing "that absolute moral truth exists; that the source of moral truth is the Bible; that the Bible is accurate in all of the principles it teaches; that eternal spiritual salvation cannot be earned; that Jesus lived a sinless life on earth; that every person has a responsibility to share their religious beliefs with others; that Satan is a living force, not just a symbol of evil; and that God is the all-knowing, all-powerful maker of the universe who still rules that creation today." This definition is not far from what we would call fundamentalist evangelical Protestantism, yet despite what some might assume, it applies to only one in twenty Americans.[28]

If so few Americans are fundamentalists, yet most Americans are Christians, what does contemporary Christianity look like? Obviously, it has a multitude of faces, but one of the most important trends in American religious observance today is the rise of megachurches that are remarkably casual in their culture and their theology. In these churches, many of which are affiliated with leaders like Rick Warren, the author of *The Purpose-Driven Life*, adults attend services in T-shirts and shorts, stopping for a latte in the coffee shop on their way in, while their children play video games in the on-site game room. But not only the outward trappings are different; listen to a sermon by Joel Osteen, the pastor of a congregation whose home is a former basketball arena, and you might think you've tuned in to an episode of *Oprah* with a bit of God sprinkled in, as much self-help as soul-saving.[29] Fire and brimstone are nowhere to be found; in their place is a more welcoming, less judgmental religious observance that seeks to accommodate itself to modern American lifestyles. God is not looking to punish you; instead, He wants you to have a healthy marriage, a fulfilling job, a nice car, and a steadily growing investment portfolio. As Alan Wolfe put it, "In every aspect of the religious life, American faith has met American culture—and American culture has triumphed."[30]

The attendees of these churches have rejected the harshness of fundamentalist religion and sought in its place something that, though scorned by traditionalists as watered-down, provides them with spiritual sustenance without making undue demands on their lives. Yet Republicans have failed to pay a price for their embrace of fundamentalists only because Democrats have been hesitant to criticize religious radicals for fear of being tagged as opponents of religion itself. They need to get over this fear and make a clear demarcation between the religious radicals and everyone else. Simply proclaiming their faith is not enough; Democrats will never win a piety contest with Republicans. Instead, they need to have spokespeople with religious credibility (and there are plenty) offer clear, unambiguous denunciations of the religious radicals, then force Republicans to accept or repudiate them.

GO SOUTHWEST, YOUNG MAN

Although pundits are constantly pleading with Democrats to worry about their weakness in the South, it is the Southwest—Arizona, New Mexico, Colorado, and Nevada—that in coming years will provide the most fruitful field from which they can harvest new electoral votes (Democrats' problems in the South and their potential in the Southwest are the topics of an upcoming book by Thomas Schaller titled *Whistling Past Dixie*). In 2004, George W. Bush won all the electoral votes from these four states, but comparing the results with those of four years previous shows significant Democratic potential. In New Mexico, the result was virtually the same as it had been in 2000: though Bush improved from losing the national popular vote by one-half of a percentage point to winning by 2.5 percent, in New Mexico he went only from a razor-thin 366-vote loss to a nearly as small 5,988-vote win. In Nevada and Colorado, Bush did worse than he had four years before. Only in Arizona did Bush make a similar improvement, as he did nationwide, going from a 6-point win to a 10-point win.

The first feature of these states that should give Democrats hope for winning the Southwest is smaller numbers of the socially conservative, evangelical voters that make up the Republican base. On issues like abortion, gun control, and gay rights, the Southwest is a region that looks distinctly progressive. The Southwestern states come by what conservatism they have via libertarian leanings, not by Christian right leanings.[31]

Yet it is the growing number of Hispanic voters that makes the

Southwest a particularly critical area for Democrats. Hispanics are at the moment overwhelmingly Democratic, but there is nothing permanent about that loyalty. Indeed, Republicans are doing all they can to win Hispanic votes, with only limited success so far. The media-sponsored 2004 exit polls showed that President Bush significantly improved his performance among Hispanics, from 35 percent in 2000 to 44 percent in 2004. Researchers quickly challenged the 44 percent result, offering lower estimates closer to 40 percent, which was confirmed by the exit poll organization—an improvement, but a smaller one.[32] But these national results obscure the fact that only in two unique states did Bush have significant Hispanic support: his home state of Texas and Florida, which has large numbers of conservative Cuban Americans.

In the decade between 1993 and 2003, the proportion of Hispanics in the United States increased by just under 4 percentage points, from 9.8 percent to 13.7 percent. Thirteen states showed increases in Hispanic population higher than the national average (see the table below for the top ten).

In these ten states, we see two solidly Republican states (Texas and Utah), three solidly Democratic states (California, Illinois, and Oregon), and all four of the Southwestern states (in bold type),

Hispanic Population and Bush Votes

	Hispanic Population in 1993 (%)	Hispanic Population in 2003 (%)	Increase (%)	2004 Bush Hispanic Vote (%)
Nevada	11.8	21.9	10.1	39
Arizona	20.2	27.8	7.6	43
Texas	27.2	34.2	7.0	49
California	27.9	34.3	6.4	32
Florida	13.1	18.6	5.5	56
Colorado	13.4	18.6	5.2	30
Illinois	8.6	13.6	5.0	23
Utah	5.3	9.9	4.6	—
Oregon	4.6	9.2	4.6	17
New Mexico	38.9	43.2	4.3	44
United States	*9.8*	*13.7*	*3.9*	*40*

Source: U.S. Census Bureau, National Election Pool

plus Florida. Each state had its own particular characteristics in 2004 (for instance, Bush's poor showing among Colorado Hispanics may be partly a result of coattails from the successful Senate candidacy of Democrat Ken Salazar). But overall, despite Bush's improved performance, we see continuing strong Democrat support from Hispanics everywhere but Texas and Florida. Without Bush on the ticket in coming years, it may be only Florida where Republicans get majority support from a sizable Hispanic population. Texas may see a particularly precipitous drop in Hispanic support for the next Republican nominee, considering that only 17 percent of Texas Hispanics call themselves Republican, compared to 28 percent of Florida Hispanics.[33] As the proportion of Hispanic voters in the Southwest grows, these states become more and more likely to move to the Democratic column.

The election of 2004 notwithstanding, evidence suggests that Democrats continue to enjoy an overwhelming advantage with Hispanic voters. While the two parties are at parity among all voters nationally, there are nearly twice as many Hispanic Democrats as Hispanic Republicans.[34] A June 2005 Democracy Corps poll of Hispanics found them picking a generic Democrat over a generic Republican for Congress by 32 percentage points (61 percent to 29 percent). The most important attributes in winning the support of Hispanics for Democrats were "on your side" and "shares your values," with Democrats enjoying the widest advantage over Republicans on "accepting different cultures." While these results make it clear that Democrats start any election with the majority of Hispanics in their camp, they still have to work to keep Hispanics there, particularly as Republicans work hard to move them to the GOP.

PARTY AND IDEOLOGY

Republicans have been extremely pleased by recent trends in party identification, in which the Democratic Party is losing strength while the Republican Party is gaining strength. In 2004, exit polls for the first time showed that an equal number of Republicans and Democrats had voted. A look at data over the last half-century shows an unmistakable trend: beginning in the mid-1960s, significant

Party Identification, 1956–2004

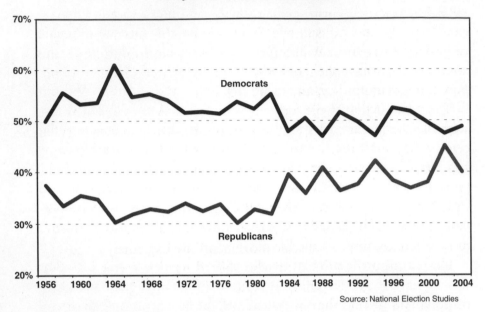

Source: National Election Studies

numbers of Americans began to move away from the Democratic Party and toward the GOP, a trend that accelerated during the Reagan years (see chart above). We have now reached the point where Democrats hold only a small advantage.

While it would be naive to deny that this is a problem for Democrats, this shift is a long-term process that is finally reaching its completion. For a hundred years after the Civil War, whites in the South were so loyal to the Democratic Party that they came to be known as "yellow dog Democrats"—they'd vote for a yellow dog if he ran on the Democratic ticket. But these voters were, in effect, Republicans in waiting. The national Democratic Party was an uneasy coalition of Northern liberals and Southern conservatives, held together by tradition more than by ideological affinity. The break came when Lyndon Johnson signed the Civil Rights Act of 1964, after which he supposedly turned to an aide and said, "I think we have just delivered the South to the Republican Party for a long time to come."[35] And he was right.

Four decades later, what political scientists refer to as "realignment" is almost complete. Southern conservatives, both officeholders and voters, have steadily migrated from their traditional home in the Democratic Party to their ideological home in the Republican Party. As they did so, they changed the GOP, moving its center of gravity away from Wall Street bankers and corporate chieftains southward, turning the party more socially conservative, more bellicose in foreign policy, and more religious.[36]

The result is that while for many years most Americans identified with the Democratic Party, at the start of the twenty-first century the two parties are roughly at parity. Yet this is not because the country has "moved to the right," as so many believe. Instead, voters who were already conservative but held a regional loyalty to the Democratic Party have moved to the GOP, where they belonged all along. This isn't to say there will be no vacillations in party identification in the near future, but large-scale movements are extremely unlikely.

If we look more closely at who shifted parties, we see that the movement to the Republicans happened almost entirely in the South. The graph that follows shows the states to which we referred as "Deep South" and "Not-So-Deep South" compared to the rest of the country.[37]

Party Identification, South and Non-South

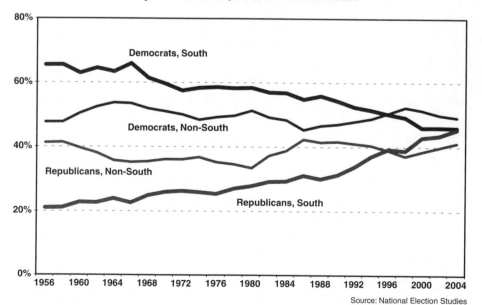

Source: National Election Studies

Outside the South, both parties are within a few points of where they have been for most of the last fifty years. In the South, on the other hand, the proportion of Republicans has nearly doubled, from the low 20s to the low 40s, while the proportion of Democrats has dropped by 20 points, from the low 60s to the low 40s. After 1996, the proportion of Democrats in the South finally fell below the proportion of Democrats in the rest of the country, and the proportion of Republicans in the South rose above the proportion of Republicans elsewhere.

Self-described ideology is another story. While the political meaning of the terms is always a matter of debate, the number of people who will place themselves in each category has changed very slowly in recent years, with the number of liberals staying about the same, while the number of conservatives has risen slightly (see graph below).

So why is it that self-described conservatives consistently outnumber self-described liberals by 10 to 15 percentage points,[38] despite the fact that on the majority of key issues the liberal position is the more popular one? Conservatives have presented an

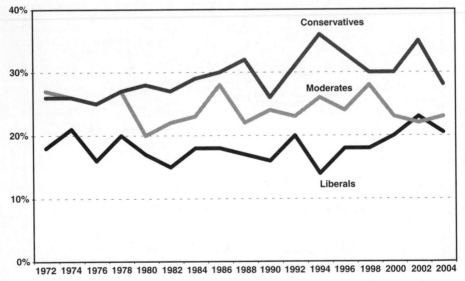

Ideological Self-Identification

Source: National Election Studies

ideology that is less about where they stand than about who they are: strong, principled, patriotic. And they have defined liberals as the opposite of all those things. So when a pollster asks someone over the phone whether he's a conservative, a moderate, or a liberal, only the most committed liberals willingly assume the label.

Many people, both liberals and conservatives, make the mistake of believing that since the number of people who will say to a pollster "I am a conservative" is larger than the number of people who will say to a pollster "I am a liberal," that means that the Republican agenda has more supporters than the Democratic agenda has. This is not the case, though; it's just the opposite, in fact. If the number of people who divide on conservative/liberal lines were the same as the number who divide on Republican/Democratic lines, then every election in recent years would have been a blowout. This hasn't happened, for two reasons.[39] First, in every presidential election since 1988 there have been more conservatives who voted Democratic than there were liberals who voted Republican, as the following graph shows.

While there is evidence of increased partisan loyalty among conservatives, loyalty among liberals is even stronger. Second, since

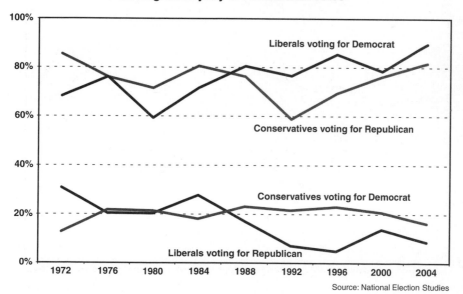

Ideological Loyalty in Presidential Votes

Source: National Election Studies

1980, moderates have become more and more inclined to vote Democratic. In every election since 1988 the Democratic candidate has outpaced the Republican candidate among moderates, even in years in which the Republican won as the graph below shows.

Even someone with the liberal pedigree of *Washington Post* columnist E. J. Dionne has interpreted the larger number of conservatives as requiring the Democrats to move to the center. "According to the network exit polls, 21 percent of the voters who cast ballots in 2004 called themselves liberal, 34 percent said they were conservative and 45 percent called themselves moderate," Dionne wrote in mid-2005. "Those numbers mean that liberal-leaning Democrats are far more dependent than conservatively inclined Republicans on alliances with the political center. Democrats second-guess themselves because they have to."[40]

Dionne would be right if everyone who talked to a pollster understood the words *conservative*, *liberal*, and *moderate* in the same way people in Washington do. Political elites tend to believe that like them, voters understand all the issue positions that com-

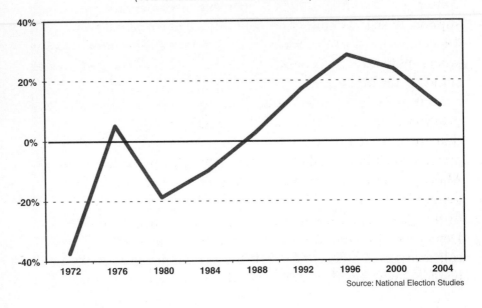

Democratic Advantage among Moderates

(Vote for Democrat minus vote for Republican)

Source: National Election Studies

prise contemporary liberalism and conservatism, and if they call themselves "moderates," that means they must be midway between the positions of the Democratic and the Republican Parties on the major issues of the day.

In fact, the people who call themselves "moderates" aren't midway between the two parties. When you examine what they believe, you find that they look much more like liberals than like conservatives. According to the National Election Studies, in 2004, 56 percent of moderates associated themselves with the Democratic Party, while only 31 percent leaned toward the Republicans. It isn't just party identification, either; on issue after issue, moderates have opinions almost exactly mirroring those of liberals. Sixty-four percent of liberals say we should increase spending on Social Security, as do 68 percent of moderates—while only 47 percent of conservatives agree. Eighty-eight percent of liberals and 84 percent of moderates say federal funding on education should be increased, compared to only 58 percent of conservatives. Seventy-three percent of liberals and 66 percent of moderates want more spending for child care—but only 38 percent of conservatives agree. Sixty-two percent of liberals and 57 percent of moderates want to spend more on aid to the poor, compared to only 39 percent of conservatives.

On some issues, moderates are in fact between liberals and conservatives—for instance, 67 percent of conservatives say they support Bush's tax cuts, compared to 37 percent of moderates and 14 percent of liberals. Yet it's exceedingly hard to find an issue where moderates and conservatives stand on one side and liberals stand on the other.

So if most "moderates" are Democrats who hold liberal policy positions, why don't they call themselves liberals? One answer is that these words have meanings outside the political realm that affect what kind of labels we are willing to place on ourselves. Many people are attracted to the ideas of "moderation" and "independence" even if their beliefs actually align fairly closely with one of the two parties. If you ask survey respondents whether they're Democrats, Republicans, or independents, around 30 percent will call themselves independents. If, however, you then ask the independents whether they lean toward one party or the other, most will say yes, to the point where the number of "true" independents falls to around 10 percent of the population.

But even if lots of people like thinking of themselves as "moderate," why should it follow that more people choose to call themselves "conservative" than "liberal?" The answer lies in the sustained campaign conservatives have waged—not merely against liberals or liberal ideas but against liberalism itself. Unlike liberals, conservatives don't simply criticize specific candidates or pieces of legislation, they attack their opponent's entire ideological worldview. Tune into Rush Limbaugh or any of his imitators, and what you'll hear is little more than an extended discourse on the evils of liberalism, in which specific events are merely evidence that the problem is the ideology—the talk-radio screamer Michael Savage titled his latest book *Liberalism Is a Mental Disorder*. Indeed, large portions of the conservative movement can be understood in these negative terms, as an effort to crush liberalism in all its manifestations. Conservatives understand that their main enemy is not a law, a government program, or a social condition they don't like. Their main enemy is a competing ideology, and that is what they spend their time fighting. When was the last time you read a book-length polemic against conservatism?

There is no doubt that the difference between the number of people who tell pollsters they are conservatives and those who say they are liberals should be a matter of concern for Democrats. If, however, they respond to that concern by "moving" to an imagined "center"—in other words, by making their positions on issues more conservative—they will find themselves in an even worse hole than they are now. The Democrats' "liberal" problem isn't about issues, it's about identity.[41]

In order to identify the areas where progressives can make the most progress, we must go beyond what people call themselves to what they really think about the nuts and bolts of political matters. To do so, we can divide issues into three broad areas with distinct characteristics: the opportunity matrix, the sociocultural matrix, and the national security matrix.

3

A PROGRESSIVE
COUNTRY

*The Three Issue Matrixes of
American Public Opinion*

Look at most of the controversies that divide global opinion, and the United States comes down on the conservative side. America tolerates lower levels of government spending than other advanced countries, and far higher levels of inequality, at least in terms of wealth. One in six American households earned less than 35 percent of the median income in 2002; in Britain, one of Europe's more unequal countries, the proportion of similarly disadvantaged households is closer to one in twenty. America is the only developed nation that does not have a full government-supported health-care system, and the only Western democracy that does not provide child support to all families. America is one of only two countries in the Organization of Economic Cooperation and Development that does not provide paid maternity leave—and the other country, Australia, is actively considering introducing it.

—JOHN MICKLETHWAIT AND ADRIAN WOOLDRIDGE, *THE RIGHT NATION: CONSERVATIVE POWER IN AMERICA* (2004)

Micklethwait and Wooldridge's facts are right—we do have lower government spending than other advanced countries do, more inequality, a poor health-care system, and inadequate child care. Yet it would be a mistake to conclude that this state of affairs is nothing more than a representation of American popular will. In fact, most Americans would be all too happy to have a national health-care system, universal child care, and many of the other benefits Europeans enjoy. What keeps these things from happening isn't popular opposition but the efforts of well-heeled interest groups and sympathetic Republicans.

Progressives who find themselves quick to accept the suggestion that America is fundamentally conservative, has always been so, and will always be so should stop to recall just how many progressive goals have been accomplished over the years. Progressives ended slavery, established the forty-hour workweek, abolished child labor, enacted food safety laws, obtained voting rights for women, established the Social Security and Medicare systems, ended Jim Crow segregation, and passed laws to protect our water and air, to name just a few. Every one of these advancements was achieved only over the vigorous opposition of the conservatives of the day. For all their shrewdness, conservatives have been stifled time and again by a powerful force: public opinion. This is why progressives have the potential to succeed more completely and more quickly than conservatives have, because their agenda is in fact supported by majorities of Americans.

As we examine the survey data that support this contention, we should be wary of putting too much stock in any one result. Polling is but one method among many of assessing public opinion, and one that has a number of inherent flaws. But by looking at enough data, we can identify the areas of strength and weakness that should guide progressives as they formulate strategies for the coming years.

THE OPPORTUNITY MATRIX

As we will see later, among the cornerstones of a rebuilt progressive identity is the idea that progressives stand on the side of working people and advocate opportunity for all. Nowhere is the contrast with conservatives clearer—and thus, nowhere is the progressive advantage greater—than in the complex of issues we can call the opportunity matrix. These issues encompass not only job prospects but all the factors that affect people's fortunes in life and determine our collective prosperity: the schools in our communities, the availability of affordable health care, the relationship of employers and employees, the quality of our air and water, and the choices our government makes with our tax dollars, to name a few.

For all their attention to social issues, conservatives remain the ally of corporate America, arguing in their words and policies that the best society arises from giving maximum leeway to and imposing minimal taxation on businesses, the theory being that eventually the benefits will trickle down to the rest of us.* This devotion to the interests of corporations determines their views not only on economics but on a variety of issues.

Unsurprisingly, those of us waiting for the trickle are not quite as rapturous about the genius of this approach as those on whom the government's largesse and protection are showered. Drawing on their own experience and what they see in the news media, majorities of Americans express skepticism about both the good faith of big business and the outcomes that are produced by the system as it currently exists, as these results from a 2003 survey by the Pew Research Center show:

	Agree	Disagree
"Business corporations generally strike a fair balance between making profits and serving the public interest."	38%	57%
"There is too much power concentrated in the hands of a few big companies."	77%	20%
"Business corporations make too much profit."	62%	32%

---

*On one appearance I made on *The O'Reilly Factor*, Bill O'Reilly accused me of being "socialistic" and wanting to overthrow the American system, then demanded that I pledge my allegiance to corporate America. "Do you love capitalistic America?" he asked. "Do you like corporate America?" Rather stunned, I asked when it had become necessary to love corporate America in order to be a patriot. O'Reilly persisted with, "No, no, no. I'm asking you. Do you like corporate America?" I responded, "I think capitalism is a great system, but I think it also needs the involvement of government in order to function properly." As though he had just discovered a picture of Leon Trotsky in my wallet, the author of *Who's Looking Out for You* shouted, "Aha!"

	Agree	Disagree
"Labor unions are necessary to protect the working person."	74%	23%
"Today it's really true that the rich just get richer while the poor get poorer."	68%	29%

Source: Pew Values Study, August 2003

Other polls reveal similar beliefs, such as the January 2003 Gallup poll that found 63 percent of Americans believing that "money and wealth in this country should be more evenly distributed among a larger percentage of the people," a positively socialistic sentiment. Despite enjoying a government safety net that is meager compared to what can be found in Western Europe, Americans do believe that their government has a responsibility to see to its citizens' basic needs:

	Agree	Disagree
"Our society should do what is necessary to make sure that everyone has an equal opportunity to succeed."	91%	8%
"It is the responsibility of government to take care of people who can't take care of themselves."	66%	31%
"The government should guarantee every citizen enough to eat and a place to sleep."	65%	33%
"The government should help more needy people even if it means going deeper in debt."	54%	42%

Source: Pew Values Study, August 2003

That these beliefs are only intermittently translated into policy doesn't diminish their importance. In fact, they are particularly significant given the unremitting conservative assault on the idea that government has any meaningful responsibilities toward the less fortunate.

If this is true, though, how is it that conservatives have had success attacking social programs like welfare, which was dramatically scaled back during the Clinton administration? The strategy they used was to shift focus away from the government's responsibility to help the needy and toward the question of individual responsibility and virtue. Republicans portrayed recipients of government assistance as undeserving, with the welfare program in particular defined as taking tax money from hard-working whites and giving it to indolent blacks. This is not to say that everyone who supported welfare reform was a racist—far from it. But Republicans knew that racism was a key resource on which they could draw in their quest to dismantle welfare, just as they had in their attacks on social programs in general.[1] In fact, people's beliefs about welfare are wildly inaccurate—they overestimate the percentages of welfare recipients who are black, the number of Americans on welfare, and the proportion of the budget that goes to welfare—a fact about which Republicans were no doubt pleased.[2] Justified or not, the argument that welfare recipients were undeserving was sufficiently resonant to allow welfare's opponents to succeed. Republicans made welfare a story with a villain: Ronald Reagan's mythical "welfare queen," a lazy black woman driving in her Cadillac to pick up her government check, her lavish lifestyle funded by the taxes of hard-working middle-class Americans.

The lesson is that when government programs are seen as serving the undeserving, they won't have wide public support. This fact can be used against conservatives, since so much of their economic policy is about larding giveaways on those who don't want to pay their fair share: the corporate raiders, the shiftless heirs, the greedy souls whose allegiance is only to themselves.

While the American public is closely divided on many of the social issues we will explore in a moment, on most of the issues in the opportunity matrix the progressive position isn't embraced just by a majority, but by a *huge* majority, including by many Republicans. For instance, in 2004, George W. Bush won the state of Florida by 52 to 47 percent. At the same time, however, Florida voters approved a ballot initiative to raise the minimum wage in their state to $6.15, one dollar over the federal minimum, by an overwhelming 71 to 29 percent. Even if every single Kerry voter voted for the minimum wage increase (not particularly likely), this means that more than 1.6 million Floridians voted for Bush *and* for a policy that he and his party vehemently oppose. The same thing happened in Nevada—Bush won the state by 2.6 percent, but an initiative hiking the minimum wage passed by 68 to 32 percent. Though conservative officeholders inevitably oppose increases in the minimum wage, national surveys routinely find support for such increases exceeding 80 percent.

Nor is the unquenchable Republican thirst for tax cuts widely shared by the public. When the CBS News/*New York Times* poll asked people in 2002 whether they would be more likely to vote for a congressional candidate who thought it was more important to cut taxes or for one who thought it more important to balance the budget, only 18 percent preferred the candidate who wanted to cut taxes, compared to 73 percent preferring the one who wanted to balance the budget. Even if we get personal, asking whether people want *their* taxes cut, a majority will prefer deficit reduction (53 to 41 percent in a 2003 survey by NPR, the Kaiser Family Foundation, and Harvard's Kennedy School). In that same survey, when people were asked what was more important to them, "lowering your taxes, or maintaining spending levels on domestic programs such as education, health care, and Social Security," only 18 percent chose lowering their taxes, while 80 percent chose maintaining domestic spending. And when asked what bothered them most about the tax system, the factors that Republicans emphasize were selected by few respondents, with 14 percent choosing the amount they have to pay and 31 percent choosing the complexity of the system, while 51 percent chose "the feeling that some wealthy people get away with not paying their fair share."

In short, while nobody likes paying taxes, Americans will support them providing two conditions are met: if they believe the system works fairly, and if they believe the government is using the money for things they support. The second condition has at least temporarily been satisfied, in no small part because of the aftermath of September 11, with its lionization of government workers and the ensuing focus on the military and homeland security. For the moment, Republicans have stopped arguing that taxes are bad because government just wastes the money—after all, with control of all three branches of government, they're the ones doing the spending. As for the first condition, Americans don't believe the system is fair, which provides a base of support for progressive tax reform.

Progressives have to make a very simple case and make it repeatedly: when it comes to the economy, Republicans have failed while Democrats have succeeded. On almost any measure you can come up with, the economy does better when a Democrat is in the White House. Economic growth? Since 1960, Democratic administrations have averaged 4 percent real growth, compared to 2.75 percent when Republicans are in the White House. Go all the way back to 1930, and GDP growth looks even better for Democrats: 5.4 percent, as opposed to only 1.9 percent under Republicans. Democratic presidents have also been better for the stock market; since 1900, the returns on the S&P 500 have averaged 12.3 percent under Democrats but only 8 percent under Republicans.[3] Republican presidents have presided over larger increases in the size of government in both spending and the number of federal employees and have had greater increases in deficits. Inflation has also been lower under Democrats, as has unemployment.[4]

This is quite an extraordinary record, and one that would probably come as a surprise to people conditioned to believe that Republicans are "fiscal conservatives"—careful, responsible, if anything too concerned with balancing the books. The economic records of the Clinton and Bush administrations, particularly the stunning failure and incompetence of the latter, have gone a long way toward reversing this belief. But progressives can continue to improve their image as economic stewards by repeating these facts, in both their particulars (Democrats are better for the stock market, Democrats are better for economic growth) and the general principle that Democrats are better for the economy. It also wouldn't hurt to stop using *fiscal conservative* as a compliment. No Republican would ever claim to be a "social liberal"—even if he or she is one—so why do so many Democrats claim to be "fiscal conservatives"? They need to define a "fiscal conservative" as someone who runs up deficits to pay for tax cuts for the elite—not something anyone would want to admit to—while a "fiscal progressive" is someone who balances the budget and gets results for the American economy and the American worker.

On economics, Republicans have successfully advanced their agenda despite being on the wrong side of public opinion. The same is true of health care, where any attempt to seriously address the problem of the uninsured or the perverse results of a profit-driven health system is inevitably met with cries of "socialized medicine!" As it happens, though, Americans are quite open to the idea of a single-payer system like those used in the rest of the industrialized world. Fifty-six percent of respondents to a July 2003 CBS/*New York Times* poll agreed that "fundamental changes are needed" to our health-care system, while a further 30 percent said, "Our health care system has so much wrong with it that we need to completely rebuild it." That October, the ABC News/*Washington Post* poll asked this question: "Which would you prefer—the current health insurance system in the United States, in which most people get their health insurance from private employers, but some people have no insurance, or a universal health insurance program, in which everyone is covered under a program like Medicare that's run by the government and financed by taxpayers?" The latter choice—a single-payer system—was preferred by 30 points, 62 to 32 percent.

This one result doesn't show that single-payer health care is a slam-dunk and could be enacted easily, but it does demonstrate that Americans are more than open to the idea if it is framed properly. Progressives have taken the wrong lesson from the defeat of the 1993 Clinton health-care plan, believing that the public isn't ready for a wholesale overhaul of the way we finance health care in this country. In fact, one of the key problems with the Clinton plan was the lengths it went to maintain the profit-driven nature of the system and to enhance the role of HMOs. It was defeated not because it was unpopular in its particulars, but because its complexity allowed the Republican/corporate alliance that opposed it to use distortion and fear-mongering to leave the administration without the public support it needed to force the bill's passage. We will discuss the health-care issue in more detail, but for the moment it's enough to note that the GOP is and must be portrayed as the guardian of a widely unpopular status quo.

On the other issues in the opportunity matrix, there is wide support for an active government that works to safeguard citizens' rights, advance their interests, and provide them with opportunity. The American people want strong environmental protection (86 percent agreed in a 2003 Pew poll that "there needs to be stricter laws and regulations to protect the environment"), investments in schools, and increased government funding of research into alternative energy sources (more than 85 percent in recent polls by Fox News and *Newsweek*), to name a few. In short, the progressive vision of an active government seeking to solve problems and expand opportunity—not the conservative vision of a government that gets out of the way so the market can work its magic—is the one Americans support.

THE SOCIOCULTURAL MATRIX: WHY PROGRESSIVES ARE WINNING THE CULTURE WAR

Conservatives love to quote something the *New Yorker* film critic Pauline Kael supposedly said after the 1972 election, when she expressed shock that Richard Nixon had not only won but won in a landslide, since she didn't know a single person who voted for him. Today, though, a different belief grips progressives, particularly those who live in places where most people share their views. Despite knowing lots of like-minded people, they believe that communities like theirs are few and far between, and the vast majority of Americans are conservatives whose values and political choices couldn't be more different from theirs. So when conservatives start wielding "culture war" issues, progressives get nervous, convinced that discussion of cultural issues will bring only defeat from the overwhelmingly conservative and traditional American electorate.

The truth, however, is that progressives are winning the culture war—in fact, it's not even close. Our recent history shows a steady movement to bring American society in line with progressive ideals about work, family, child-rearing, sexuality, and a dozen other subjects. Despite the conventional wisdom that we are becoming steadily more polarized, on many issues we are actually growing closer together—because we're all becoming more progressive.[5]

Consider marriage and family, perhaps the arena that raises conservative hackles to the greatest heights. Conservatives once believed that a marriage meant a woman became a man's property; they also once believed that only members of the same race should marry, a belief that held sway until not too long ago. Interracial marriage was illegal in sixteen states when the Supreme Court struck down all such prohibitions in 1967.[6] In 1982, a third of white Americans still believed interracial marriage should be illegal; two decades later the number had declined to one in ten.[7] (Always in the forefront of social change, Alabama got around to removing its antimiscegenation law from the books in 2000 in a ballot initiative, though 40 percent of Alabamians voted to keep the ban.)

Social conservatives may not like it, but in recent years the vast majority of Americans have thrown off the Puritan legacy in which external authorities and arbitrary traditions determine the choices we make in our own families. In 1969, Governor Ronald Reagan of California signed the nation's first no-fault divorce law, meaning couples no longer had to prove that one spouse had been adulterous or violent in order to obtain a divorce. While conservatives blame the rapid spread of no-fault laws over the following two decades for increases in divorce rates, few people are nostalgic for the restrictions on personal liberty of the pre-no-fault age. How many Americans think that if two people want to get divorced, the government should poke around in the details of their marriage to see whether they "deserve" it or not?

The goals of the women's liberation movement, virulently opposed by conservatives, have become accepted as core values of a modern society: that men and women should be treated equally in the workplace, that both partners in a marriage have an equal right to a career, and that men have a responsibility to share in child care and housework (though most men may not live up to it). In 1977, fourteen years after the publication of *The Feminine Mystique*, 38 percent of Americans still agreed that "women should take care of running their homes and leave running the country up to men," a "traditional" belief about family and gender roles. Two decades later, the proportion agreeing had fallen to 15 percent.[8]

The conservative prejudices of the past have become confined to an ever-shrinking proportion of the population, and voicing these prejudices in public has become impossible for office holders or anyone seeking to participate in public debate. In 1987, a Pew poll found only 48 percent of Americans agreeing with the statement "It's all right for blacks and whites to date each other." By 2003, the number was 77 percent. This change occurred both across generations—with each generation more tolerant than the one before it—and within generations, as the same cohort became more tolerant over time.

On issues of "sin," the country continues to embrace personal liberty and not the harsh judgment of social conservatives. As many as half of Americans admit to having tried marijuana, and four out of five believe doctors ought to be able to prescribe it for their patients.[9] Eleven states have medical marijuana laws on the books. One in three Americans believes it should be entirely legal, while nearly half believe possession of small amounts should be legal.[10] Though Republican governments may funnel millions of dollars to laughable "abstinence" programs in schools preaching the cold virtue of chastity until marriage, the overwhelming majority of Americans are not virgins when they marry,[11] and the proportion of adults who express to pollsters the conservative view on sex—that it's morally wrong to have sex before marriage—has never in the last twenty years been more than a third of Americans.[12]

The idea of a strict family hierarchy enforced by ruthless punishment is also growing antiquated. When the TV psychologist Dr. Phil interviewed George and Laura Bush during the 2004 campaign, he asked whether they spanked their daughters; almost simultaneously, Laura said, "Not very often," and George said, "Not really." It would hardly be a stretch to conclude that while they had spanked them at least occasionally, Bush concluded that saying so was not wise, and so he equivocated with "Not really." When a politician as conservative and politically astute as George W. Bush won't admit to spanking his children, you know there's something going on.[13]

The conservative icon William F. Buckley wrote in 1955 that the job of a conservative was to stand "athwart history, yelling Stop."[14] Half a century later, it should be obvious that history will keep moving no matter what conservatives yell at it. And most critically, on the "cultural issues" conservatives use to keep their base aroused, young people are overwhelmingly progressive: they favor gay rights, as many as half say they've dated someone of another race, they are environmentalists, they favor gender equality, and they are strong advocates of personal liberty. In fact, as Leonard Steinhorn has observed, today's "generation gap" isn't so much between the young and the rest of us, as between the old and the rest of us. It is the pre–baby boom generation that holds most closely to "traditional values" on matters of race, sexuality, and religion.[15]

Which brings us to the issue of gay rights, and specifically same-sex marriage. After the 2004 election, social conservatives were proud that in eleven states, ballot initiatives outlawing gay marriage succeeded at the polls, some by wide margins. They proclaimed loudly that the country had demonstrated its devotion to traditional conservative values. Yet here as on so many other "cultural" questions, American public opinion has become increasingly progressive. Conservatives are in a constant race to stay ahead of public opinion, moving ever leftward as they keep one step ahead of evolving mores and beliefs. So while at any given moment it may appear that progressives are the ones "out of step" with the American people, the direction of change is unmistakable. It is only because the questions have changed so dramatically that conservatives can find themselves in a temporary majority.[16]

We can appreciate this progression if we step back and consider the extraordinarily rapid evolution of beliefs about equality for gays and lesbians that occurred around the turn of the twenty-first century. In April 1997, the actress Ellen DeGeneres and the character she played on the sitcom *Ellen* simultaneously came out of the closet. The event was positively earth-shaking: a Lexis-Nexis search for March, April, and May of that year produces 1,465 news stories about DeGeneres's coming out, including 758—or over 25 stories per day—in April.

Yet just a few years later, the brouhaha over DeGeneres's coming out seems absurdly overblown. Gay characters are all over television, and not just on the one or two "gay-themed" shows like *Will & Grace* or *Queer Eye for the Straight Guy*. Numerous ensemble dramas have gay characters whose sexuality is only occasionally used as a plot driver. The consequence is that more and more Americans have gay people they know, even if that person is only a character on one of their favorite shows. In 1992, 42 percent of Americans told the CBS/*New York Times* poll that they personally knew a gay person; by 2004, the number had risen to 69 percent in a *Los Angeles Times* poll. And nothing changes opinions about gay rights faster than learning that someone you care for is gay.

While the initiatives on election day 2004 may have all run against gay marriage, what's truly remarkable is that we were discussing the topic at all. When Howard Dean began running for president, he was largely dismissed by the national press corps as unelectable, not because he opposed the Iraq war (a position that began to look more sensible with each passing day), but because he had signed a law establishing civil unions in Vermont. His support of civil unions was thought to be so radical that it would make him instantly unacceptable to voters in large portions of the country. Yet within months, Dean's position was not only echoed by other candidates, it became the median position of the American voter. All of the other Democratic contenders eventually voiced their support for civil unions. Then, days before the election, civil unions were endorsed by none other than George W. Bush, who said in an interview that although he still favored a Constitutional amendment banning gay marriage, he felt that states should be able to pass civil union laws if they pleased.

Few politicians have a better understanding of the national zeitgeist than Bush does; by splitting the difference between his more conservative supporters and gay marriage advocates, he knew just what he was doing. But what is so striking is how quickly a radical idea became a moderate compromise. According to the 2004 exit polls, 25 percent of voters believed gays should be allowed to marry, 35 percent believed they should be able to form civil unions, and 37 percent believed their relationships should have no legal status. Add the first two together and you see that 60 percent of Americans favor at least civil unions.[17]

Though members of the Radical Religious Right crowed that fears of gay marriage swung the election to Bush (a notion with no empirical support), in fact the issue of gay rights will in the coming decades do tremendous harm to the conservative coalition. As time passes, American public opinion becomes more and more welcoming of gays as individuals and as a class deserving of the full rights of citizenship. Just a few years ago, the idea that we would even be debating marriage rights for gays was unthinkable (and indeed, in one of the great ironies of recent years, it was the right that raised the specter of gays being allowed to marry as a scare tactic, at a time when gay activists themselves believed it was too pie-in-the-sky to advocate publicly). According to the Human Rights Campaign, at the end of 2004, 43 percent of Fortune 500 companies provided domestic partner benefits to their employees, a number that is going nowhere but up. Among the largest hundred companies, the figure was 69 percent, and among the top fifty it was 76 percent. Forty-nine of America's fifty largest companies include gays and lesbians in their nondiscrimination policies. These aren't just "new economy" companies—the most significant turning point on the issue of corporate domestic partner benefits may have been in June of 2000, when the big three automakers together announced that they would add benefits for same-sex partners, after an agreement with the United Auto Workers to study the issue. In addition, despite the controversy over "Don't Ask, Don't Tell" at the beginning of the Clinton administration, a two-to-one majority of Americans now believes gays should be able to serve openly in the armed forces.[18] While a decade ago upward of 70 percent of the public opposed gay couples being allowed to adopt children, the public is now evenly split on the question.

As on issues of race, two parallel evolutions have been taking place in public opinion. The first is that individuals have become more tolerant over time. The second is that new generations of adults are more tolerant than their parents were, what social scientists call a "cohort effect."[19] The change grows stronger over time as members of the less-tolerant older generation die off and their views become more and more rare. Consider a December 2003 poll for NPR, which found that while 76 percent of Americans older than sixty-five were opposed to gay marriage, only 45 percent of those between eighteen and twenty-nine were opposed. When the poll asked whether people supported "civil unions, giving them the legal rights of married couples in areas such as health insurance, inheritance, pension coverage, and hospital visitation privileges," 59 percent of the respondents between eighteen and twenty-nine were in favor, compared to only 39 percent of those sixty-five and older. In addition, supporters of civil unions outnumbered opponents among all groups under the age of fifty. A 2001 poll of high school seniors by Hamilton College found that 66 percent supported gay marriage, 68 percent supported gays adopting children, 79 percent favored protections against employment discrimination, and 77 percent agreed that "gay people contribute in unique and positive ways to society."[20]

American society is in the midst of a virtuous cycle: the more people there are who are accepting of gays, the more gay people feel comfortable being open about who they are. The more openly gay people there are, the more people know someone who is gay. The more people there are who know someone who is gay, the fewer people there are who can sustain antigay prejudice, and the more accepting society becomes.

But the stance of those in the Radical Religious Right toward homosexuality is unlikely to change any time soon. Since they believe the Bible absolutely prohibits homosexuality, they don't see any room for compromise.[21] As American opinion evolves, their views will grow further and further from the mainstream. Whether it takes ten years or forty years, there will come a day when gay Americans have full legal rights, and antigay prejudice becomes a hallmark of fringe thought. At some point, the national Republican Party will repudiate its own history on this issue, just as it has on the issue of race. In all likelihood, it will go through a period when it speaks the right words to the national audience but continues to mine antigay sentiment in the South for votes. One day, however, Republicans will stop doing even that.

Nonetheless, the idea that progressives are out of step on social issues persists—even when it comes to issues on which their positions have clear majority support. After the 2004 election, some journalists, particularly Tim Russert of NBC News, began asking Democrats whether they might consider changing their position on abortion. Russert, who never fails to go after Democrats with a sledgehammer while treating Republicans with deference and respect, failed to mention that it is the Republicans who are out of step with public opinion on the issue of abortion. It is the Republicans whose party platform advocates making abortion illegal, something few Americans agree with. It is the Republicans who have only purely pro-life politicians in their congressional leadership, while the Democratic Senate leader is at odds with most of his party on the issue.

In fact, the Republican position on abortion is held by only around one in five Americans. On this issue, most of the public is conflicted—not wanting to ban abortion but not wanting it to be too easy to get; agreeing with some restrictions but not with the extreme position that dominates the Republican Party. As in so many areas, the answer you get on a survey depends on how you ask the question, but a look at a range of public opinion data shows a clear majority of Americans in favor of legal abortion.

OPINIONS ON ABORTION

"Do you think abortion should be legal in all cases, legal in most cases, illegal in most cases, or illegal in all cases?" (ABC News/ *Washington Post*, April 2005)

Legal in all cases:	20%
Legal in most cases:	36%
Illegal in most cases:	27%
Illegal in all cases:	14%

"Which of the following best represents your views about abortion—the choice on abortion should be left up to the woman and her doctor, abortion should be legal only in cases in which pregnancy results from rape or incest or when the life of the woman is at risk, or abortion should be illegal in all circumstances?" (NBC News/*Wall Street Journal*, May 2005)

Woman and her doctor:	55%
Only rape, etc.:	29%
Always illegal:	14%

"Which of these comes closest to your view? Abortion should be generally available to women who want it. Abortion should be available but under stricter limits than it is now. Abortion should not be permitted." (CBS News, April 2005)

Generally available:	36%
Stricter limits:	38%
Not permitted:	24%

"In 1973 the *Roe versus Wade* decision established a woman's constitutional right to an abortion, at least in the first three months of pregnancy. Would you like to see the Supreme Court completely overturn its *Roe versus Wade* decision or not?" (Pew Research Center, June 2005)

Yes, overturn *Roe v. Wade*:	30%
No, don't overturn *Roe v. Wade*:	63%

Here, too, we should not forget that there are important regional differences. When the 2000 National Annenberg Election Survey asked whether people thought the government should ban abortion, only 22 percent said yes; however, the figure in Louisiana was 38 percent, while that in Vermont was only 10 percent. Yet in recent years the debate over abortion has been dominated by arguments not about whether it should be banned but over issues like "partial-birth" abortion or parental consent laws. Knowing their ultimate goal is not shared by the public, the pro-life movement has chosen these issues as a way of chipping away at abortion rights where they can. As Thomas Frank has pointed out, though, Republicans *intentionally* lose battles over abortion, the better to keep their base agitated and maintain the crusade.[22] When the Supreme Court struck down Nebraska's "partial-birth" abortion law because it contained no exception to protect the health of the mother,[23] congressional Republicans wrote a national law, *making sure to include no such exception*, so that it was guaranteed to be struck down. When that occurs, they will rail against "activist judges" and tell their supporters that the fight must go on, and on, and on.

Yet pro-life activists won the battle over "partial-birth" abortion the moment they devised the name.[24] As the right has understood for so long, the one who chooses the terms of the debate is nearly always the one who wins. In addition, progressives have another problem in the abortion debate. The language they speak—one of rights under threat—operates at an abstract level. As the pre–*Roe v. Wade* days of back-alley abortions become more distant, the pro-choice side has more and more trouble connecting the arguments it makes to people's own experiences, fears, and emotions.

According to the *American Prospect* editor Sarah Blustain, part of the problem is that many Democrats fear that acknowledging that an abortion is nothing to be pleased about cedes too much ground. "To this generation, the 'choice' of a legal abortion is no longer something to celebrate," Blustain wrote. "It is a decision made in crisis, and it is never one made happily. Have you ever talked to a woman who has had an abortion? . . . I promise you, such a woman does not talk about exercising the 'right to choose.' You may accuse her—and me—of taking such rights for granted, and maybe you'd be right. But mainly she will tell you how sad she is, how she wished she hadn't had to make that 'choice,' how unpleasant the procedure was. She is more likely depressed than defiant."[25]

I would add that whether depressed or defiant, her predominant emotion is likely to be relief. Bill Clinton understood the complexity of this issue, which is why when he talked about protecting abortion rights, he said he wanted abortion to be "safe, legal, and rare." This formulation acknowledges that no one wants more abortions to occur but also demands that women's rights be maintained. Progressives can expose the hypocrisy of conservatives who say they oppose abortion but also don't want teenagers to learn about contraception—a policy that when implemented nearly inevitably results in more abortions. In fact, rates of abortion declined significantly during the Clinton presidency.[26]

Columnist E. J. Dionne suggests a story one can tell about abortion that links progressive values, personal interests, and even some conservative values. A young woman who works in a factory finds herself with an unintended pregnancy. Imagine that she makes good wages, has health insurance, and knows that she can return to her job after a maternity leave. Will she choose to have an abortion? Probably not. But what if she is living month to month, doesn't have health insurance, and will lose her job if she takes time off? Will she have an abortion then? Probably.

Dionne's story shows how progressives can refocus the abortion debate. What if progressives framed all discussion of abortion around the question "How can we reduce the number of abortions?" The alternatives debated will not be about whether a fetus has rights or whether abortion is murder but about which policies will most effectively reduce the number of abortions. The discussion will then tilt in favor of progressive solutions. We could make "abortion reduction" a watchword, attaching it to policies on sex education, health insurance, and workers' rights.

Yet at the same time that some Democrats take a position on abortion easily caricatured as doctrinaire, others—particularly Democratic politicians—approach the issue by apologizing for their own beliefs. How many Democrats have said they are "personally opposed to abortion" but nonetheless pro-choice when it comes to making laws? If you say you're "personally opposed" to abortion but are pro-choice in policy, people will conclude that you're just a hypocrite. Either you're pro-choice or you're not. Either you think abortion is murder or you don't. And don't say you aren't willing to "impose your views" on other people—that's what policy making is about, imposing your views on other people. This doesn't mean you have to accept the Republican argument that anyone who is pro-choice just loves abortions and thinks everyone should have one once a month. Democrats believe, and need to say, that they understand an abortion is not cause for celebration and is usually associated with sadness, for a variety of reasons, but they also believe that it is the woman's decision to make. If you say you "personally oppose" abortion, you aren't convincing people that you think like them; you just look spineless.

On the abortion issue, conservatives have demonstrated that if you are smart about the arguments you make and the debates you shove to the forefront, you can win victories even while on the wrong side of public opinion. They are also aided by the fact that the most ardent pro-lifers are more passionate and committed, more likely to protest and write letters and vote on this single issue than are the most ardent pro-choicers.

This is also true of another of the principle "cultural" issues, gun control. Few gun control advocates can match the apocalyptic fervor of the NRA's shock troops, who see even the mildest restrictions on weapon ownership as the prelude to a communist takeover. Faced with the noise created by gun advocates, many people assume that the progressive position on gun control is wildly unpopular, but, in fact, most Americans want reasonable gun restrictions. Although there are regional differences, even in the most pro-gun region, the public is evenly split on whether the government should do more to restrict gun purchases.

OPINIONS ON GUN CONTROL

"In general, would you say you favor stricter gun control, or less strict gun control?" (Harris Interactive, September 2004)

Stricter control:	60%
Less strict control:	32%

"What do you think is more important—to protect the right of Americans to own guns, or to control gun ownership?" (Pew Research Center, February 2004)

Protect the right to own guns:	37%
Control gun ownership:	58%

"Do you think that gun control laws in this country should be more strict than they are now, less strict, or are gun control laws about right now?" (*Time Magazine*, October 2004)

More strict:	49%
Less strict:	8%
About right:	38%

"Would you like to see gun laws in this country made more strict, less strict, or remain as they are?" (Gallup, February 2004)

More strict:	53%
Less strict:	12%
Remain as they are:	34%

Overall, are you satisfied that [the assault weapons ban] has expired, dissatisfied that it has expired, or does it not make a difference to you either way?" (NBC/*Wall Street Journal*, September 2004)

Satisfied law has expired:	12%
Dissatisfied law has expired:	61%
No difference either way:	25%

Smart progressives will understand that it's unlikely that handguns will ever be banned in the United States. It's equally true that in some parts of the country, particularly the Rocky Mountain region and parts of the Midwest, gun control as a general matter is not particularly popular. Yet it's also true that those on whom the Republican Party relies on this issue are at the extreme of American opinion. As the chart below shows, even in the most pro-gun regions of the country, most people support some reasonable restrictions on gun ownership.

On gun control, abortion, and most other issues that make up the sociocultural matrix, conservatives are in the minority. And the conservatives who care most about these issues—and who are most vocal about them—are more dogmatic, more prone to extremist beliefs, more tolerant of radicals in their midst, more prone to embarrassing utterances, and less willing to compromise. The sociocultural issues are therefore the ones that offer some of the best opportunities to isolate conservatives from the rest of the electorate.

Grover Norquist calls his federation of conservative activists the "Leave Us Alone Coalition." The business interests want to be free of regulation and taxation, the gun groups want to be free to own whatever weaponry they please, and so on. But the conservative coalition is now dominated by a group that wants much more than

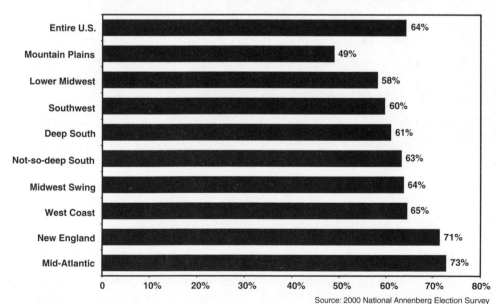

Should the Government Do More to Restrict Gun Purchases?

Region	Percentage
Entire U.S.	64%
Mountain Plains	49%
Lower Midwest	58%
Southwest	60%
Deep South	61%
Not-so-deep South	63%
Midwest Swing	64%
West Coast	65%
New England	71%
Mid-Atlantic	73%

Source: 2000 National Annenberg Election Survey

to be left alone. They want the government—in matters both real and symbolic—to embody and advance their worldview and their agenda. They won't take no for an answer, and they've given up being quiet. Their new visibility, however, is their greatest weakness.

THE NATIONAL SECURITY MATRIX

National security is an area particularly well-suited to the black-and-white delineations favored by many conservatives. "You are either with us," said George W. Bush after 9/11, "or you are with the terrorists." Congenitally intolerant of ambiguity of any sort, conservatives quickly fetishized Bush's "moral clarity," his love of the simple and refusal to "second-guess" himself—what most of us see as reacting to changing circumstances and admitting that somewhere in the past we might have been mistaken. Reporters went along as well, scolding John Kerry for his appreciation of "nuance" and advising him that if he wanted to earn their praise, he'd best banish anything smacking of complexity from his thoughts and utterances.

Here more than in any other area, the conservative need to appear manly provides the philosophical underpinning of policies affecting millions. Marginalized are the conservative isolationists of old, replaced by a tough-talkin', butt-kickin' American avenger, part Crusader and part professional wrestler. That virtually all of the Republican leadership of today found ways to avoid actual danger when their country called on them in Vietnam matters not a whit[27]—these are hard men who don't hesitate to deliver death from above to all who might get in our way.

In 2004, the Democratic primary electorate decided, with precious little deliberation, that by virtue of his Vietnam service John Kerry was the man to put an end to Republican attacks on the patriotism of Democrats. This was virtually the entirety of Kerry's alleged "electability." After all, a couple of draft-dodgers like Bush and Cheney would never question the patriotism of someone with a chest full of medals, would they? It appeared that the Kerry campaign itself was possessed of this belief as well.

But, of course, they would. *That's what they do.* The Democrats could raise George Patton from the grave and nominate him, and the

Republicans would attack him for being unpatriotic and weak on defense. The only question is whether the attack would work. For it not to work, the Democrat needs two things: to be seen as personally strong—not because he plays football or goes hunting, but because he has powerfully felt convictions and displays political courage—and to have a national security philosophy that can be understood.

After the defeat of 2004, some Democrats pined for a return to the "muscular liberalism" of Harry Truman and John F. Kennedy, ready to shed American blood if necessary in the battle against communist totalitarianism. Truman and Kennedy, however, must be understood in the context of where Republican thought was at the time. Those Democrats posed a contrast with a Republican Party that had a strong isolationist wing showing little enthusiasm for foreign adventures.

In 2006, the situation is utterly different. Though some Republican isolationists remain, the party is in the grip of a messianic vision in which the American military functions as God's mighty sword, smiting evildoers and bringing the blessings of democracy to poor people in dusty far-off lands, whether they know they want it or not. Next to the neoconservatives always wondering which country to invade next, it's awfully hard not to look timid. And Democrats' problem is that without the White House, they can *say* they're tough, but they can't *show* it. Meekly assenting to George W. Bush's phenomenally misconceived Iraq war doesn't make you look tough, it makes you look like a pushover, particularly when the results turn out to be so disastrous.

Naturally, the Iraq debacle didn't change President Bush's opinion on anything, but it has made many Americans wonder whether we're going about this in the right way. Progressives shouldn't hesitate to remind people that those who doubted the wisdom of invading Iraq—and who had their patriotism questioned as a result—turned out to be right on all counts, and the Republicans who supported the war turned out to be wrong on all counts. Iraqis did not welcome the U.S. occupation with flowers and candy. The war has dragged on for years with steadily increasing American casualties. It has brought untold numbers of new recruits to Al-Qaeda. There were no weapons of mass destruction or an Iraqi plan to attack the United States. The war destroyed America's credibility in the world—who would believe an American president who claimed to have evidence that a country like North Korea had dangerous weapons and evil intentions? And the public has grown steadily dissatisfied, with majorities now believing the war was a mistake.

Nonetheless, there are some factors of public opinion working against progressives. While Bill Clinton and the Republican Congress made some modest defense cuts in the wake of the Soviet Union's implosion, after September 11 defense expenditures rocketed back up, to the point where the United States now spends as much on its military as the rest of the world combined. It is hard to see how in the immediate future a Democrat could find a politically palatable way to propose meaningful overall spending cuts. This does not mean, however, that the public has an unquenchable thirst for more defense spending—a December 2004 poll by the University of Maryland, for instance, found that only 34 percent of Americans favored increasing defense spending.

Nor has the public unconditionally embraced the Bush administration's unilateral foreign policy vision. When a November 2004 Democracy Corps poll asked people to choose whether "America's security depends on building strong ties with other nations" or "America's security depends on its own military strength," the first statement beat the second by 52 to 40 percent. A similar question in an August Pew Research Center poll, asking whether American foreign policy should "be based mostly on the national interests of the U.S., or should it strongly take into account the interests of its allies?" found those choosing the latter, outnumbering those favoring mostly U.S. interests by 49 to 37 percent. In a separate question, 59 percent said the Bush administration was too quick to use the military in handling international problems.

These results suggest that the American people understand that as Bill Clinton said at the 2004 Democratic convention, wisdom and strength are not opposing values. Progressives need to articulate a foreign policy vision based on the progressive principles that enjoy wide support: a commitment to human rights, an unwillingness to send Americans to die without good cause, and an understanding of the importance of strong alliances between democratic nations. Despite the fourth-grade-level appeal of the Bush administration's we'll-fight-them-there-so-we-don't-have-to-fight-them-here rationale, most Americans don't believe that the Iraq war made America safer from terrorism.[28] And as the war dragged on, they began to place more emphasis on securing the homeland rather than on military action overseas, something Democrats had been calling for (and the Bush administration had been utterly negligent on) since September 11. When a January 2005 Pew poll asked whether "building our defenses at home to prevent future terrorist attacks" or "taking military action to destroy terrorist networks around the world" should be a higher priority, Americans chose building defenses at home by 60 to 28 percent.

The Iraq debacle has discredited Republican foreign policy and provided progressives with an opportunity to formulate and advocate an alternate vision based on safeguarding American lives and promoting American values. An intense focus on issues like securing the "loose nukes" of the former Soviet Union—perhaps the most serious threat to American security in the world today, and one almost completely ignored by the Bush administration—could go a long way toward convincing Americans that progressives are serious about national security.

But even if Americans agree with progressives on the particulars of foreign and security policy, they will need to be convinced that progressives have the toughness and the strength to do what is necessary to defend the country. This is an impression that must be built up via a wide variety of issues, many of which are completely unrelated to matters of war and peace. The problem Democrats have on national security isn't that Americans have rejected the solutions they have offered, it's that Americans approach national security issues already believing that Democrats are weak—not just on national security issues but in general. Saying, "We like war, too!" will do nothing to address this problem. Democrats have to convince people that they have strong convictions for which they are willing to stand up, and then they'll be far more likely to get a fair hearing on national security issues.

GETTING PAST THE ISSUES

The values of our society, like those of all societies, are in a constant state of growth and change. If we look over our history though, it becomes obvious that this growth is not in a conservative direction but in a progressive direction. The American people continue to become more open, more tolerant, and more committed to equality and liberty. This is not to say there isn't backsliding and backlash along the way or much more work to be done, but the movement is clear and inexorable.

The public opinion data we have examined point toward a clear conclusion: America is, in fact, a progressive country. Most of the items on the progressive agenda have support from a majority of the American people. It is the Republican stronghold of the South, and the conservative evangelicals who dominate political life there, that are the most out of step with the rest of the country.

If progressives were to conclude that this advantage is all they need to be successful, however, they would be making a terrible mistake—the same mistake Democrats have made in election after election. Their issue advantage provides not a guarantee of victory but a context out of which victories can be constructed. Progressives need to banish the idea that if only voters could be convinced to look at the issues, then everything would be fine. Their issue advantage is a starting point for public persuasion, not an end point. As the *American Prospect* editor Michael Tomasky has suggested, the Democratic advantage has in practice actually been harmful, because it allows them to keep telling themselves that all they need to do is get people to focus on issues:

> So a Democratic presidential candidate's pollster goes out into the field and comes back with data proving that 54 percent of the people are with us on this issue, and 61 percent of them are with us on that one, and so on. And so the pollster tells the candidate, "Just talk about the issues, and everything will be ducky."
>
> Republican pollsters, meanwhile, conduct the same polls, and they study the same data.
>
> They tell their candidates, "Actually, boss, we can't really win on the issues, so we'd better come up with something else."

Well, after the past six weeks, we all know what that something else is. It's character. That is, make the election about the other guy's character. . . . In a rational world (speaking of things liberals want to believe in!), they would win campaigns on the issues. And in fact they did win two, but that was only when they had an unusually articulate and charismatic candidate named Clinton (and when it was possible to win with 43 percent of the vote, as Clinton did in 1992, or when the Hobbesians nominate a septuagenarian hatchet man, as they did in 1996).

But the world is the world. Republicans understand the world, and Democrats do not. Republicans know that voters will respond emotionally to character questions, and they know that the media will lap them up like a thirsty dog. Democrats keep thinking that voters will do something as improbably nutritional as study a health care plan (as, surely, a scattered few do), and that the media will show themselves eager to write articles and broadcast discussion segments about health care plans. Both assumptions are folly.[29]

In other words, Democrats look at public opinion data and decide to argue based on *logos*, while Republicans look at the data and decide to argue based on *ethos*. But the way the American people relate to politics and make political decisions is not rational. There is nothing rational about it. If it were rational, Michael Dukakis, Al Gore, and John Kerry all would have been president. Electoral success isn't about plans, it isn't about résumés, it isn't about experience, and it isn't about ideas. It's about connecting on an emotional level through *ethos* and *pathos*—how people feel about a candidate, and how he makes them feel about themselves.

Progressives need to understand that campaigns are not about issues. Issues are a resource, fuel that can be used to drive forward the story a campaign wants to tell. We will discuss the stories progressives should be telling in chapter 6. Before they can tell those stories, however, they need to have a better sense of who they are and who their opponents are. They have to redefine both progressivism and conservatism.

4

KNOWING WHO
YOU ARE

Redefining Progressivism

Recent elections have become like prizefights in which the Democrats are wearing soft, cushy boxing gloves, the better not to hurt anyone. They stroll to the center of the ring and say to the Republicans, "Let's be civil about this, shall we? By the way, what are you doing with that knife?"

At the end of the match, the Democrats are lying on the canvas, blood coursing from their multiple stab wounds. And what do they do in response? They stare at their hands and say, "Boy, I really need some better gloves. Maybe if they had stronger laces. Or maybe if they were a different color . . ." Are we religious enough? they ask. Do we need to find a Southerner to be our standard-bearer? Do we need to change our position on abortion? On gun control? On trade? Here's a radical idea: stop looking for a nicer pair of boxing gloves, and pick up a knife of your own.

This is not a plea for Democrats to "move left." The belief that the key to winning electoral majorities lies in subtle tweaking of party platforms—in either a leftward or a rightward direction—is the kind of naive thinking in which conservatives would never indulge. It is no accident that Republican losses are not greeted with debates on whether their party should "move to the center" or "be true to its beliefs," because they understand that the laundry list of issue items that make up their party platform has only a marginal impact on whether they win or lose.

Nonetheless, these debates persist. Some centrist Democrats seem consumed with the idea that what their party needs is to purge its left flank, to banish Michael Moore into exile (as though Moore has actual political followers), and return to the "Third Way" ideology of the Clinton years. This argument is heard most often from the centrist Democratic Leadership Council, which Clinton once led. Many on the left, in turn, view the DLC as a bunch of turncoats who have sold out the Democratic Party's traditional supporters for gobs of corporate cash.

But the problem with the DLC is not its ideology—there is plenty of room in the Democratic Party for progressives and centrists, whose disagreements are far less significant than what they have in common. The problem with the DLC is that it is at heart a group of policy wonks who allowed Bill Clinton's victories to convince them that the Third Way is political genius that represents the one true path to enduring Democratic success. Clinton's victories didn't happen because of his ideology, though; they happened because Bill Clinton is the most talented politician of our lifetime. Today, the DLC offers Clintonism without Clinton, and it sometimes seems to forget that it no longer actually controls any levers of power. As an approach to governing, the Third Way has a lot to commend it, but as a political ideology for an opposition party, it only exacerbates the problems Democrats face.

In addition, people forget just how populist Bill Clinton's 1992 campaign was. He may have favored the death penalty, missile defense, and NAFTA, but he also promised universal health care. He aired ads blaming George Bush for layoffs and jobs moving overseas. He talked over and over again about "people who work hard and play by the rules." In short, though he had some conservative positions, Clinton understood that the core of his appeal was a connection to and an advocacy for working people.

Today, the first order of business for progressives is to define themselves for the public, to articulate the fundamental principles that animate their beliefs about government and society. They need to identify positions on issues that flow directly from these principles and advocate them forcefully. They need to learn new ways of talking about their beliefs. In short, they need to redefine progressivism, focusing less on *logos* and more on *ethos*.

Some Democrats nonetheless find the temptation to look for the solution to defeats in tweaking of the issue agenda irresistible (particularly when prodded by the press, which greets any Democratic loss with tut-tutting about how Democrats are out of touch and need to move to the center—a lecture they don't feel the need to deliver to Republicans when they lose). But particularly at the presidential level, much of voter decision-making is based not on evidence but on impressions and gut feelings—Bush makes me feel safe, Clinton understands my problems. This is what Democrats fail again and again to understand. Recalibrating their issue agenda simply doesn't register with voters.

It doesn't register because most Americans *have no idea* what the specific issue agendas of the two parties are. Saying so may sound elitist, but it is a fact backed up by decades of political science research.[1] It is sometimes difficult for those engrossed by politics to grasp, but most people are not particularly interested in public affairs, for any number of reasons. Some of these are nonvoters, but even many people who vote pay only fleeting attention to the political world. To take just one example, in most years, most Americans are unable to identify which party controls the House of Representatives.[2]

As a consequence, they make decisions based on a combination of actual information and inferred information. The latter is derived from what scholars call *heuristics*, information shortcuts that allow us to make educated guesses about where candidates stand and what they might do. The most useful heuristic is party affiliation: for instance, even if I have never heard either congressional candidate in my district speak about abortion, I can assume that the Democrat is pro-choice and the Republican is pro-life. Although the heuristic won't be accurate 100 percent of the time, it will lead me in the direction I want to go far more often than not.

Yet party is a very specific kind of heuristic, a clear piece of data.

Other kinds of heuristics are more malleable and thus more open to influence. We use a candidate's "character" as a shortcut, a way of predicting what that individual will do and how he or she will react to events and circumstances we can't yet foresee. Even if we are not consciously thinking about our decision in this way, when we are left with the impression that a candidate is trustworthy, intelligent, or genuine, we believe that these qualities will correlate with the kinds of policy moves we favor. Since people do it all the time in their daily lives, they are very adept at making judgments about character quickly and with only the barest pieces of evidence to go on.

The question is not whether citizens will make character assessments—they will—but whether the character assessments they make are well-grounded and relevant. Many progressives recoil when they hear some Christians say that they voted for George W. Bush because he is born-again.[3] For those people, however, Bush's religion suggested that he would act in a particular way and pursue particular policies, so it provided an adequate information shortcut (whether this conclusion was a reasonable one, given Bush's record, is another matter).

As we saw in the previous chapter, the issue terrain overwhelmingly favors progressive candidates. Republicans understand this; consequently, they focus elections on character in part because they have no choice. Yes, in certain regions of the country their issue agenda is overwhelmingly popular, but in national elections they have found ways to talk about issues that aren't really about issues at all. They have worked long and hard to build up an image of their party that can serve as a default in the absence of other information, establishing an *ethos* about both the party in general and their candidates in particular. Voters in 2004 may not have been able to tell you the differences between Bush's and Kerry's plans for Iraq, but they knew that Bush was strong and Kerry was weak. This was the message of the Bush campaign, delivered relentlessly, hammered home in every ad, every speech, nearly every utterance.

In contrast, Kerry was much more likely to take the laundry-list approach. Consider this television ad from early in the general election campaign:

As President I'll set a few clear national priorities for America. First, we will keep this country safe and secure. Second, I'll put an end to tax incentives that encourage American companies to ship jobs overseas. And third, we'll invest in education and health care. My priorities are jobs and health care. My commitment is to defend this country. I'm John Kerry and I approved this message because together we can build a stronger America.

Without a unifying theme, what you get is this list of carefully poll-tested issue positions. Each one garners overwhelming support from the public, but as an argument for Kerry's candidacy this ad has almost no persuasive value. By trying to say everything, it says virtually nothing. One Kerry staffer told the *New Republic* after the election, "I remember one day [senior communication strategist Joe] Lockhart saying, after watching the evening news, 'We have no message.'"[4]

In contrast, conservative identity is so firmly established that it provides an easy template for every campaign. When a Republican says that he is strong on defense and the Democrat is weak, he is not laboring to convince voters of something they haven't contemplated before, he is activating the sets of associations that are already present in their minds. These associations—what psychologists call *schemas*—are networks of connected ideas that are established through consistent reiteration. Because we can't have every piece of information in our memory available for easy reference, we link pieces of data together. For many voters, merely calling someone a "liberal" is like pushing a button in their heads that lights up a set of related ideas: weak, permissive, wants to raise taxes, loves big government.

Constructing these schemas takes time and endless repetition—just what conservatives have been doing for decades. If progressives want to succeed over the long term, they need to construct a positive schema for "progressive" and a negative schema for "conservative." Issues have a part to play in this reconstruction, but only if they are wielded with an eye toward more generalized ideas about who conservatives and progressives are. Mark Schmitt, who writes the blog the Decembrist, put it well when he observed in 2004 that the very separation between issues and character is mistaken; the better way to understand it would be to say that issues are *about* character:

> If I were running the issues department of the Kerry campaign, or any campaign, the sign above my desk would not be James Carville's "It's the Economy Stupid": my sign would say, *"It's not what you say about the issues, it's what the issues say about you."* That is, as a candidate, you must choose to emphasize issues not because they poll well or are objectively our biggest problems, but because they best show the kind of person you are, and not just how you would deal with that particular issue, but others yet to rear their heads. The best illustration of that is John McCain. The most admired political figure achieved his status in large part by his crusade for campaign finance reform. I've seen all the polls on this for seven or eight years, and "campaign finance reform," as an issue, is of interest to at most 5% of the public. I'd like for it to be otherwise, but it's not. And yet, for McCain, campaign finance reform is the perfect issue. It's tells a story about his independence, and his persistence, and it gives him a populist message without having to embrace more liberal economic policies.[5]

We can apply this principle not just to candidates but to a broader ideology like progressivism. The issues progressives choose to push in a high-profile way should be chosen not just because they're right, but for what they say about progressivism. In other words, issues should be thought of as a way of arguing through *ethos*.

Let's take the example of a constitutional amendment to do away with the Electoral College. Progressives often complain that conservative positions are simple enough to fit on a bumper sticker, while progressive positions are nuanced and complex, giving conservatives an advantage in public debate. But here is a case where just the opposite is true. The progressive position is this: every American should have an equal say in who his or her president is. Simple as that. What's the conservative position? A series of indefensible claims. *It's part of the American political tradition.* Well, so was slavery and the disenfranchisement of women, until we decided they weren't consistent with our values. *The Founders didn't believe in direct democracy.* True enough. The whole point of the Electoral College was to put a brake on the passions of the public—but I'd like to hear conservatives get up and defend the idea that the masses are too stupid to elect their president. *The Electoral College forces presidential candidates to seek votes in the entire country instead of just piling up votes in big cities.* This is just false—presidential candidates go only where the polls are close, which means most Americans—including those who live in states like California, New York, and Texas—get no attention whatsoever.

Some will contend that amending the Constitution is extraordinarily difficult, and given the inevitable opposition of Republicans—whose power depends on the Electoral College—it stands little chance of gaining the supermajority necessary to become law. That doesn't matter, though. Not only is doing away with the Electoral College the right thing to do, advocating it helps build the identity of progressivism. It's about fairness, it's about equality, it's about eliminating special privileges. It doesn't matter if the special privilege is a tax break enjoyed by a corporation or the disproportionate votes allocated to the people of North Dakota. The principle is the same—in the progressive vision of America, everyone is treated equally and has an equal voice. Force conservatives to defend the Electoral College, and they'll wind up defining themselves in the way progressives want them defined.

This is an issue on which the progressive position is principled, simple, easy to understand, and in accord with American values. The conservative position is power-driven, complex, illogical, and antidemocratic. As an added benefit, strong majorities of the American people already favor eliminating the Electoral College (the figure in a 2004 Gallup poll was 61 percent). A debate on the Electoral College—no matter what its practical outcome—would help convince voters that progressives believe in democracy, while conservatives want to rig the game so they can win.

MAPPING OUT A RHETORICAL STRATEGY

If progressives are to make issues say something about them, they have to approach each debate by mapping out a rhetorical strategy that serves both short-term and long-term goals. The question isn't only how the present debate will enable them to carry the day, but how the arguments they make serve the larger goal of enhancing the image of progressivism and discrediting conservatism.

Fortunately, the most effective short-term arguments are also usually those that have the most long-term benefits. We should start with an understanding that we can divide our motivations in the political world into two large groups, interests and values. In other words, each citizen is open to persuasion on two basic questions, "What's good for me?" and "What's good?"

As an example, let's take President Bush's 2003 effort to eliminate taxes on stock dividends. Among the standard talking points was that more than half of all American adults now own stock. What they didn't say, of course, was that most of these are people who have some mutual funds or 401(k) accounts, out of which they get little to nothing in dividends. The point, however, was to take a policy whose benefits were targeted narrowly at wealthy investors and convince everyone else that it was in their interests as well.

This was the interest justification. The value justification was the argument that taxing dividends amounts to "double taxation" because the corporation pays taxes, then the shareholder pays taxes—whether it affects you or not, it's just wrong. This argument was also utterly phony, since almost any tax on anything is double, triple, or quadruple taxation—for instance, you get taxed on your income and then you buy groceries and the supermarket pays taxes; that's double taxation, too.

But Republicans had an interest justification and a value justification that both grew from a core Republican principle, that taxes are inherently bad. Winning approval for the tax cut may have been a nearly foregone conclusion given their control of Congress and lockstep Republican unity, but the debate had a further benefit: it reiterated for voters who Republicans are and what they believe. As such, it served both their short-term goal of getting a piece of legislation passed and the long-term interests of conservatism.

Let's apply this to a progressive priority, national health care (we can leave aside for the moment what sort of health-care plan we're discussing; we'll take up this question later on). Progressives advocate health insurance that doesn't disappear when you change jobs and can't be taken away by an HMO whose only goal is profiting from you and your family. This is the interest justification. The value justification is only slightly different: here in the wealthiest country on earth, no parent should have to choose between paying the mortgage and taking his child to the hospital when the child gets sick. No family should be one illness away from bankruptcy.

Underneath those two broad justifications, there are specific arguments about costs, public health, economic productivity, and so on. Each argument is tied to the interest justification or the value justification, both of which grow directly from the core progressive principle.

Obviously, progressives regularly make arguments that fit into this general structure. What they need is to make sure that *every* argument they make does so. In approaching each issue, they need to ask three simple questions: What is the most persuasive interest justification we can make? What is the most persuasive value justification? And what core principle does our position on this issue express? In constructing those arguments, we need to begin with the values justification, in order to tell voters not only what the policy will mean to them but what it means to us.

WE'RE ALL VALUES VOTERS

While many commentators reacted to the 2004 election by exclaiming that self-interest no longer determined how people vote, the truth is that the connection between self-interest and voting was always tenuous at best. In fact, political scientists have rejected the idea that Americans vote purely on their self-interest since the early 1980s.[6] But most of us—including reporters and pundits—continue to believe that while our own opinions are motivated by principle, other people want only what's best for themselves.[7] One fascinating study by sociologist Nina Eliasoph found that citizens talked about larger principles and the common good when speaking in private, but when talking to groups or to reporters, they found themselves speaking only of their own particular interests. "They assumed that the public forum was a place for plaintive individuals to expose their side of the story, to 'speak for themselves.'" Eliasoph's review of local press coverage bore out her subjects' impulse: citizens tended to be quoted only when they were explaining their opinions or participation as a function of their own narrow self-interest (or that of their children) but not when they were speaking in terms of the broader community. She called this "momism," the idea that you have a legitimate voice when speaking as a mom but not when speaking as a citizen.[8]

So when exit polls in 2004 revealed that when voters were asked what issue mattered most to them, "moral values" was the most common response given, reporters sat up and took notice. The question was poorly constructed for a number of reasons, and the 22 percent who picked the "moral values" option did not represent a higher number than had cited similar justifications for their votes in the past, including years when Democrats won. In addition, frequent church attendees comprised no more of George W. Bush's votes in 2004 than they had in 2000,[9] and the gay marriage initiatives on the ballots in eleven states made no difference to the outcome (two were in states Kerry won easily, eight were in states Bush won easily, and analyses indicated that Ohio's initiative gave Bush at best a modest boost, without which he would have won anyway). Always on the lookout for a new and seemingly unexpected story line, though, the press seized on "moral values," declaring that Bush had won because a wave of highly religious voters flocked to the polls to register their opposition to abortion and gay marriage.

Within hours, the most radical religious conservatives announced that they'd won the election for Bush, and he'd better pay up in return. Radical clerics like Jerry Falwell suddenly came out of the woodwork, popping up again on our television screens to proclaim not only their apocalyptic faith and message of hate but their undying fealty to the Republican Party. James Dobson, the head of Focus on the Family,[10] immediately took credit for Bush's victory on behalf of his followers. Bob Jones wrote a letter to Bush that read, "In your re-election, God has graciously granted

America—though she doesn't deserve it—a reprieve from the agenda of paganism. . . . Don't equivocate. Put your agenda on the front burner and let it boil. You owe the liberals nothing. They despise you because they despise your Christ." As their first order of business, they publicly humiliated the pro-choice Republican senator Arlen Specter, who was forced to engage in a pathetic ritual of genuflection to convince them not to oppose his ascension to the chairmanship of the Senate Judiciary Committee.

The newly vocal Radical Religious Right—simultaneously proclaiming its power and influence and wailing in victimhood that in America Christians are everywhere oppressed—made secular voters and lots of progressive religious people very nervous. What they may not understand is that these figures make moderate religious people nervous, too. The more the Radical Religious Right is seen as the face of the Republican Party, the better it is for progressives. This offers the opportunity to change the story of religion and American politics from one in which Republicans are the religious party and Democrats the secular party to one in which Republicans are the party of religious conservatives and Democrats are the party of seculars, religious progressives, and religious moderates.

Ironically, it is often commentators who themselves are *not* particularly religious who warn Democratic candidates that they'd better start shouting hosannas on the stump, whether it's true to who they are or not. Yet it's far from clear that dropping in some God-talk would do Democratic candidates much good. As Trinity College professor Mark Silk observed, talking about your own religious beliefs isn't necessarily the way to appeal to religious voters. A look at recent history bears him out: Bill Clinton could speak the language of the pulpit better than anyone, even George W. Bush, yet the church attendance gap was wider during his elections than it had been in the years before. Bush may warm the hearts of hardcore evangelicals with his religious talk, but most of them were going to vote for him anyway, and Democrats won't win their votes by simply dropping a few references to hymns into their speeches.

The idea that Americans are dying to hear more about religion from their candidates also doesn't hold up to scrutiny. An August 2004 Pew poll found that 10 percent of voters thought John Kerry discussed his faith too much, while 15 percent thought he discussed it too little, but 56 percent thought he talked about it the right amount. The numbers for Bush were not all that different—11 percent thought he discussed his faith too little, 24 percent thought he discussed it too much, and 53 percent thought he discussed it the right amount. Given that Bush discussed his faith far more often than Kerry, these results suggest that most Americans are comfortable with a fairly wide range of religious confession on the part of their politicians.

The degree to which Bush discusses religion is actually somewhat overstated. Early in the 2000 primaries he called Jesus his favorite philosopher and, when asked for details, said, "Well, if they don't know, it's going to be hard to explain"—a message that says to some voters, "I'm one of you," but says to others, "I'm not one of you." But as Bush grew more skilled as a candidate and a politician, explicit talk of Jesus left his public utterances, replaced by subtle allusions to hymns and scripture (understood by those in the know but unnoticed by everyone else) and extremely vague statements that referenced religion in only the most general terms. While I don't have many good things to say about Bush,[11] his direct discussion of religion, while extraordinary in its frequency, has for the most part been admirably ecumenical, careful to include not only Jews and Muslims but every now and again atheists as well. As a consequence, the number of people who are alienated by his religious rhetoric is far smaller than it might be.

The lesson for progressives is not that they should mimic Bush or simply talk about religion more than they are comfortable with. They have to find a language that assures voters, religious or not, that their political positions are driven by deeply held moral values. There are moral absolutes, and progressives should not be afraid of proclaiming them. It is morally wrong to tax work but not wealth. It is morally wrong to do nothing while 45 million Americans go without health insurance. It is morally wrong to allow polluters to befoul our land and air. By talking about the moral components to these issues, progressives can attract religious voters without alienating secular voters. And in fact, there was a brief moment in the 2004 campaign when John Kerry and John Edwards began talking about the values underlying their progressive ideology (something Edwards had done throughout the primaries). For some reason, though, they quickly dropped this rhetorical line without explanation.

The result was that voters didn't see them as people driven by fundamental beliefs. To take one example, Kerry wasted an extraordinary opportunity on health care, the issue on which Americans consistently gave him the biggest advantage over Bush. When talking about health care, he would always get mired in the particulars of his plan. So when voters bothered to think about it, they would ask themselves, does Kerry have a good plan? And few knew, because few pay attention to the details of plans. Kerry could have made health care a frontal assault on Bush's values, the values of someone who would let millions of people lose their health coverage while he was busy giving tax cuts to the elite, who would promise a patient's bill of rights and then break his promise, who would see parents being forced to choose between paying the bills and taking their kids to the doctor and say, too bad, I've got fat cats to take care of. Kerry could have said that Bush wants health care to be a privilege, something you get if you're lucky, and you could lose at any time, while he and other progressives believe health care should be something that every American has, that no family should live in fear of the financial devastation that can come from a serious illness, that a president who sees 45 million Americans without coverage and doesn't bother to do anything about it has shown what his moral values really are.

Kerry didn't say those things, but the opportunity will recur, given the fact that the Republicans currently in power don't exactly feel an urgent need to come up with proposals on health care. The principle is the same for any issue: using values as a starting point to talk about health care or economics or foreign policy gives voters a picture of who you are at your core. Only when progressives start doing that can they begin to counteract the impression so many have that they don't know who they are or what they stand for.

The values at the heart of the progressive creed are nearly universal; if voters can be convinced that progressives really are on the side of working people and are motivated by a belief in things like opportunity and fairness, it becomes much more difficult for conservatives to convince them that progressives are alien from them. The traditional conservative argument has been, "He may say he's on your side, but I'm one of you, and he's not." This argument is persuasive only if voters have a sneaking suspicion that maybe progressives aren't really on their side.

As columnist Michael Kinsley pointed out, placing an opinion in the realm of "values" is often an attempt to make it immune from criticism—it's one thing to attack someone's opinion, but attacking his or her values is considered out of bounds.[12] Conservatives have done such a good job of framing their positions in terms of values that the press corps has adopted the same frame: a strongly pro-life person is a "values voter," but a strongly pro-choice person is just somebody with an opinion; values play a role in elections in heavily Republican states but not in heavily Democratic states.[13]

Progressives need to change the frame that says that conservative positions reflect values but progressive positions don't. The way to do that is by using the language of morality, and yes, the word *values*, when talking about their positions. When pundits tell them to "talk about values," they're really telling them to move to the right. But progressives don't need to talk about values, they need to talk about *their* values. When they do, they'll find fertile ground in public opinion. A poll by Zogby International after the 2004 election found that when people were asked which "moral issue most influenced your vote," 42 percent said the war in Iraq, while only 13 percent chose abortion, and 9 percent said same-sex marriage. When they were asked what was "the most urgent moral problem in American culture," 33 percent picked "greed and materialism," 31 percent chose "poverty and economic justice," 16 percent said abortion, and 12 percent said same-sex marriage.[14] In other words, Americans do think about progressive priorities as moral issues. Progressives need to start talking about them that way.

When they do, they'll find their arguments resonating more strongly with voters. Research has shown that when politicians frame their appeals in terms of values, voters are more likely to think about the issue involved in the same terms. As a consequence, they make judgments that are less likely to be overcome by consideration of other issues. In other words, while an appeal to a voter's interest is often weighed against other issues that might offset it—his health care plan sounds good, but I'm not too hot on the tax plan—a values appeal is more likely to be seen as fundamental and to trump other interest-based appeals.[15] Whether something is a "values" issue depends on how it is framed. So conservatives want "values voters" defined in a very narrow way, as people opposed to abortion and gay rights. If we define everything else as outside the realm of values, only Republican appeals have this power to overcome other issues.

WHAT CONSERVATIVES SAY ABOUT LIBERALS

After the 2004 election, I attended a number of earnest panel discussions, some involving only progressives but some with conservatives as well, contemplating the meaning of the election and what progressives should do in response. Without fail, someone would bring up the notion that progressives show contempt and disdain for the good people of the "heartland." Unless they stop disrespecting people in the country's vast middle, it was suggested, they would continue to lose elections. The one thing I didn't hear—even when I stood up and asked for it—was any evidence that such contempt and disdain could actually be found in any meaningful quantity.

The idea that people on the coasts hold people in the heartland in contempt did not merely arise spontaneously, when heartlanders took a good, hard look at what coastal dwellers were saying about them. It was a *conservative strategy*, a means of stoking anger and resentment and maintaining the conservative class war. It has been particularly effective in the South, where insecurity and resentment of those who supposedly "look down on us" has been a core part of the political and social culture since even before the Civil War.

The importance of this conservative class war cannot be overstated. Without discrediting the idea that Democrats stood for working people, the Republicans would never have been able to transform themselves from a minority to a majority party. They did so by redefining the "elite" in America, convincing Americans to stop thinking about those who hold money and power and instead focus their resentments on college professors and Hollywood actors. Listen to conservative talk radio and what you hear is an endless recitation of the crimes of the alleged "liberal elite." The Republican Congress can appropriate $2 million of taxpayer money to buy George W. Bush a yacht, as they did in November of 2004,[16] and it will occasion not a mention, but should an obscure college professor somewhere say something that can be interpreted as unpatriotic, it will be trumpeted from sea to shining sea as evidence that liberals hate America and the Americans who love it. Extraordinary amounts of time, energy, and money are devoted to locating and publicizing alleged outrages of political correctness or anti-Americanism committed by individual liberals, none too inconsequential to become grist for the demonization mill.

This tactic dates back to the administration of Richard Nixon, who during his first term devised a "blue-collar strategy" based on a secret report drawn up by Department of Labor official Jerome Rosow titled "The Problem of the Blue-Collar Worker." As labor historian Jefferson Cowie describes it, the strategy was to "recast the definition of 'working class' from economics to culture":

The President and his staff agreed that the body of evidence they unearthed and popular milieu around them supported three basic, interlocking propositions. First, the white working-class vote was politically up for grabs and Nixon could be the leader to knit them into a new political coalition— essentially giving mainstream party legitimacy to Wallace-ite sentiments. Second, while Rosow's report brought up significant bread and butter issues and argued that any concern for workers had to include two million blacks "who share many of the same problems as whites in their income class," it was neither the entire working class nor its material grievances on which the administration would focus; rather, it was the "feeling of being forgotten" among white male workers that Nixon and his advisors would seek to tap. Finally, policy and rhetoric would be formulated that did not require federal expenditures or even wage increases—the politics of recognition and status would be enough.[17]

Cowie quotes from the Nixon campaign's 1972 "Assault Book": "As the campaign progresses, we should increasingly portray McGovern as the pet radical of Eastern Liberalism, the darling of the *New York Times*, the hero of the Berkeley Hill Jet Set; Mr. Radical Chic. The liberal elitists are his—we have to get back the working people; and the better we portray McGovern as an elitist radical, the smaller his political base. By November, he should be postured as the Establishment's fair-haired boy, and RN [Nixon] postured as the Candidate of the Common Man, the Working Man."

Sound familiar? It should, because Nixon's "blue-collar strategy" has provided the template for every Republican presidential campaign since. Those campaigns showed that the antielite argument— if repeated often and loudly enough—was sufficiently powerful that the GOP could move steadily to the right and continue to win elections. Resentment, properly nurtured, could make policy all but irrelevant.

Today those resentments still burn, and there is only one direction in which it is acceptable in public debate for contempt to be directed: from conservatives and those in the "heartland" toward liberals and those who live on the coasts. Had John Kerry had the audacity to criticize Texas as a petri dish of un-American values, commentators across the political spectrum would have bludgeoned him for being divisive and insufficiently respectful of millions of Americans. Yet George W. Bush routinely heaped scorn on Massachusetts. "In twenty years as a senator from Massachusetts," he would say, Kerry "has built a record of—[pause for comedic effect]—of a senator from Massachusetts." This was inevitably greeted with loud guffaws from the crowd of true believers. When he was in the West, Bush would say, "My opponent says he's in touch with the West, but sometimes I think he means Western Massachusetts." If he was criticizing Kerry's spending proposals, he would say, "His spending promises will cost about four times that much, more than $2.2 trillion. That's with a 'T.' That's a lot even for somebody from Massachusetts!"

Or consider this television ad, aired in Iowa by the conservative Club for Growth during the 2004 primary season:

ANNOUNCER: What do you think of Howard Dean's plans to raise taxes on families by nineteen hundred dollars a year?

MAN: What do I think? Well, I think Howard Dean should take his tax-hiking, government-expanding, latte-drinking, sushi-eating, Volvo-driving, *New York Times*–reading . . .

WOMAN: . . . Body-piercing, Hollywood-loving, left-wing freak show back to Vermont, where it belongs.

MAN: Got it?

You may have heard of this ad; its appearance was a minor story, discussed by cable anchors with amused smiles. But imagine for a moment the outrage that would have resulted had a liberal group aired an ad telling George W. Bush to "take his tobacco-chewing, trailer park–living, NASCAR-loving, *Field & Stream*–reading, grits-eating, right-wing freak show back to Texas, where it belongs." The controversy would have dragged on for days if not weeks, with commentators ruminating on how liberals can't hope to win elections if they keep showing contempt for ordinary people in the heartland.

Because it has been so often repeated, the idea that people on the coasts are condescending toward people in the heartland has taken hold not only among many Americans but among the chattering classes as well. And a related idea—that places where there are lots of Republicans are the "real" America, while places where there are lots of Democrats are something else—has become a staple of news "analysis," usually delivered by journalists who are themselves disconnected from the way most Americans, liberal or conservative, live.

In fact, it is this very disconnection that leads them to define what is authentically American in ways that are precisely in line with the conservative class war. Because they have internalized the conservative critique of the "liberal media elite," they believe that the things they are indifferent to, uninterested in, or unfamiliar with must represent the true, authentic America. They don't watch NASCAR, so it must be the most American of sports. They don't listen to country music, so it must be the rhythm to which real Americans tap their feet. No reporter would dream of criticizing a candidate for being unfamiliar with, say, the New York subway system, but the politician who displays an ignorance about the mechanics of a feed lot is sure to be chastised for his lack of connection with the good people who form the backbone of our nation.

To take just one example, read how Stuart Rothenberg, one of the most-quoted nonpartisan election analysts in America, described the "values divide":

> The Democrats have two separate, though not unrelated, problems in trying to deal with their cultural positioning. The first is that the party represents and reflects the broad cultural attitudes of the two coasts—essentially metropolitan New York City and California—rather than the values of the rest of the country.
>
> Notice that I didn't suggest that the Democrats don't have values. They do. Everyone knows that, and they knew it before Kerry spent much of his acceptance speech in Boston—and the Democratic convention as a whole—talking about the importance of values.
>
> The Democrats' problem is that, politically at least, they have the wrong values. While the two coasts represent consumerism, secularism, personal gratification and celebrity, much of the rest of the country values traditional family life, patriotism, religion, modesty and deferred gratification.[18]

Put aside how patently ridiculous Rothenberg's description of America is (one can't help but wonder whether he has ever met any actual Americans). Have you ever read something written by a "nonpartisan" as openly contemptuous of people from the "heartland" and the values they supposedly hold? Of course not. Only coastal dwellers can in the pages of our media be subject to such scorn.

There is a strain of elitism and stereotyping that runs through the Washington press corps—but it is nearly always wielded in ways that benefit Republicans and harm Democrats. Consider a speech

CNN political correspondent Candy Crowley made after the 2004 election, in which she related how when she sat down at a restaurant in Iowa with John Kerry, he ordered green tea but was told by the waitress that they had only Lipton's. "I advised the senator that he would need to carry his own green tea in Iowa and probably several other states, as well," Crowley quipped to her audience, going on to say that the episode stuck with her because it showed just how out of touch Kerry was with regular Americans.[19]

Yet it turns out the only one out of touch was Candy Crowley. As it happens, Lipton's makes six different varieties of green tea, which account for 20 percent of the company's sales in the United States. And if you happen to be in Dubuque, you can get it at that snobby elitist grocery known as K-Mart.[20] Crowley assumed that people in the heartland couldn't possibly drink green tea, but her ignorance manifested itself not in condescension toward Iowans but in contempt for Kerry. Crowley and her colleagues exalt a mythical, stereotypical heartland American, a character of simple tastes, simple ideas, and simple beliefs, whose very pores emit the aroma of authenticity. Naturally, this character has nothing but scorn for people like John Kerry, the type who, as David Brooks wrote, doesn't "know what makes a Pentecostal a Pentecostal" or "know what a soybean looks like growing in the field."[21] None of them would be caught dead drinking green tea or, heaven forbid, a latte. Odd, though, that of the states that voted most heavily for Bush in 2004, Starbucks has 36 stores in Utah, 34 in Idaho, 8 in Wyoming, 20 in Nebraska, and 27 in Oklahoma—not to mention the 536 in Texas (easily more than the 349 in New York).[22]

In short, the twin assaults on the "liberal elite" and the "liberal media elite" have convinced reporters—whose perspective shapes the national discussion—that conservatives are real, authentic, ordinary Americans, while liberals are effete, phony, and less than completely American. Any effort to promote economic fairness can, in a feat of acrobatic logic worthy of the Flying Wallendas, be dismissed as an elitist attempt to force working people to accept things they really don't want, like health coverage and good wages.

Few conservative commentators wield this club with more verve than the bow tie–wearing, Ph.D.-holding George Will, who regularly mocks the pretentiousness and condescension of intellectuals for regular folks. "Why does the left disparage what everyday people consider their fundamental interests?" asks Will, who knows about as much about "everyday people" as a golden retriever knows about thermonuclear physics. He offers the laughable assertion that "moral" issues are important because no one in America has any more economic problems; since Americans have been "emancipated from material concerns," we can focus on more important things, like Janet Jackson's exposed breast.[23]

Nothing is more fashionable in conservative circles than this Blue Collar Heartland Chic, the endless praising of common folk whom the typical right-wing pundit knows only from his or her imagination. Connecticut-bred Ann Coulter proclaims of Kansas City, "It's like my favorite place in the world. Oh, I think it is so great out there. Well, that's *America*. It's the opposite of this town [New York]. They're Americans, they're so great, they're rooting for America. I mean, there's so much common sense!"[24] Of course, Coulter doesn't choose to live in Kansas City, her favorite place in the world, but perhaps common sense is best viewed at a distance.

David Brooks has built a career on analyzing the consumption distinctions between the authentic heartland denizens on their riding mowers and the shallow blue-staters, latte froth drizzling from their pretentious lips onto the Arts & Leisure section of their Sunday *Times*.[25] You can hear Blue Collar Heartland Chic in the words of Michael Barone, who wrote a whole book on the superiority of "Hard America" over "Soft America," or Peggy Noonan, clear and away America's most ridiculous opinion columnist. Though she was a brilliant speechwriter for Ronald Reagan, in her columns Noonan reaches such breathtaking heights of inanity that she stands alone in the landscape of political commentary, channeling the thoughts of people living and dead or asserting that dolphins were sent by God to shepherd Elian Gonzales to the shores of Miami.[26] Noonan heaps scorn on the "intellectuals, academics, local clever people who talk loudly in restaurants, and leftist mandarins of Washington, Los Angeles, New York, and other cities," who do not provide soldiers to fight in Iraq. Instead, those soldiers "came from a bigger America and a realer one—a healthy and vibrant place full of religious feeling and cultural energy and Bible study and garage bands and sports-love and mom-love and sophistication and normality."[27] Cities, apparently, are places where sports are ignored, moms go unloved, and garage bands are nowhere to be found.

Perhaps no one embodies Blue Collar Heartland Chic more than Bill O'Reilly (though as a New Yorker, he is honest enough to put the emphasis more on the blue collar than on the heartland). O'Reilly's persona is built on his being a tough-talking regular guy who isn't afraid to stand up to the powers-that-be, armed only with courage and common sense—plus a television show, a radio show, and a syndicated column. O'Reilly delights in bringing on a hapless scholar with no television experience whom he can interrupt and call "perfessor" with a contemptuous sneer, the better to show how stupid "pinhead" intellectuals are. Though not as predictably down-the-line Republican in his issue stances as some of his Fox colleagues are, his boundless concern for the little guy does not extend to anything that might actually serve the little guy's interests. Instead, O'Reilly's advocacy is more concerned with stirring up resentment at the "eggheads" and the "liberal media." As the jacket copy of his book *Who's Looking Out for You?* reads, "Bill O'Reilly is mad as hell—and he's not going to let you take it anymore." Or, as another conservative talk radio host put it in the title of his book, *They Think You're Stupid.*[28]

As a starting point to countering the argument that the "elite" about which people should be resentful and angry is not those who hold money and power—after all, most of them are conservatives—but rather, those who are highly educated or who work in the entertainment industry, progressives should engage in a little rhetorical appropriation. No one called Bush's tax cuts "elitist," though they plainly were. No one calls the Republican position on health care "elitist," though it plainly is. Conservatives call progressives "elitist" so much in part to keep the charge from being turned back on them. So progressives should do just that. *Elite* evokes something that *wealthy* or *rich* do not: the idea of undeserved privileges. Most people want to be rich, but few want to be part of an elite. Progressives need to rejoin the idea of "elitism" to those who work against the interests of working people by using the word to describe Republican policies.

No single idea has been more critical to Republican successes in recent years than creating the perception that liberals are the elite. But this is also part of a larger matrix of contrasts that conservatives have attempted to build between the two competing ideologies. Among its contentions are the following:

CONSERVATIVE CONTRASTS

Conservatives are outsiders.	Liberals are insiders.
Conservatives are plucky underdogs fighting the status quo.	Liberals hold power and depend on the status quo.
Conservatives are brave and strong.	Liberals are cowardly and weak.
Conservatives are regular people.	Liberals are elitists.
Conservatives love America.	Liberals hate America.
Conservatives believe in individual initiative.	Liberals think government should solve every problem.
Conservatives believe in personal responsibility.	Liberals coddle the unworthy.
Conservatives believe in the free market.	Liberals want government to run everything.
Conservatives love freedom.	Liberals want to tell you what you can do with your own life.
Conservatives believe in the family.	Liberals want to undermine the family.
Conservatives believe in right and wrong.	Liberals are moral relativists.

We could go on, of course. Could one make a similar list of current liberal beliefs about the two groups? One certainly could, but one would quickly find oneself going further and further afield from what one actually hears in mainstream debate. Some people might believe, for instance, that conservatives want a permanent underclass of exploitable workers, while liberals want everyone to have opportunity, but few politicians or commentators will come out and say it so starkly. Conservatives, on the other hand, do not hesitate to state these contrasts in the bluntest of terms. Liberals are more likely to argue that conservatives are wrong about issues, have made serious and damaging mistakes, and have used their power in the government and the media to hoodwink Americans into going along with a dangerous agenda. For their part, however, conservatives say liberals are not just wrong but are outright traitors who want to destroy our country and all it represents (let liberals get a bit aggressive—as they did in criticizing George W. Bush during the 2004 campaign—and conservatives pretend to be shocked at the "political hate speech"). Consider the titles of some offerings from Regnery, the premier conservative publishing house: *Invasion Within: Overcoming the Elitists' Attack on Moral Values and the American Way; Outrage: How Gay Activists and Liberal Judges Are Trashing Democracy to Redefine Marriage; Reckless Disregard: How Liberal Democrats Undercut Our Military, Endanger Our Soldiers, and Jeopardize Our Security; Persecution: How Liberals Are Waging War against Christianity; Useful Idiots: How Liberals Got It Wrong in the Cold War and Still Blame America First; Unholy Alliance: Radical Islam and the American Left*. The message couldn't be clearer: liberals are not patriotic Americans with different views about the nature of government and the path toward a better country but sinister enemies with whom there can be no compromise.

Unlike most of the arguments that liberals make, those listed previously are powerful in part because they provide contrasts between the two ideological groups, telling people something about conservatives and liberals at the same time. Every conservative argument has a mirror image, the awful thing they want people to believe about liberals. Progressives need to build the same kind of contrasts—starting with defining what it is they believe.

5

SAY IT LIKE YOU
MEAN IT

Defining Progressive Identity

It is within the context of the conservatives' sustained effort to define liberals as everything anyone in their right minds should hate that progressives must begin to reconstruct a public identity. So just what do progressives believe? What is at the core of progressivism? The fact that we even need to ask this question is a testament to what a poor job liberals have done in recent decades in articulating and communicating their beliefs. As I said in the introduction, ask an ordinary person what conservatives believe and chances are he'll offer a few simple ideas that conservatives constantly emphasize; ask him what liberals believe and he'll repeat a conservative caricature. It isn't surprising, given that the only ones undertaking a systematic effort to define liberalism are the conservatives.

The worldview that progressives share has at its heart a vision of community, equality, tolerance, mutual responsibility, individual freedom, systems that operate fairly, and a government that serves the many and not just the few. How can we put all these ideas together into a single statement of belief? The answer is that *progressives believe we're all in it together*. What does it mean to say we're all in it together? It means every individual's freedom and opportunity must be valued. It means we have responsibilities to one another. It means we believe government's purpose is to protect its citizens and improve their lives. It means that we look for solutions that work for all of us.

Apart from summing up the progressive vision, this establishes a contrast with conservatives, who believe we're all on our own and we're all out for ourselves. The idea that we're all in it together unites the worldviews of the more affluent, highly educated progressives and the blue-collar workers who may be more conservative on some social issues. It also tells a story about who progressives are and why they advocate the things they do. From there, we can construct a hierarchy of progressive identity, traveling through abstract principles down to specific policy goals:

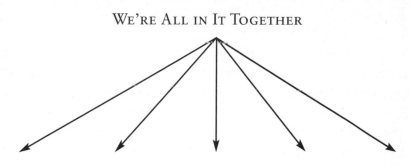

WE'RE ALL IN IT TOGETHER

Government That Works for Everyone	Opportunity	Security	Individual Freedom	Progress
Fair taxes	Support for education	Social Security	Equal rights for all	Energy independence
Corporate accountability	Student loans	Universal health care	Privacy	Community Internet
Consumer protection	Small business loans	Family leave	Freedom of expression	Investment in medical research
Workplace protection	Living wage	International cooperation	Safe and legal abortion	
Fair elections	Support for unions	Real homeland security	Access to contraception	Investment in infrastructure
Honest government			Civil rights	
Environmental protection				

While at first glance it may look complex, this pyramid is actually quite simple: a single summation of progressivism that leads to five fundamental principles, under which we can place almost any issue. In fact, it is more coherent than the Four Pillars of Conservatism. There is no particular reason why traditional values and small government should go together—indeed, they are often at odds. But the idea that we're all in it together is something to which the progressive position on nearly any issue can ultimately be traced.

The purpose of arraying various issues this way is to be able to trace a specific position or goal back to the principle it serves, and from there back to the fundamental notion lying at the heart of progressivism. The point is not that this entire pyramid will be put on a bumper sticker, but that it offers a way of picturing progressive values that suggests how one can talk about them. Nor is it the case that one could not imagine a single progressive position that could not fit under one of the five principles or be traced back to the idea that we're all in it together, just as there are some conservative positions completely unrelated to the Four Pillars. But it is comprehensive and encompassing enough, and true enough to the fundamentals of progressivism, that any progressive should be able to see it as a fair summation of what he or she believes.

Some might protest that this sounds too collectivist, that conservatives will just caricature it as socialistic. It has long been understood that Americans tend to be more individualistic than are residents of other Western democracies; even Alexis de Tocqueville noted that American individualism made efforts to unite communities difficult. This is one explanation for the fact that a strong socialist movement could never be established in the United States as it was in Europe.

But conservatives will attempt to caricature *anything* progressives say about themselves. The idea that we're all in it together happens to be the truth of what progressives believe, so they have to make a case for it. And it would be a mistake to conclude that appeals to the common good are destined to fail. Americans may believe that we are each responsible for our own fate, but they also believe we have obligations to one another. The idea that we're all in it together puts our own liberties and interests in a larger context that shows how each of us benefits from policies that serve us all. For instance, why do progressives believe in student loans? Because we believe everyone deserves educational opportunity. And we believe everyone deserves opportunity because we're all in it together—when a young person gets an education, she gets a better job, she offers more opportunity to her children, she helps to build her community, and we all gain in the end. Our values and our interests are united as each of us benefits from creating a moral society. The idea that we're all in it together must be presented not as a call for people to subvert their own interests but to see where and how their interests and their values converge.

With this hierarchy in mind, we can begin to formulate the contrasts that define both progressives and conservatives. If we think again about that person on the street, the goal is that when he is asked what defines progressivism, his first response will be that progressives think we're all in it together. When he wonders what makes a progressive different from a conservative, he should be able to draw on a series of contrasts that enhance the image of progressivism and discredit conservatism.

Both are critically important, and this is yet another area in which conservatives have been winning. While conservatives spend untold time and energy convincing the public that being a liberal is shameful, liberals haven't bothered to discredit conservatism. You will never catch a Republican saying he or she has some liberal policy positions, but Democrats regularly tout themselves as "fiscal conservatives" or say they have some "conservative values," as John Kerry did in 2004. To take another example, in debating Social Security in 2005, Hillary Clinton said, "It just is beyond me how people who call themselves conservative could have the gall to support economic policies that are sending the younger generation into the biggest deficit and debt hole that any generation has ever inherited."[1] Her statement assumes that a "conservative" is someone who is fiscally responsible and would never saddle our young people with debt. In other words, it says to the opposition, "Your ideology is great—everyone should be a conservative. Your only problem is that you're not being conservative enough."

If this project is to succeed, progressives need to pledge to never again use the word *conservative* with anything but a pejorative connotation. We can then begin to build a series of critical contrasts between the two ideologies:

PROGRESSIVE CONTRASTS

Progressives are working people.	Conservatives are the elite.
Progressives believe the government should work for all of us.	Conservatives believe the government is there to serve special interests.
Progressives want opportunity for all.	Conservatives want only those who are members of the club to have it.
Progressives want to create security.	Conservatives want to undermine security.
Progressives believe in respecting other people's beliefs and choices in life.	Conservatives want to force you to live according to their beliefs.
Progressives believe in progress.	Conservatives are stuck in the past.
Progressives want everyone to pay their fair share of taxes.	Conservatives want to tax work but not wealth.
Progressives think businesses should be good citizens— treating their employees and their communities with respect.	Conservatives think corporate profits are more important than the interests of people, communities, and the country.
Progressives think America is strongest when we act with our friends and allies.	Conservatives are too childish to realize that alliances make us stronger.
Progressives believe in a democracy in which every American has an equal voice and an equal vote.	Conservatives want to rig the game in their favor.
Progressives believe everyone— including corporations—has to take responsibility for their actions.	Conservatives believe in giving the powerful a free pass to harm people.
Progressives believe the government should pay its bills.	Conservatives believe the government should just borrow money and leave it to future generations to pay the bill.
Progressives are problem solvers.	Conservatives are ideologues.

Some progressives might look at this list of contrasts and say, "Do we really want to sink to their level? Isn't this just a cruel caricature of conservatism? Can't we just make our case without saying unkind things about our opponents?" To that I can only respond, you sure must enjoy losing.

The fact is that conservatives will continue to make their contrasts whether progressives choose to counter them or not. Politics is about subtlety and precision, but it is also about broad strokes. This list is neither exhaustive nor permanent—there are other contrasts one could make, and others that may become important in the future. But it provides a starting point for building in the public mind the identity of progressives as people who believe we're all in it together and thus advocate policies that enhance opportunity, security, freedom, and progress. Let us examine each in turn:

Progressives are working people. Conservatives are the elite.

There may be no single idea that conservatives have worked harder to subvert than the notion that progressives and Democrats stand for working people. Why do I refer to "working people," as opposed to "regular people" or "ordinary people"? First of all, no one wants to be regular or ordinary. Second, it encompasses the working poor and the middle class. Third, it puts the emphasis on people's responsible contributions to their families, their communities, and their country. There are still many people who identify with the Democratic Party because of its traditional support of working people, not because of its positions on abortion or gay rights. Holding those voters requires keeping the opportunity agenda at the heart of the progressive message.

Some might say, didn't Al Gore try to be a populist, talking about "the people versus the powerful"? Didn't John Kerry do the same thing? It didn't work for them, so why should we think it will work for someone else? The answer is that it did work for them; it just wasn't enough to bring them to victory. This wasn't because of the argument itself but because of the inconsistency and the manner in which it was made and the mismatch between the message and the messengers. As Gore's pollster Stanley Greenberg has shown, an economic populist message was extraordinarily effective for Gore:

not only did polling show that his economic message performed dramatically better than Bush's, but the period of the campaign when Gore was actually stressing economic populism—during and after his convention—was the period in which he went from a significant deficit to his largest lead of the campaign.[2] As for Kerry, the Bush campaign successfully attacked his character and heightened the salience of terrorism, the one issue on which polls consistently showed Bush had the advantage.

And neither candidate was able to convey to voters that a concern for working people was not just one among many priorities but their most fundamental value, something that would have translated into real action had they been elected. They approached the idea largely through the lens of policy proposals (Kerry perhaps more than Gore). As such, they failed to establish trust through the use of *ethos*, argument based on the character of the speaker. It wasn't that people didn't agree with what they were saying; voters just had a little trouble believing that this particular candidate would actually be there for them when the chips were down. Consider a contrast: did middle- and working-class people like Bill Clinton because of his expansion of the Earned Income Tax Credit? Of course not. They liked him because he felt their pain. He may have expanded the EITC because he felt their pain, but it was his sincere concern for them that they understood. Through his rhetoric, his style, and his policies, he was able to establish trust through *ethos*. The EITC expansion, like other policies, was seen as an outgrowth of his values.

Too often, when Democrats talk about potentially potent class arguments, they forget that nearly everyone wants to be rich. For instance, the Gore campaign criticized Dick Cheney in 2000 for the $36 million golden parachute he got when he left Halliburton. But the more cutting critique would have been that he got the money despite the fact that he laid off nine thousand workers and cut retirees' medical benefits, something that was rarely mentioned. During their debate, Joe Lieberman joked that Cheney had done very well in the Clinton economy. But what if he had said, "Dick, I wonder if you ever considered giving some of that money back to the nine thousand workers you laid off. Did you ever sit down with one of those workers and his family?" Few people would have voted against Dick Cheney because he's rich. But had they known that he got rich by throwing hardworking Americans out of their jobs, it might have been a different story.

The other principle problem of Gore's and Kerry's arguments was that they sought to appeal to people's very real economic anxieties but told a story in which their intended audience was a collection of victims. This is not how people like to think of themselves. A better message would have been one based not on resentment but on hope, that working people are not victims but heroes-in-waiting, who need only to have obstacles removed from their paths so they can achieve all they are capable of. If the "working people" message is built only on resentment of the upper class, it will fail, because people like to think that they are doing pretty well and, more important, that in the future they will become wealthy. Progressives need to establish themselves as partners in the story people tell about their own future success. Doing so requires a message based on hope and opportunity.

Standing for working people is not a statement of an agenda; it is a value from which agenda items flow. It's not only about appealing to people's self-interest; it's about appealing to what people believe government should do, and about the kind of public servants they'll trust to do the right thing. It's also a positive message that needn't necessarily contain its negative. To borrow Al Gore's phrase, being for the people doesn't mean being against the powerful—unless the powerful are trying to screw the people.

The idea of standing for working people has a strong economic component, but it isn't only about economics. And it's worth noting that while there is a spectrum of ideology on the left side of the political divide, what unites nearly everyone from the center to the left is this populist perspective. While there are left-leaning hawks and doves, the pro-choice and the pro-life, the advocates of gun control and those for gun rights, they all believe that government should be on the side of working people.

Finally, it's absolutely essential that progressives begin to reverse the perception that they constitute America's "elite," the holders of unearned privileges and scorn for regular people. The key to doing so is not only to talk about their support for working people but to define conservatives as the elite. They must do this by bringing up the inequities that result from conservative policies and by explicitly calling conservatives the "elite" and their ideas "elitist." Once again, this argument moves from *logos* to *ethos*, making a case not only about what conservatives do but about who they are.

Progressives believe the government should work for all of us. Conservatives believe the government is there to serve special interests.

Although many seemed to discover it only in 2004, it has been true for decades that when it comes to the role of government, Democrats talk about programs while Republicans talk about values. This has been the case in large part because since the New Deal, Democrats have been the defenders of government. When Democrats come before the voters, they point to Democratic programs that have wide public support. Though they were the opponents of government, Republicans wisely steered clear of directly attacking popular programs. Instead, they offered more abstract arguments, claiming that government is inefficient, wasteful, and corrupt (and examples aren't hard to find).

Though they were taking seemingly opposite tacks, both parties had a majority of the American people on their side, because Americans simultaneously hate government and love the things government does for them. Researchers have been aware of this paradox since 1964, when a study by Lloyd Free and Hadley Cantril found that a majority of Americans were "ideological conservatives," but an even larger majority were "operational liberals."[3] When asked general questions about government, they said that it shouldn't do too many things, that it should let the market operate largely unfettered, that it was more likely to do harm than good. Yet when asked one by one about specific programs, a majority expressed strong support for nearly all the things that government was doing. This paradox is captured in the oft-told tale about the congressman who is accosted by an elderly constituent who wags her finger in his face and tells him, "Tell the government to keep its hands off my Medicare!" Or in a more recent version, George W. Bush charged in 2000 that Democrats "want the federal government controlling the Social Security, like it's some kind of federal program."

In fact, when you ask Americans about specific government programs, they'll say they want more money and effort spent on just about everything the government does, from education to environmental protection to transportation to health care to the military (the only exception is programs targeted specifically at poor people, such as food stamps). In the last decade or so, 50 to 55 percent of Americans have said they want a smaller government with fewer services, hardly an overwhelming majority. This figure was affected somewhat by September 11, with a slightly greater number wanting a more active government since the terrorist attacks,[4] but the Republicans continue to sing their antigovernment song. The president himself regularly tells his audiences how good it is to get out of Washington, as though the job he worked for years to reach and keep is some sort of distasteful chore he'd rather just pitch so he can hang out with good, honest folk, watching baseball games and going to backyard cookouts.

Many liberals have a kind of civics-class view of campaigns, assuming the best thing would be if all voters read each candidate's platform and made up their minds that way, without all this bunk about "character" and "values." Back in the real world, that's not how it works. Republicans have successfully defined Democrats as the defenders of big, inefficient, wasteful, corrupt government. The answer for Democrats is to change the question, so that it's not "Should government be big or small?" but rather, "Who is government going to serve?"[5] Progressives can then supply the answer: conservatives say government should serve a chosen few, we say government should serve all of us— because we're all in it together.

Events in recent years have made it more difficult for conservatives to make their traditional arguments about "getting government off your back." After September 11 and Hurricane Katrina, Americans are more inclined to want government to protect them and become angry when it fails to do its job. As the Republican Party becomes more controlled by religious conservatives who are looking for government not to get out of the way but to enforce their beliefs on everyone, their claims about small government become increasingly hollow.

Progressives want opportunity for all. Conservatives want only those who are members of the club to have it.

Opportunity provides the link between underlying American individualism and the progressive belief that we're all in it together. With this contrast, we emphasize that progressives advocate policies that help everyone—not those with connections or a famous name, but everyone. In this, conservatives are undone by their own defense of aristocracy and crony capitalism. While Americans may believe strongly that each of us is responsible for our own fate, they also believe that success must be earned. So while progressives defend the social safety net, they should also go after unearned privileges as a way not only of highlighting the principle of equality but of undermining conservatives' claims of individualism. The unfairness of legacy admissions to universities and no-bid Pentagon contracts for well-connected companies resonates strongly both with people who believe in equality and with those who are committed to individual achievement.

Progressives want to create security. Conservatives want to undermine security.

Though President Bush's attempt to initiate the privatization of Social Security failed miserably, progressives should understand that they are working to roll back enormous progress Republicans have made in recent years on redefining what government is capable of. As the political scientist Jacob Hacker has observed, Republicans have had a great deal of success selling insecurity:

> President Bush keeps saying the "economy is strong, and it's getting stronger." But Americans don't believe it. Unfortunately, Americans also don't believe that government can effectively address the problem of rising insecurity. In a recent series of focus groups, the Economic Policy Institute (EPI) found that middle-class Americans "believe traditional relationships that formerly provided some security are disappearing." Yet they

also believe that "government is corrupt and neither trust-worthy nor a source of solutions." The middle-class response to rising insecurity, according to the EPI's focus groups, is blunt and resigned: "It's up to me."

All of which suggests that there may well be a method to the madness of Bush's calls for an "ownership society." The Republican agenda is to replace existing protections with highly individualized private accounts and then let the chips fall where they may. This strategy may help the affluent and fortunate, but it won't provide strong guarantees of economic security to most Americans. A recent analysis by Yale econo-mist Robert Shiller drives this home, predicting that nearly 50 percent of Americans who opt into private Social Security accounts based on the formula recommended by Bush's Com-mission to Strengthen Social Security would fail to break even, while the tenth of account holders who are least fortunate would lose around $50,000 in net retirement wealth.

Yet, while the ownership society can't guarantee economic security, it fits perfectly with the idea that "it's up to me"—that Americans are on their own in the new world of work and family. And, the more Americans believe that, the more likely it is that they will support conservative politicians who want to shift even more risk onto their shoulders. Call it the vicious cycle of insecurity—if Americans feel no one can help them, they will back leaders who won't. In the '30s, Democ-rats saw economic security as the keystone of a broad coali-tion in support of their party. Today, Republicans appear to see economic *insecurity* in much the same way.[6]

So it isn't just that Republicans aren't offering you anything, it's that there's nothing to be offered. The diabolical brilliance of this strategy is hard to deny. Instead of directly attacking Democratic economic policies on substantive grounds, it attacks the very idea that government can do anything for you in the realm of econom-ics. Once you've bought it, you'll sign on to anything Republicans want to do, no matter how inequitable, so long as it doesn't directly harm you. One more huge tax giveaway to the rich? Sure, whatever, doesn't matter much to me. Dismantle Social Security? If you've already convinced me it's doomed, who cares? The idea that there is an alternative that might actually help you begins to seem outside the realm of possibility.

If progressives are to succeed in protecting the programs they enacted in the past and in creating new avenues for government to improve the lives of Americans, they must counter this argument with their own case on the creation of security. To do so, they first have to shine the light on the point Hacker makes: conservatives are selling insecurity. They don't want you to be secure in your job, they don't want you to be secure in your health care, they don't want you to be secure in your retirement. Progressives, on the other hand, want to create and enhance security, because security creates opportunity.

Imagine what kind of opportunities you could seize, what kind of bold risks you could take if you knew your health care wouldn't be in jeopardy, if you knew you could get a loan to start a business, if you knew you could pay for college for your kids. How many people who had a great idea for a small business didn't want to take the risk because they were worried about losing their family's health coverage? The kind of security progressives want can unleash the entrepreneurial spirit that lies within so many Americans.

This message is infused with hope and oriented toward the future. It says not just "they're screwing you" but "they're holding you back from achieving what you could." If progressives are to make this argument successfully, though, the first thing they need to do is stop apologizing for government. Start talking about the things people *want* government to do, and you can move the conversation to areas where progressive solutions resonate.

Progressives believe in respecting other people's beliefs and choices in life. Conservatives want to force you to live according to their beliefs.

As our society changes, we are constantly negotiating the limits of freedom and tolerance. One of the great conservative successes of recent years has been the controversy over "political correctness," after which many Americans became convinced that it was liberals who were the tyrannical force in society, trying to tell you what you can say or even what you can think. While there were certainly some excesses of sensitivity, the campaign to publicize the issue followed the conservative template: locate individual cases where someone (no matter how obscure) acted stupidly, then repeat the story endlessly on talk radio and in conservative media outlets, painting all liberals with the brush of a few misguided nineteen-year-olds. The consequence was that conservatives managed to reposition themselves as rebellious freethinkers, standing up bravely for liberty in the face of the oppressive powers-that-be. Remarkably, conservatives were able to adopt the persona of the rebel, an anti-establishment pose lending them a patina of coolness.

The excesses of the Bush administration and the prevailing interpretation of the 2004 election provide the opportunity for progressives to reverse this story, stripping it away to show that conservatives aren't fighting The Man, they *are* The Man. Now it is the conservatives who are looking into your bedroom to see if you are having the kind of sex that meets with their approval, sending the FBI to your local library to see what books you've been taking out, and forcing their religious agenda on your kids in sex-ed and biology class. The newfound prominence of the most radical religious elements, those who want to impose their beliefs on everyone and install a virtual theocracy—like the town alderman in Tennessee who wanted to ban sports in public parks on Sunday mornings, because people should be in church[7]—puts progressives back in the position of arguing for personal freedom. They should make the grim, joyless, puritanical ideology of the Radical Religious Right the face of conservatism. Progressive morality is about how we treat one another; conservative morality is about them telling you how to live your life.

Progressives believe in progress. Conservatives are stuck in the past.

Progressives need to remind people—over and over—that conservatives opposed nearly every societal advance and expansion of freedom that today we universally acknowledge as the right and proper thing to have done. Conservatives opposed the elimination of slavery, then opposed the elimination of Jim Crow. Conservatives opposed the enfranchisement of women, then later opposed the movement to grant them equal economic rights and freedom from discrimination. Conservatives opposed efforts to clean up the environment. Conservatives opposed the elimination of child labor and the creation of the forty-hour workweek and the paid vacation.

And it is conservatives who continue to oppose the social, technological, and moral progress advocated by progressives. They rail against stem cell research and equal rights for gay Americans, unable to greet change with anything but fear and retrenchment, always nurturing the next backlash and seeking out the next scapegoat. Progressives, on the other hand, are the advocates of advancement, the champions of progress, the ones exploring for novel solutions to our problems. While conservatives believe the best America existed at some vaguely defined point in the past, progressives believe the best America lies in the future.

Progressives want everyone to pay their fair share of taxes. Conservatives want to tax work but not wealth.

For years, conservatives have successfully argued that taxes are just bad, an oppressive force from which we need "relief." When the argument is framed as "Are taxes good or bad?" progressives get backed into a corner where they have no choice but to defend taxes themselves. Shifting the argument to "Is everyone paying their fair share?" forces Republicans to defend the status quo, since the last thing they'll be doing is advocating a more progressive system. Indeed, as I write, the Bush administration is debating whether to do away with tax progressivity altogether. Fairness is a powerful concept that resonates strongly with people; when framed in this way, the progressive position has strong support. Consider the results of an April 2005 Gallup poll that asked whether people thought different groups were "paying their fair share in federal taxes, paying too much or paying too little":

	Paying Too Much	Paying Too Little	Paying Their Fair Share
Lower-income people	51%	10%	36%
Middle-income people	41%	5%	52%
Upper-income people	7%	68%	22%
Corporations	4%	69%	21%

In other words, people have a fairly accurate grasp of the reality of the tax system—that wealthy people and corporations find ways to avoid paying their fair share. Even George W. Bush used this argument in 2004, when he charged that "the rich hire lawyers and accountants for a reason when it comes to taxes. That's to slip the bill and stick you with it." The fact that Bush was saying this as a way of arguing *against raising taxes on the rich* may make your head spin, but he was tapping into a real public sentiment.

But it is vital to understand that Americans' feelings toward the rich run more to envy than to resentment. To some, this fact demonstrates the diabolical genius of American capitalism, tamping down class-based complaints by endlessly repeating that since anyone can be successful, if you aren't you have no one to blame but yourself. But the American Dream—that with hard work anyone can succeed—is deeply ingrained in the American psyche, no matter how selectively it works in real life and no matter the persistence of an American aristocracy. So when progressives are telling the story of economics, they have to make villains not out of "the rich" per se, since that is a group most Americans would love to join. Instead, the villains should be those who got rich by cheating or by exploiting the labor of honest people—and won't pay their fair share. Progressives need to argue that conservatives are working on behalf of people who are morally unworthy, the Ken Lays of the world.

The idea that conservatives want to tax "work but not wealth" perfectly captures the Bush administration's tax policies: cutting taxes on capital gains, inheritances, and stock dividends, while doing little or nothing to reduce most of the taxes most people pay, particularly payroll taxes.[8] At some point in his second term, George W. Bush will probably attempt to enact tax "reform" that will almost certainly follow the template of the tax cuts he passed during his first term, in which the taxes that the wealthy pay—on inheritances, on stock dividends, on high incomes—were cut or eliminated. The conservative tax vision is one in which only work is taxed, and the only people who pay taxes are those who work for a living. Despite the political risks of enacting a plan amounting to a legislative version of Leona Helmsley's assertion that "only the little people pay taxes," chances are that Bush and the Republicans will be unable to stop themselves. With a unified message, Democrats and progressives could use the issue against Republicans for a decade or more.

Progressives think businesses should be good citizens—treating their employees and their communities with respect. Conservatives think corporate profits are more important than the interests of people, communities, and the country.

For years, conservatives defined themselves as "pro-business" and liberals as "antibusiness." Progressives need to change the argument to one of good business versus bad business. Lord knows there are plenty of opportunities—barely a month passes without some new revelation of corporate malfeasance or undeserved tax loopholes. The fact that Democrats let the Enron scandal pass without suturing it to George W. Bush's forehead was a case of political malpractice so appalling it should get their licenses revoked.[9] While they said it was a terrible thing, they didn't say that Enron happened because of conservative policies.

The good news is that this contrast has already been established. Most Americans continue to believe that Democrats are the party of ordinary people on *economic* issues, just not on much else. In October 2004, a CBS/*New York Times* poll asked, "Do you think George W. Bush is more interested in protecting the interests of ordinary Americans or more interested in protecting the interests of large corporations?" Fifty-nine percent of people said he was more interested in protecting large corporations, and only 33 percent said he was interested in protecting ordinary people. Yet a healthy number of those 59 percent ended up voting for him anyway. In the same poll, 65 percent said John Kerry was interested in protecting ordinary people, while only 21 percent said he was interested in protecting corporations.

So progressives need to find and highlight companies acting true to progressive values at the same time as they criticize corporate criminals. Consider the contrast between Wal-Mart and Costco. Costco gives its workers excellent wages and benefits and still makes healthy profits. Because it treats its workers with respect, it has far lower rates of turnover and theft than other retailers do.[10] Wal-Mart, on the other hand, embodies conservative values: it pays its workers poverty wages, fights any hint of unionization tooth and nail, lectures its employees on "time theft" (i.e., spending a moment doing something other than working, like tying your shoes or going to the bathroom), and, as a number of lawsuits have revealed, has discriminated against female employees and forced its employees to work for no pay, sometimes actually *locking them in the store* while they work off the clock. Though the company makes a quarter of a trillion dollars in revenue per year—that's trillion, with a "T"—and the Walton family members who control it are worth $20 billion each, according to a report by the Democratic staff of the House Education and Workforce Committee, a Wal-Mart store with two hundred employees costs the taxpayers approximately $420,750 per year in social service costs, because wages and benefits for Wal-Mart employees are so meager that people are forced to turn to food stamps, Medicaid, and other services just to get by. While in the early twentieth century Henry Ford decided to pay his workers enough so that they could afford to buy the cars they built, Wal-Mart pays its employees so little they can barely afford to shop anywhere but Wal-Mart.

Progressives need to look for vocal allies in the business world whose practices embody progressive values and spend time talking about and through them. Simply addressing an issue repeatedly goes a long way toward convincing people you are concerned about it and are not reflexively opposed. Witness how in 2000 George W. Bush took education, an issue on which Democrats traditionally had a huge advantage, and fought Al Gore to a draw. Was it because people were convinced his education plan was a good one? Hardly—few people knew anything about it. By visiting schools and airing ads about education, however, Bush convinced people he was a "different kind of Republican" who truly cared about the issue. Progressives can do the same thing on economics, by looking for creative ideas to help small businesses and advocating for them in a high-profile way.

Progressives think America is strongest when we act with our friends and allies. Conservatives are too childish to realize that alliances make us stronger.

Foreign policy and national security are the areas that present the greatest challenge for progressives in bolstering their public identity. It will not be easy for progressives to articulate their views on foreign policy and national security in a way that won't be caricatured by conservatives as weak. So in order to convince Americans that they are just as serious about defending America as anyone, progressives should do three things. First, they should make themselves the defenders of the men and women in uniform. They should wage visible campaigns to improve pay and benefits for military personnel, an easy case to make at the moment, given the Bush administration's pathetic record in this area. The fact that a soldier puts her life on the line on her government's orders while back home her family is forced to turn to food pantries because her pay is so low is an abomination. The fact that the Bush administration attempted to cut combat pay and veterans' benefits is a betrayal.

Second, progressives should not be afraid to proclaim the importance of working with other countries. While the Bush administration may display contempt for alliances, in fact, the American public expresses strong support for international cooperation. According to a 2004 poll by the Pew Research Center, 54 percent of Americans said improving relations with allies should be a top priority. By 49 to 37 percent, they believed the United States should strongly take allies' interests into account when making foreign policy, rather than deciding mostly on America's interests. Fifty-six percent believed the United States' alliance with Western Europe should stay as strong as it had been in the past, while only 33 percent believed we should pursue a more independent course. Given the fact that the Bush administration has worked to elevate bellicosity to a value of the highest order, it might appear as if the American public wants nothing more than to flex its muscles, but this does not appear to be the case.

Third, progressives need to understand, as I stated previously, that their perceived weakness on national defense is not really about defense, it's about a *general* perception of weakness that transcends any particular issue. Once that perception of weakness is addressed and corrected—a process that will take time—progressives will find that the American people are more and more responsive to their plans and ideas about national security.

The worst mistake would be to assume that the way to establish "credibility" on national security is to simply adopt the Republican position on issues like the Iraq war. Incredibly, many Democrats believe that despite the fact that those in their party who supported the war turned out to be spectacularly wrong, it is the ones who opposed the war who are supposed to lack "credibility" on national security. Who looked weaker on Iraq, Howard Dean or John Kerry? The answer is clear: it was Kerry, who couldn't explain his own position and wound up being hurt by *both* his initial support and his later opposition to the war. Do the Democrats who voted for the war and continue to argue that we must "stay the course" look strong or credible on national security? Not a bit. They look like chumps. As of this writing, the American people by a margin of nearly two to one have come to believe that the war was a mistake. The lesson is that whatever you are going to argue on national security, you have to argue it not as though you're trying not to offend anyone or trying to maintain your "credibility," but as though you actually believe that the course of action you advocate is the one that will keep Americans safe.

Progressives believe in a democracy in which every American has an equal voice and an equal vote. Conservatives want to rig the game in their favor.

This contrast should be obvious to anyone who has been paying attention to politics in recent years. As reliable as the rising of the sun, each election brings new incidents of Republicans attempting to prevent African Americans from voting, whether through official channels (illegal voter purges, challenges to registrations in African American neighborhoods) or less visible means (mailings to African Americans threatening them with jail if they try to vote or telling them to wait until after election day). Whether it's the re-redistricting in Texas to gerrymander more Republican seats, the impeachment of Bill Clinton over a consensual affair, the recall of Gray Davis in

California, the defense of the Electoral College, or the refusal to grant voting rights to the citizens of the District of Columbia, the conservative principle is the same: they will do what it takes to win, even if it means ignoring or undermining democratic principles.

So when fighting on one of these issues, progressives need to argue not just that what conservatives are doing at a particular moment is wrong, but that this is what conservatives do: they try to keep people from voting unless they're going to vote the right way. Progressives, in contrast, want everyone to vote and want every vote to count.

Progressives believe everyone—including corporations—has to take responsibility for their actions. Conservatives believe in giving the powerful a free pass to harm people.

As we discovered in the 1990s, personal responsibility can be a powerful idea, one that resonates with traditional American themes of individuality and self-reliance. Wielded against criminals and the poor, it transformed cruel and insensitive policies into expressions of principle. No less a personage than George W. Bush said, "For too long, our culture has sent the message, if it feels good, do it and if you've got a problem, just go ahead and blame somebody else. Each of us must understand that's not right. Each of us must understand that we are responsible for the decisions and choices we make in life."[11]

This message can easily be turned back on conservatives and brought directly in line with the question of whose side the government is on. Conservative efforts at "tort reform" and deregulation can be countered with the idea of responsibility: when a corporation hurts someone, even if it's big and powerful, it has to take responsibility, even if we have to use the courts to force it to do so. If corporations aren't willing to act responsibly, then the people, through their government, can force corporations to do so. When they step out of line, they have to be held accountable.

Progressives believe the government should pay its bills. Conservatives believe the government should just borrow money and leave it to future generations to pay the bill.

For decades, Republicans were the advocates of fiscal responsibility, introducing constitutional amendments to force balanced budgets and railing at Democratic pork-barrel projects. Since the 1990s, however, the roles have switched: Republicans now offer weak justifications of budget deficits as they dole out more pork to their home districts than Democrats ever dreamed of. Ronald Reagan increased the budget deficit more than his thirty-nine predecessors combined; Bill Clinton created the first surplus in decades; George W. Bush created the largest deficit in American history. Bush wants to borrow $2 trillion to privatize Social Security.

Progressives should henceforth use *fiscal conservative* to describe someone who is willing to pile up huge debts for things he wants now, sticking our children and grandchildren with the bill. A "fiscal progressive" is someone who is careful with the public's money, invests it wisely in projects that benefit the country, and doesn't leave debt for others to pay back.

This can be linked to a counterintuitive but potentially persuasive idea: conservatives just don't know how to handle the nation's economy. As we noted before, looking over the last half-century, Democratic administrations have outperformed Republican administrations on average in GDP growth, job growth, unemployment, real disposable income growth, stock market value, and deficit reduction. In short, Republicans are disastrous for the economy.

Progressives are problem solvers. Conservatives are ideologues.

While it's essential that the public understand that progressives have strong values that animate their ideas about how government should act, the public should also understand that conservatives are held in the sway of a radical ideology that leads them to ignore reality and advocate policies that exacerbate the problems they claim to want solved. For instance, under the pro-choice administration of Bill Clinton, the number of abortions declined significantly. But George W. Bush's priority has been "abstinence only" sex education—which studies have found doesn't reduce teen sexual behavior but *increases* unsafe sex[12]—rather than reducing teen pregnancy and the number of abortions.

Why do Republican presidents perform so poorly when it comes to the economy? Because they're governed by ideology. When times are good, they cut taxes for the elite; when times are bad, they cut taxes for the elite. They always promise that the benefits will trickle down, but they never do. Progressives want an economy that works for everyone, and they are willing to do what it takes to achieve it; conservatives have an ideological commitment to tax cuts for the elite that is immune to facts.

By stressing the areas where conservatives are in the grip of an uncompromising ideology, progressives can begin to insert wedges between the factions of the conservative coalition. Highlight the retrograde social agenda of the Radical Religious Right, and the libertarian wing becomes uneasy. Call attention to the elitist character of conservative economic policy, and religious conservatives may grow dissatisfied that their issues don't generate more practical results. As the former Republican strategist Marshall Wittmann wrote,

> When I was at the Christian Coalition, I witnessed first-hand the alliance of the deregulation, no-tax crowd with the religious conservatives. Ironically, the rank and file of the religious right are hardly the country club set. They are largely middle-class Americans who don't rely on trust funds or dividend checks for their livelihoods. But the leaders of the religious right have betrayed their constituents by failing to champion such economic issues as family leave or access to health insurance, which would relieve the stresses on many working families. The only things the religious conservatives get are largely symbolic votes on proposals guaranteed to fail, such as the gay marriage constitutional amendment. The religious right has consistently provided the ground troops, while the big-money men have gotten the goodies.[13]

The religious conservatives may blame liberals for what they see as the excesses of Hollywood, but it is large corporations, most controlled by conservatives, that are the prime purveyors of the coarse entertainment culture, none more so than Rupert Murdoch, the conservative media baron and owner of both the Fox television network, with its relentlessly ribald offerings, and the Fox News Channel, with its relentless cheerleading for the GOP. Progressives should force conservative free-market fundamentalists to defend the worst cultural offerings presented to the American people.

Progressives also need to focus attention on the good things government has done over the objections of conservatives who couldn't see past their ideology to the interests of the American people. The G.I. Bill, Social Security, Medicare, unemployment compensation, student loans—these and many more were opposed by conservatives when they were enacted, because conservatives have trouble imagining that government can accomplish anything. The conservative wants to drill for more oil, but the progressive wants to use American ingenuity to discover new and better sources of energy. The progressive believes in progress, hope, and the possibility of a better day.

We could add more to this list of contrasts, but it provides a starting point to see how issues can be framed to create bright-line differences in the public mind between progressives and conservatives. We may also without too much effort locate specific issues progressives can push to the front of their agenda to highlight each one. The point is not that voters will have memorized each and every one of these contrasts, but rather that after they have been emphasized again and again, they will resonate.

Although we have been talking about progressives and progressivism and not about Democrats per se, much of this discussion applies to the Democratic Party as well. Democratic candidates who come before the primary electorate should be asked this simple question: "Why are you a Democrat?" I'd be interested to hear a DLC, "Third Way" Democrat's answer, because I'm not sure what it would be. It wouldn't be "Because Democrats believe we're all in it together," or "Because Democrats are the party of working people." So just what would it be? If a candidate can't answer that question in one sentence, he or she doesn't deserve any progressive's support.

GETTING BEYOND THE ISSUES

"In no other country is the Right defined so much by values rather than class," write John Micklethwait and Adrian Wooldridge.[14]

This may be true in the beliefs of those who vote Republican, but in its policies the GOP is as firmly class-oriented as could be. Until the unlikely event that the party ceases working on behalf of the most well-heeled Americans to the detriment of the rest of us, Republicans must be made to bear responsibility for their elitist agenda. The fact that they haven't is only partly a product of their shrewd emphasis on "values" issues; it comes just as much from Democrats' failure to describe in a convincing way the goals and the consequences of the conservative agenda.

So progressives need not only to talk about values but to reconnect policy to the very idea of values, to demonstrate how every government decision, every policy position—whether that of progressives or conservatives—expresses a set of values. The vast majority of citizens don't approach politics as a checklist of issues, looking to place themselves in one box or the other.

After the 2004 election, Christopher Hayes wrote an unusually blunt assessment of the undecided Wisconsin voters whose doors he knocked on, trying to persuade them to vote Democrat. Among the things he learned was that many people who aren't particularly interested in politics don't readily make connections between the conditions in their lives and their communities and what happens in the political realm:

> Perhaps the greatest myth about undecided voters is that they are undecided because of the "issues." That is, while they might favor Kerry on the economy, they favor Bush on terrorism; or while they are anti-gay marriage, they also support social welfare programs. Occasionally I did encounter undecided voters who were genuinely cross-pressured—a couple who was fiercely pro-life, antiwar, and pro-environment for example— but such cases were exceedingly rare. More often than not, when I asked undecided voters what issues they would pay attention to as they made up their minds I was met with a blank stare, as if I'd just asked them to name their favorite prime number.
>
> The majority of undecided voters I spoke to couldn't name a single issue that was important to them. This was shocking

to me. Think about it: The "issue" is the basic unit of political analysis for campaigns, candidates, journalists, and other
members of the chattering classes. It's what makes up the sub-
headings on a candidate's website, it's what sober, serious people wish election outcomes hinged on, it's what every
candidate pledges to run his campaign on, and it's what we
always complain we don't see enough coverage of.

But the very concept of the issue seemed to be almost completely alien to most of the undecided voters I spoke to. (This
was also true of a number of committed voters in both
camps—though I'll risk being partisan here and say that Kerry
voters, in my experience, were more likely to name specific
issues they cared about than Bush supporters.) At first I
thought this was a problem of simple semantics—maybe, I
thought, "issue" is a term of art that sounds wonky and intim-
idating, causing voters to react as if they're being quizzed on a
topic they haven't studied. So I tried other ways of asking the
same question: "Anything of particular concern to you? Are
you anxious or worried about anything? Are you excited about
what's been happening in the country in the last four years?"

These questions, too, more often than not yielded bewilder-
ment. As far as I could tell, the problem wasn't the word
"issue"; it was a fundamental lack of understanding of what
constituted the broad category of the "political." The unde-
cideds I spoke to didn't seem to have any intuitive grasp of
what kinds of grievances qualify as political grievances. Often,
once I would engage undecided voters, they would list concerns, such as the rising cost of health care; but when I would
tell them that Kerry had a plan to lower health-care premiums, they would respond in disbelief—not in disbelief that he
had a plan, but that the cost of health care was a political
issue. It was as if you were telling them that Kerry was prom-
ising to extend summer into December.

To cite one example: I had a conversation with an undecided
truck driver who was despondent because he had just hit a
woman's car after having worked a week straight. He didn't
think the accident was his fault and he was angry about being

sued. "There's too many lawsuits these days," he told me. I was set to have to rebut a "tort reform" argument, but it never came. Even though there was a ready-made connection between what was happening in his life and a campaign issue, he never made the leap. I asked him about the company he worked for and whether it would cover his legal expenses; he said he didn't think so. I asked him if he was unionized and he said no. "The last job was unionized," he said. "They would have covered my expenses." I tried to steer him towards a political discussion about how Kerry would stand up for workers' rights and protect unions, but it never got anywhere. He didn't seem to think there was any connection between politics and whether his company would cover his legal costs. Had he made a connection between his predicament and the issue of tort reform, it might have benefited Bush; had he made a connection between his predicament and the issue of labor rights, it might have benefited Kerry. He made neither, and remained undecided.

In this context, Bush's victory, particularly on the strength of those voters who listed "values" as their number one issue, makes perfect sense. Kerry ran a campaign that was about politics: He parsed the world into political categories and offered political solutions. Bush did this too, but it wasn't the main thrust of his campaign. Instead, the president ran on broad themes, like "character" and "morals." Everyone feels an immediate and intuitive expertise on morals and values— we all know what's right and wrong. But how can undecided voters evaluate a candidate on issues if they don't even grasp what issues are?[15]

Cynicism pervades American political culture, driven in no small part by a news media whose meta-narrative relentlessly hammers home the message that all politics is deception and the system is fraught with corruption. This makes practical appeals inherently suspect—if a politician says, "Elect me and you'll get X, Y, and Z," people are unlikely to believe him. He may be sincere, but people don't think the political system will produce results for them in a reasonable amount of time. On the other hand, a politician who convinces people they can trust him because of who he is and what he believes doesn't generate the same suspicion (nor, as it happens, does he have the same burden of delivering on his promises).

Consider the television ad aired more than any other during the 2004 campaign. "Ashley's Story," paid for by a Republican group called Progress for America, told the story of a young girl who had "closed up emotionally" after her mother was killed on September 11—until George W. Bush came to town. "Our president took Ashley in his arms and just embraced her. And it was at that moment that we saw Ashley's eyes fill up with tears," says a family friend in the ad. "He's the most powerful man in the world," says Ashley, "and all he wants to do is make sure I'm safe, that I'm okay." Fortunately for Bush, the cameras were there to capture him holding Ashley in his arms. This ad tells us nothing about whether Bush's policies on terrorism—or any other issue, for that matter— were wise or effective, but it establishes him as both caring and powerful, the man who will keep our children safe from harm.[16] Progress for America spent $14 million airing the ad in battle- ground states; there may have been no more effective advertisement in the campaign.

In his discussion of Wisconsin voters, Christopher Hayes also mentions in passing something that seems rare: he encountered plenty of conservatives who were planning to vote for Bush but also for Wisconsin senator Russell Feingold, who is one of the most progressive members of the Senate. Why? They "admired the back- bone and gutsiness of their Democratic senator." Feingold is unapologetic about his progressivism and often goes out on a limb to do the right thing. While there can be no doubt that many senators had grave reservations about the USA Patriot Act when it passed just after September 11, only one—Russ Feingold— actually voted against it. Even voters who disagreed recognized that it took extraordinary political courage, and it pays off when Feingold runs for reelection. In 2004, John Kerry won Wisconsin by just under 12,000 votes, while Feingold won his race by more than 330,000.

The late Paul Wellstone did the same thing: he turned potentially damaging legislative votes into positives by framing those votes as acts of courage. When in 1996 he was being hammered by his opponent for voting against welfare reform (the opponent called him "Senator Welfare"), Wellstone aired an ad explaining his stance by saying that though his vote might cost him the election, his parents taught him to always stand up for what he thought was right. The result was that even those who disagreed with him on that one issue saw Wellstone as a man of principle whom they could trust.[17]

Voters respond to candidates like Russ Feingold and Paul Wellstone not because they agree with every one of these individuals' stands on issues—most people don't know what most of those stands are. What they do know about those candidates, however, tells them Feingold and Wellstone they are the kind of people they'd like to have representing them. When progressives lead with their values, stand on principle, and offer clear contrasts between themselves and conservatives, they win.

For too long, progressives have believed that their commitment to all Americans could be presented to voters as a list of programs and promises instead of a statement of values and beliefs. In doing so, they allowed conservatives to define them and found themselves shouldering sole responsibility for government's failures. Until progressives understand that politics is not about what you'll do but about who you are, they will continue to fail.

6

TELLING THE STORY

Politics and the Power of Narrative

Conservatism has become a Hollywood movie, liberalism has become literature. Like the movie blockbusters, contemporary conservatives centralize action, extol the power of the individual to bend the world to his or her will, demonize enemies to the point where anything short of annihilation would be a surrender, operate from an absolute confidence in the hero's rightness while treating opposition to it as a form of treason, and promise the comforting catharsis of eventual victory that confirms everything that has gone before. Contemporary liberals, on the other hand, like the best literature, centralize thought and deliberation rather than action, fasten on human interconnectedness and the inability of any one individual (or nation) to command events, attempt to understand the complexity of life, operate from a decidedly wary position when it comes to absolute certainties, and promise no final victories.

—Neal Gabler[1]

The political world presents an overwhelming volume of information, much more than nearly anyone can hope to assimilate, understand, and draw upon. Likewise, despite how poorly the typical citizen performs on current-events quizzes, the problem is not so much that we have too few thoughts or beliefs about political issues but that we have too many.[2] In wading through the murky, rushing waters of politics, we need to find a way to categorize and store what comes at us so that it all makes sense and we can resolve the competing impulses that pull us in opposite directions.

As in so many areas, the way we do so is to construct stories that explain and organize the political world. Indeed, some psychologists believe that stories form the basis of all memory.[3] Perhaps above all, stories enable us to create order. They organize events in time, sort the critical from the irrelevant, and help us reach back to draw upon what we have learned.

A quick look at our information environment makes the importance of narrative more than clear. How do we teach our children history? We tell them about the Boston Tea Party to enable them to understand the American Revolution or about Rosa Parks and the Montgomery bus boycott to explain the civil rights movement. Successful preachers, from Jesus on down, have told stories to lead their flocks to wisdom or salvation. Presidents use dramatic tales (the Tonkin Gulf incident, the "attack" on the *Maine*) to convince the public to go to war. Advertisers offer thirty-second dramas to convince us of the life-transforming effects of the latest shampoo or member-stiffening elixir.[4]

The news itself is presented to us as a succession of "stories," most of which contain the elements common to most narratives. In recent years, reporters have become particularly fond of the use of *exemplars*, ordinary citizens who are used as vehicles through which a story may be told, to the extent that each day's paper or broadcast is little more than a succession of personal vignettes bracketing the actual news of the day. A typical news story begins and ends with the ordinary person—the individual welfare recipient, the family considering its retirement options, or the soldier on the front line—while the middle of the story contains the denser policy information that affects the lives of the broader class of people whom the exemplar represents. The stories told by the exemplars often shape how we perceive events, even when they are unrepresentative. As the Republican pollster Frank Luntz once instructed GOP officeholders, "A compelling story, even if factually inaccurate, can be more emotionally compelling than a dry recitation of the truth."[5]

So attentiveness to the stories we tell in politics is absolutely essential to any project of political persuasion. When a story is repeated often enough, it becomes part of our understanding of the world. Its elements can be evoked simply and easily, so that each of us fills in what we know of the story without having to be told the details. When we answer questions or make decisions, we are drawing on the stories that exist in our memory and selecting among them. The question for political persuaders is what stories people have at their disposal and which they will use when they approach a political issue.

POLITICAL STORIES GOOD AND BAD

In a July 2004 interview on *60 Minutes*, John Kerry was asked whether he thought President Bush injected his religious beliefs into politics too much. He replied, "Abraham Lincoln wisely avoided trying to invoke God on the side of the North or assist the South, but prayed that he was on God's side. I think that that's the lesson that John [Edwards] and I would bring to this. We are both people of deep faith."

If the story about Lincoln sounded familiar to some, it was because Kerry's running mate had mentioned it in a primary debate a few months earlier, when *New York Times* reporter Elisabeth Bumiller asked the candidates one of the dumbest questions ever posed in a debate, "Really quick, is God on America's side?" This was Edwards's response: "Well, there's a wonderful story about Abraham Lincoln during the middle of the Civil War bringing in a group of leaders, and at the end of the meeting one of the leaders said, 'Mr. President, can we pray, can we please join in prayer that God is on our side?' And Abraham Lincoln's response was, 'I won't join you in that prayer. But I'll join you in a prayer that we're on God's side.'"

The story about Lincoln invokes the nation's most revered president and demonstrates the speaker's faith while rebuking those who use God for their own narrow purposes. In Edwards's telling, it has a setting, context, characters who speak, a moment of tension (when Lincoln refuses the prayer), and a dramatic twist. Kerry's telling, on the other hand, is not really a story at all—it's more a *description* of a story. The moral is still there, but it loses all of its narrative power.

Literary theorists point to two distinct elements of narrative: the events or plot of the story, and the manner in which the story is told. Many theorists use the Russian terms *fabula* and *sjuzet*, or roughly "story" and "discourse," to refer to these two ideas. In the previous example, Kerry and Edwards are working with the same *fabula*, but only Edwards gives it a *sjuzet*. Edwards probably learned the importance of narrative as a litigator—after all, a trial is less a debate than a storytelling contest. The side that offers the more compelling and plausible story is the one that wins. In fact, research indicates that this is exactly how jurors think about trials: they construct a story about the case as it proceeds, often filling in story elements that are not presented in the trial from their own experience and beliefs.[6] Election campaigns are not much different.

Successful politicians don't just need good stories, they need to be good storytellers. Kerry—and he is hardly alone in this—often succumbs to the impulse to argue like the debate champion he once was, marshalling evidence and offering point-by-point refutations of the other side's arguments. But voters aren't debate judges carefully marking their scoresheets. They are an audience listening to the stories they are told, relating them to the ones they already know, and constructing their own narratives as they move toward decisions. To reach them, progressives need to assimilate storytelling as an essential part of the way they talk about issues.

This was Ronald Reagan's genius; the stories he told were usually crafted by others, but he could tell them with a skill unmatched among politicians. What made Reagan such an adept storyteller wasn't just being a good actor—although that certainly helped. As the communication scholar Kathleen Hall Jamieson wrote in her 1988 book *Eloquence in an Electronic Age*, Reagan employed a series of techniques that drew voters into the stories he was telling. He used visually compelling props and sets whenever possible. He used the stories of ordinary people to construct arguments for policies—a practice that has since become standard operating procedure but was revolutionary when Reagan first used it. (In his 1982 State of the Union address, Reagan told the story of Lenny Skutnik, who dove into the Potomac to save survivors of a plane crash; Skutnik was sitting in the hall with the First Lady. Every subsequent State of the Union address has featured the same technique.) He evoked common visual experience, "build[ing] his arguments from a visual scene he and the nation recently ha[d] experienced." Finally, Jamieson wrote, "Better than any modern president, Reagan understands the power of dramatic narrative to create an identity for an audience, to involve the audience, and to bond that audience to him."[7] Reagan's stories told us something about the subject of the story, something about Reagan, and something about us, the listeners.

We can see these elements at work in the film made for Reagan's 1984 convention, titled *A New Beginning*. In the most affecting section of the film, pieces from two speeches Reagan gave at the fortieth anniversary of D-Day are edited together with Reagan's voice-over:

> [*voice-over*] Sixty-two of the Rangers who scaled the cliffs at Pointe du Hoc, now back 40 years later to the scene of their heroic action. [*cut to Reagan at podium*] These are the boys of Pointe du Hoc. These are the men who took the cliffs. [*back to voice-over*] It was a very moving experience. They were what General Marshall called our secret weapon: the best damn kids in the world. [*cut from the veterans to Ronald and Nancy walking through the graveyard*] Where do we find them? Where do we find such men? The answer came almost as quickly as I'd asked the question: where we've always found them in this country. In the farms, the shops, the stores and the offices. They just are the product of the freest society the world has ever known.
>
> [*back to Reagan at podium*] "Someday, Lis, I'll go back," said Private First Class Peter Robert Zannata, of the 37th Engineer Combat Battalion, and first assault wave to hit Omaha Beach. Lisa Zannata Henn began her story by quoting her father, who

promised that he would return to Normandy. She ended with a promise to her father, who died 8 years ago of cancer: "I'm going there, Dad, and I'll see the beaches and the barricades and the monuments. I'll see the graves, and I'll put flowers there just like you wanted to do. I'll feel all the things you made me feel through your stories and your eyes. I'll never forget what you went through, Dad, nor will I let any one else forget. And Dad, I'll always be proud."

Through the words of his loving daughter, who is here with us today, a D-Day veteran has shown us the meaning of this day far better than any president can. It is enough for us to say about Private Zannata and all the men of honor and courage who fought beside him four decades ago: We will always remember. We will always be proud. We will always be prepared, so we may always be free.

The story of World War II is told not through grand tales of generals and armies but through a single veteran and his loving daughter. It is the very ordinariness of the veterans that makes their story extraordinary. Reagan establishes their heroism, then situates that heroic spirit within each of us, with the answer to the question, "Where do we find such men?" This section of the convention film is only incidentally about World War II—its main point is to tell us something about ourselves as Americans.

Twenty years later, George Bush's convention film, *The Pitch*, concerned only one topic: September 11. Though it is unlike the Reagan film in that the hero in this case is the president himself, it was crafted with nearly as much skill:

How do you tell the story of a presidency? How do you tell the story so far? The story is in part, but inescapably the story of a *man*, which leads inescapably to the fact of who he is.

The great mystery of any presidency is that the sovereign people of these United States choose a leader and then only, afterwards, in the day by day, do they find out who that person really is. History reveals this. History throws you what it throws you, and you never know what's coming.

Some things about George Bush are well known: his lack of

pretension, a sincerity both of action and purpose, a tendency toward candor. There's a sense of humor that is natural. He has even been known to kid around with folks.

But some things about him aren't well-known at all. When you know him and work with him, what you're struck by is not the secrets that you have to keep, but the truths you love to tell. He doesn't like to talk about them. But maybe when we look back at this era and this man, we will ask, what do a bullhorn and a baseball have in common? What truths can they tell? Which is another way of saying, what did George W. Bush do? Who did he become? And how did that help us?

The film then shows a series of events around September 11— not decisions Bush made or actions he took, but interactions with individuals, including the endlessly repeated pictures of him vowing revenge atop the rubble of the World Trade Center. The film's final section recounts, with swelling music and slow-motion video, Bush's appearance in Yankee Stadium, culminating in his throwing out the first pitch:

It's hard for a picture to capture the presidency. But maybe a story can tell us something about its meaning. It was October 2001. America had just been hit and America was uneasy. And some were afraid. He knew. There was a baseball game, the World Series. And it was held in New York. New York was trying to come back. And he knew.

And, suddenly, the White House was calling the mayor's office, which was calling Yankee Stadium. It was the first night of the big series in New York. And look who arrived at Yankee Stadium. Derek Jeter bumped into him before he walked out to the mound, and he said, hey, Mr. President, where are you going to throw from? The president said, I hadn't thought about it. I guess the base of the mound.

And Derek Jeter said, this is New York. And in New York, you throw from the mound. And the president laughed. He was wearing a heavy Secret Service bulletproof vest and he could hardly move his arms. But he knew. So George Bush took the mound.

What he did that night, that man in the arena, he helped us come back. That's the story of this presidency. With the heart of a president, he told us, you keep pitching. No matter what, you keep pitching. No matter what, you go to the game. You go to the mound. You find the plate, and you throw, and you become who you are.

Many Democrats no doubt watched *The Pitch*, and responded, "Big deal—we should reelect him because he threw a baseball?" But the story has political power, and not just because of the high production values and deep, lush voice-over from the actor-politician Fred Thompson. It shows Bush successfully completing a physical task despite alleged danger, thereby establishing his courage and manhood (something Bush spends a lot of time working to establish) and transports us back to the days immediately after September 11. One might argue that the Bush campaign's incessant invoking of September 11 was a way to short-circuit rational thinking on the part of the electorate, but one has to grant that it worked. For most of us, the experience of September 11 was highly emotional; to invoke it is to prompt us to recall our shock, our fear, our sadness, and our anger. It also prompts us to recall how we felt about President Bush in the subsequent days, feelings that are overwhelmingly positive, if not for all Americans, then for most. This film, and indeed the entire Bush reelection campaign, was about *pathos* and *ethos*, the invocation of powerful emotions and the establishment of Bush as the heroic leader.[8] Against these, John Kerry's argument about his greater potential competence on the issue of terrorism—his use of *logos*—was pathetically ineffectual.

Reagan's example is the most relevant to progressives as they seek new stories that embody their values and their philosophy. Too often, progressives have told stories that feature ordinary people only as victims and never as heroes. Although stories of injustice done to the powerless by the powerful are important, it's also critical to regularly tell stories in which ordinary people are held up as role models, overcome obstacles, and even triumph in the end. There's nothing wrong with sad stories, but you have to show people the happy ending in order to convince them that your ideology is a hopeful one that offers them a path toward a future they'd like to be a part of.

Although many elements comprise an effective story, a few are particularly critical. First, the story must have characters, individual people whose actions shape the events. For far too long, progressives have talked about social trends and impersonal forces, arguments that, whatever truth they contain, leave listeners without much understanding of the ways policy affects individual people. On the first day of a freshman writing seminar, budding fiction writers will be instructed, "Don't tell me, show me." Characters show us the story. And stories in which characters experience things we have experienced and feel emotions we have felt are particularly resonant and moving. Any parent could describe how the experience of having children changes the reactions one has to stories involving parents and children, even the most mundane. The most effective stories connect with who we are and—like Reagan's—who we would like to be.

Rhetoric that stays at the abstract level is virtually incapable of achieving anything like *transportation*, the term literary theorists use to describe that familiar feeling when we lose ourselves in the story we are watching or reading. In order to approach that feeling of being transported, we need concrete, familiar elements, particularly people, whom we can understand and identify with. Compare these two passages from speeches at the 2004 Democratic convention, making essentially the same argument:

> And that's why Republicans and Democrats must make this election a contest of big ideas, not small-minded attacks. This is our time to reject the kind of politics calculated to divide race from race, region from region, group from group. Maybe some just see us divided into those red states and blue states, but I see us as one America: red, white and blue.

> The pundits like to slice and dice our country into red states and blue states: red states for Republicans, blue states for Democrats. But I've got news for them, too. We worship an awesome God in the blue states, and we don't like federal agents poking around our libraries in the red states. We coach

Little League in the blue states and, yes, we've got some gay friends in the red states. There are patriots who opposed the war in Iraq, and there are patriots who supported the war in Iraq. We are one people, all of us pledging allegiance to the stars and stripes, all of us defending the United States of America.

The first is John Kerry, and the second is Barack Obama. Obama starts in the same place Kerry does, at the abstract level, but then he gets specific, offering a portrait of Americans worshiping God, coaching Little League, having gay friends. The concrete, identifiable images are what give Obama's argument so much more power. Concrete, personal content is absolutely crucial to good storytelling. Consider how often someone tells you a story, and your immediate response is, "Something just like that happened to me . . ." By relating our stories back and forth, we locate the connections that bond us to other people. This common habit tells us something not only about our social interactions but also about how our memory works. When encountering a story, we ask ourselves, if only unconsciously, "Has something liked that happened to me, or to someone I know?" The concrete elements enable us to make that connection between the story being told and our own stories.

Not to pick on John Kerry, an honorable man with a lifetime of service to his country, but his failures on the narrative front were so numerous that they provide excellent lessons in what not to do. To take another example, though Kerry was endorsed early on by the International Association of Fire Fighters, he never took the opportunity to use the symbolic power of the men and women so justifiably lionized after September 11. The firefighter is vigilant, skilled, protective, and ready at a moment's notice to exercise extraordinary courage and daring in the service of others. Unlike some, he doesn't go looking for trouble but is ready when it comes (he's also a government employee and a member of a union). Though one could spot yellow "Firefighters for Kerry" T-shirts at nearly every event, Kerry never wove the story of the firefighter into an argument for his candidacy. It could have been one of the central stories he told.

One of the first things we do when we hear a story is sort the good guys from the bad guys, to figure out whom we should be rooting for and which outcome is the preferred one. This will then shape our reactions to the events of the story. This is what sociologist William Gamson found when he conducted a lengthy study listening to people talk about policy issues. People thought about justice and injustice, Gamson wrote, only when they could figure out who the bad guys were:

> The heat of a moral judgment is intimately related to beliefs about what acts or conditions have caused people to suffer undeserved hardship or loss. The critical dimension is the abstractness of the target. Vague, abstract sources of unfairness diffuse indignation and make it seem foolish. We may think it dreadfully unfair when it rains on our parade, but bad luck or nature is a poor target for an injustice frame. When we see impersonal, abstract forces as responsible for our suffering, we are taught to accept what cannot be changed and make the best of it. Anger is dampened by the unanswerable rhetorical question: Who says life is fair?
>
> At the other extreme, if one attributes undeserved suffering to malicious or selfish acts by clearly identifiable persons or groups, the emotional component of an injustice frame will almost certainly be there. Concreteness in the target, even when it is misplaced and directed away from the real causes of hardship, is a necessary condition for an injustice frame. Hence, competition over defining targets is a crucial battleground in the development or containment of injustice frames.[9]

With regard to narrative, what this means is that good stories have villains as well as heroes, and if rousing indignation at injustice is the point of the story, that villain can't be an abstraction like "the system" (for conservatives, the government, with its heartless bureaucrats, is a villain on which nearly any ill, societal or personal, can be blamed). Fortunately for progressives, efforts to make profound changes for the betterment of citizens will usually run into quick opposition from powerful foes. Anger at the underlying problem can easily be focused on these foes—the insurance companies blocking expanded health care, for instance, or the corporations resisting progressive tax reform.

A second and closely related element of good story construction is that it contains a central conflict in which clear moral distinctions are made. As we saw in the previous chapter, values-based appeals are vital to political persuasion, not only because they impart a sense of what you stand for, but because they lead people to consider their own values as they approach a political issue. When they do, the conclusions they make are more likely to become non-negotiable and trump other issues that might push them to support the other side. So the stories progressives tell must not only impart information but must also contain an obvious moral lesson, telling us why one course of action might be good for me personally and why, given my values, it's the right thing to do.

Next, a good story will have emotional content that moves its listeners—the primary element of *pathos*. We are sometimes tempted to believe that in a perfect world, emotion would be banished from the business of politics. With a dispassionate eye, voters would examine party platforms and candidate qualifications and come to reasoned, considered judgments on who our leaders should be and what policies should be pursued. After all, it is all too easy for cynical politicians to rouse people by appeals to anger, fear, or prejudice, leading them away from both their own interests and the truth itself.

This view is dangerously naive. While there is no question that emotional appeals in politics often play on people's worst instincts, any political persuasion depends on both the mind and the heart. In fact, reason and emotion are not necessarily opposed to each other; some researchers have found that heightened emotional states often lead us to seek out information, resulting in more informed decision making,[10] while others suggest that emotional appeals have their greatest effect on those most involved in an issue, resulting in "passionate reasoning."[11] Politics can make us angry or inspired, afraid or hopeful, despondent or overjoyed; as Oliver Wendell Holmes said, eloquence may set fire to reason. Only by understanding which emotions are being activated at a given time can we hope to harness the emotional content of politics to progressive ends.

We have discussed many things that conservatives do better than liberals, and the careful use of emotional appeals is certainly another to add to the list. Indeed, a look over recent presidential campaigns shows a progression of Democratic candidates desperately pleading with voters to eat the political broccoli of position papers and policy proposals, while Republicans respond with the red meat of fear and anger. This is not to say, however, that liberals don't sometimes get it right. Consider this ad, aired in early 2005 by a progressive group opposed to conservative efforts to limit medical liability for doctors and insurance companies. It features a young father discussing the death of his son; on the page the script is powerful, but on screen, the effect is devastating, particularly the ad's last line:

> My son Ian was left severely brain damaged by medical errors. He died before his fifth birthday. The insurance company didn't even want to pay for his care. Now President Bush is siding with the insurance, HMO, and drug companies, trying to end what they call "frivolous lawsuits," while 100,000 Americans like Ian die each year because of medical errors. Mr. President, let's fix the health care mess, but please stop blaming the victims. My son's life was not frivolous.

There are lots of good, rational reasons to oppose conservative efforts at "tort reform," but this ad sets the terms of debate in a simple, easy-to-understand way: it establishes the controversy as one between insurance, HMO, and drug companies on one side, and victims on the other. Although it does contain factual information, it offers that information within the context of a compelling, emotionally charged story that makes it nearly impossible for any viewer, particularly any parent, to avoid feeling sympathy for the victims. Finally, it reframes conservative language ("frivolous") as a cruel insult to those for whom we are feeling sympathy. Just as the best art has both a complexity that challenges the intellect and an emotionality that touches the soul, political messages need to be logically persuasive and laden with emotion.

Progressives also need to get over their squeamishness about telling stories that have the potential to make people angry or even afraid. Like anything else, negativity in politics can be used for ill or good. It can be honest or dishonest, fair or unfair, relevant or irrelevant. There are things voters *should* be angry about and things they should be afraid of. Scholarly research has consistently found that we tend to pay more attention to negative information than to positive information; the explanation from evolutionary psychology is that looking out for danger was essential to survival (ignore a tasty raspberry bush and you'll go hungry for a day; ignore a saber-toothed tiger and you won't be passing on your genes). As the political scientists Michael Cobb and James Kuklinski put it, voters "assign relatively more weight and importance to events that have negative, as opposed to positive, implications for them or those dear to them. When making decisions, they place more emphasis on avoiding potential losses than on obtaining potential gains. Similarly, when individuals form impressions of situations of other people, they weight negative information more heavily than positive. . . . Impressions formed on the basis of negative information, moreover, tend to be more lasting and more resistant to change."[12]

Popular entertainment is full of inspiring stories of politicians who decide that for a change, they're not going to do the photo-ops and speak the carefully considered words. They'll just tell it like it is, be who they are, stay positive, and the voters will come to them. Like Jimmy Stewart in *Mr. Smith Goes to Washington*, they'll stand up for what's right, and in the end they'll emerge victorious.

In the real world, things don't work that way. In the real world, the Republican Party would tear Jefferson Smith to shreds. His idea for a "national boys camp" would lead to a whisper campaign about pedophilia, and he would return home not a hero of democracy but a broken, humiliated man with whom no one would want to be seen.[13] Surely, there can be no one left who doubts that Republicans will ever hesitate to get mean when power is on the line. Progressives don't have to match them dirty trick for dirty trick, but they do need to understand that a program of effective storytelling must incorporate stories that highlight not only the good things progressives want people to believe about them but the bad things they want people to believe about conservatives.

Finally, a good story will frame the discussion in a way that defines the problem, establishes causes and effects, and makes one policy course the only acceptable solution. In the wake of the 2004 election, some in the mainstream media and the blogosphere began focusing on the frames underlying political discourse. This idea was spurred on by the University of California linguist George Lakoff, whose book discussing conservative and liberal frames, *Don't Think of an Elephant*, became a best-seller. Although most of the public was not aware of it, scholars have been investigating the function of frames in news discourse and political rhetoric for three decades.[14] The metaphor of the frame puts a focus on what is left in and left out of the way we conceive certain issues and events. Every news story or political argument contains a frame, an unspoken structure that determines the nature of the questions that are asked. For instance, scholars have investigated the difference between "issue frames," which discuss political events in terms of the details of policy proposals, and "strategy frames," which center on political strategies, hidden motives, and details of public opinion.[15] Experimental research, particularly that conducted by Amos Tversky and Daniel Kahneman, showed that how options are framed—for instance, whether a course of action is framed in terms of potential losses or in terms of potential gains—can dramatically affect the choices people make.[16]

As conservatives have understood for years and progressives are finally coming to realize, the language choices we make when we talk about policy can create frames that guide debate and help determine the outcome of policy conflicts. One oft-cited example is the phrase "tax relief," which defines taxes as an oppressive burden from which we need relief. This language leads us to ask not how we can make taxes more fair or even what the proper degree of taxation is but, more simply, how can we get some relief?

What has made the conservative language effort so effective is the stunning semantic unity conservatives achieve. Once the tune is written, everyone on the conservative side sings from the same hymnal. Some conservative organizations keep jars in their offices: use the wrong language in conversation—refer to the "inheritance tax" instead of the "death tax," for instance—and you have to put a dollar in the jar. If you reiterate your framing often enough, you may succeed in getting even your opponents to adopt it; this is what conservatives have done with "tax relief," an expression that is used regularly not only by Republicans but by liberals and journalists as well. This is not to say that paying closer attention to language choices will provide some sort of magic key to electoral and policy success, but good stories use language in ways that frame issues to your side's advantage.

There are many other story features we could add—good stories contain familiar elements so they are easy to understand, feature dramatic events or surprises, and draw on values held both widely and deeply, to name a few. Of course, every story won't follow precisely the same template, but in the immortal words of Larry Speakes, the spokesman for Ronald Reagan, "If you tell the same story five times, it's true."[17] The fact that Speakes made this argument as a way of excusing his boss's fabrications may be repugnant, but it does get at an important point. Repeated often enough, stories can become part of the way we understand the world so that they carry a resonance, *ringing* true whether or not they in fact *are* true in a factual sense. When progressives find good stories, they have to keep repeating them until voters assimilate them as core elements of their understanding of the political world.

WHO ARE YOU?

Democrats will continue to struggle until they understand that voters must identify with *them*—not with their plans, not with their positions, but with them. Voters have to look at the people they're voting for and say, "He's like me." As we mentioned, Democrats have traditionally talked about programs while Republicans talk about values. The result is that the Democratic argument comes down to "I'll help you out," while the Republican argument is, "I'm one of you." In other words, Republicans argue with *ethos*.

The power of this argument explains why conservatives have invested so much energy in convincing Americans that Democrats are not, in fact, one of them. Republicans have traditionally done this by clear demarcation of in-groups and out-groups, associating

Democrats with counterculture youths (Spiro Agnew called Democrats the party of "acid, amnesty, and abortion" in 1972), African Americans, or gays. The campaign against the "liberal elite" wraps all these out-groups into one package, a group not only alien from you but working on behalf of other groups also alien from you.*

To counter this image, progressives need to find stories that go beyond showing that Republicans *care only* about the elite to showing that Republicans *are* the elite. For instance, in 2000, Al Gore spent endless amounts of time hammering home the point that George W. Bush's tax plan larded most of its benefits on the richest 1 percent of Americans. It was true, and people largely believed it, but lots of those who believed it voted for Bush anyway. The same was true in 2004: voters understood that Bush's economic policies were aimed at the rich, but they reelected him. What was not in evidence was anything analogous to Bush's father's oft-cited amazement upon seeing a supermarket scanner when the devices had been in use for years: a story that demonstrated how different he was from regular people. In contrast, the Bush campaign didn't bother poring over John Kerry's economic plans to find reasons they wouldn't help people; they aired ads showing Kerry windsurfing, an activity of the idle rich.

Such stories about Bush wouldn't have been too hard to find, either. Bush's biography was brimming with incidents in which the ordinary rules didn't apply to him because of his family's wealth and influence. His life was so disconnected from the lives of ordinary people that at an event in early 2005, when a woman told him she was a single mother who worked three jobs, he responded, "Uniquely American, isn't it? I mean, that is fantastic that you're doing that,"[18] as if her situation demonstrated not economic desperation but can-do American spirit. Yet despite occasional slips like this one, many Americans look at Bush and believe him to be

---

*As one crosses the Mason-Dixon line, the idea of an exclusive in-group culture becomes stronger and stronger. Candidates in the Northeast, for instance, seldom claim to be proud owners of "Pennsylvania values" or "Rhode Island values." Candidates in the South, however, not only boast about their "South Carolina values" or "Alabama values," they accuse their opponents of not having them, whatever they might be.

one of them for two reasons: first, because it's an act he has been honing for years, and second, because his opponents have attacked the elitism of his policies without attacking him as an elitist.

Progressives need to craft stories that define realms of identity in which they and voters reside together—and conservatives stand outside. They also need those stories to be told by credible story-tellers. With all due respect, the people the Democratic Party has been nominating for president lately, despite all their commitment and governing skills, just haven't been credible messengers.

Democrats were understandably frustrated that although their candidates had the right policies, George W. Bush won two presidential races in no small part because he was the one whom people would rather have a beer with. The answer to that quandary is not to rail at voters for being shallow but to find candidates who have the right policies *and* are appealing personalities. That's what Bill Clinton was—and he won two elections with relative ease.

Listen to John Edwards talking in 2005 about a small business owner he met and you hear that unity of message and messenger. I return to Edwards not to convince readers that he should be the Democratic nominee in 2008 should he choose to run, but because among current Democratic leaders he seems the have the clearest understanding of the importance of narrative:

> You know, I can still feel her handshake—determined and strong like a truck driver. She spent 14 years working at a wash house—working for the minimum wage—earning a little more than $200 a week. She would always try to do better, but no one would give her a chance.
>
> Well, she kept pushing and pushing. She got her GED and a loan. And now she owns her own pizza franchise. We asked her how many people worked there. She said that there are "eight of us." Not "seven people work for me." There were "eight of us." She was asked about the cost of her employees and she said that it was an honor to be able to give them their paychecks. You could hear in her voice the respect she has for other people.
>
> There was hope in that room. America was in that room. It was a million miles from that mill in Robbins [the North

Carolina town where Edwards grew up], but sitting with Loretta and the others—it was a very familiar place. That natural respect for other people. That belief in effort. And that hope that if you just keep going, try some more, things will get better—isn't this what America's all about?

So we're going to let the Republicans stand with their friends on Wall Street and the big oil, big insurance companies and the HMOs. And who are we going to stand with? We're going to stand with the teachers, nurses, factory workers, tech workers and small business owners. We're going to stand with Loretta.

This story embraces the value of hard work, something Republicans often extol, but it also lauds a communal spirit as a part of success—the loan Loretta got and the sense of obligation and respect she has for those who work for her. Critically, it has a happy ending—its message is not one of resentment but one of hope and opportunity. Finally, it clearly delineates between the good guys and the bad guys. Reporters may have tired of hearing Edwards repeat that his father worked in a mill and he was the first one in his family to go to college, but his background creates a context in which the stories he tells about the struggles of ordinary people have greater sincerity and credibility. In other words, he persuades through the use of *pathos* and *ethos*.

Democrats need to understand that regardless of whether they make personality a focus of their campaigns, Republicans will—and reporters will as well. In fact, reporters are obsessed with discovering the "real" person behind the candidate and tend to turn campaign coverage into an extended psychoanalysis session, probing the candidate's past and present to figure out what makes him tick.[19] As Jonathan Chait observed, "One of the curiosities of political journalism is that reporters tend to be assiduously even-handed about matters of policy (which can revolve around disputes over objective fact) but ruthlessly judgmental on questions of character (which are inherently subjective). In fact, most reporters don't know or care much about policy. They see politics primarily through the lens of the candidates' personal traits."[20]

In the past, I have written skeptically about the press's obsession with "authenticity."[21] In reporters' hands, the quest for authenticity becomes an excuse for double standards and an endless cynicism in which every utterance from a politician's mouth is assumed to be phony and disingenuous. At the same time, reporters reward the candidate with the most convincing portrayal of the authentic; what they value is not so much the authentic over the contrived but good acting over bad acting.[22]

That said, we should acknowledge that candidates who can speak to voters in their own language and convey sincerity are all too rare and should be highly valued. Voters' evaluations of personal traits—whether they believe a candidate is honest, strong, or cares about people like them—often predict which candidate they will choose much better than whether they agree with the candidates' positions on issues. In fact, voters often arrive at a positive impression of a candidate, then project their own beliefs onto that candidate, assuming that since they feel positively about him, he must agree with them on the issues.[23] Only a few of us are thoroughly versed in complex policy matters, but everyone knows how to glean impressions of people upon meeting them and judge whether they are likable and trustworthy. These impressions will linger long after the details of a policy speech are forgotten. A candidate who assumes that once voters hear his health-care plan, they'll come to like and trust him is headed for defeat.

We all have multiple, overlapping identities that can influence how we interpret the world and make political decisions. When you vote, are you a progressive, a parent, an American, a resident of your town, a man, a woman, a Christian, a Jew, a baseball fan, an intellectual? Some of these identities will be more important than others. The two questions this raises are, first, when you are considering politics in terms of each of those identities, what are you thinking? And second, which of those identities will be most important when you pull the curtain in the voting booth? Unlike progressives, conservatives have spent lots of time thinking about the way people define themselves and how conservatives can integrate their ideology, their party, and their candidates into those identities.

"You persuade by reason, but you motivate people by tapping into their values that run much deeper," said the legendary

Republican pollster Richard Wirthlin. Describing the campaign Wirthlin helped devise for Ronald Reagan, Thomas and Mary Edsall wrote, "At the core of the 1984 campaign strategy was the recognition that televised images—Reagan filmed at the Daytona 500, surrounded by bleachers of white working-class southerners; Reagan, beer in hand, among the working-class regulars in a Boston bar—could now be used to project the values Republicans were successfully appropriating."[24]

Those images told a story about who Reagan was, a story that helped pull working-class voters toward the GOP, despite the fact that their economic interests would have led them in a different direction. This was—and continues to be—possible because the cultural and political divides in America operate both *between* and *within* people. There are those who are implacably conservative and others who are implacably progressive, but put together these groups make up perhaps 40 percent of the electorate. The rest of the public has both conservative and progressive impulses and may swing one way or another, depending on what issues are foremost in their minds and what perspective they bring to bear at a given moment.

Compelling stories can help bring the right perspectives to bear by focusing our attention on one set of issues at a time, confining the policy alternatives we will consider. Just as we might potentially give our mental energy to any issue, we might at any given time be led by any of the values we hold within ourselves. For instance, conservatives and progressives both value equality, but when it comes to economics, conservatives usually put their commitment to equality aside and focus on another of their values, individual liberty. So when progressives are writing the stories that define them, they have to ask which progressive values they are trying to express and encourage others to consider. In turn, these values will define who progressives are.

THE CONSERVATIVE MASTER NARRATIVE

Once upon a time, conservatives told a dour tale in which suffering was inevitable and the present order of things was, if unfortunate, utterly natural. They viewed human nature as fundamentally bad, prone to all manner of deadly sins without the threat of swift punishment and eternal damnation. Barry Goldwater dismissed those who worried about the prospect of his itchy finger on the nuclear trigger as being gripped by "a craven fear of death"; Goldwater's apparent lack of such fear played no small part in his crushing defeat in 1964. But soon afterward, conservatives successfully changed their story to a much more hopeful one, whose heroes were entrepreneurs and risk takers looking to the future. Even if it manifested itself in naive or disastrous forms, this story was infinitely more appealing than the story told by the Social Darwinists of years before. The liberal Woodrow Wilson became the conservative George W. Bush, each asserting that with a pure heart and a strong will, America could bring the blessings of freedom to the entire world, banishing oppression once and for all. Regardless of its sincerity or plausibility (Bush's belief that he could "rid the world of evil" has to stand as one of the more audacious presidential proclamations in history[25]), one had to admire the sentiment. In the domestic realm, conservatives argue that if we can get government out of the way, the market will bring untold blessings to all who are possessed of virtue and who show faith in its magical perfection.

Yet alongside these optimists is a crowd of malcontents enacting a continuous kabuki of complaint, a cry of victimhood oblivious to the ever-burgeoning power and wealth amassed by conservatives. To hear them tell it, they are always the underdog, always besieged and kept down by those with the real power. The act of hanging an American flag on one's porch is likely to bring a Molotov cocktail thrown through one's front window by roving gangs of thought police, a cross worn on a necklace sure to bring instant arrest, the ordering of a Budweiser greeted with withering contempt from the microbrew cognoscenti. The triumph of liberal totalitarianism, with the abolishment of the family and religion and free speech and all that honest people hold dear, is forever around the next corner, at the bottom of a slippery slope down which we find ourselves eternally tumbling. Like end-timers assuring us that although they were wrong last year and the year before, *this* New Year's Eve will surely bring Armageddon, they are slowed not a bit by being proved wrong again and again, the coming American Sodom always a result of next year's wedge issue.[26]

This combination of wistfulness for a past that never was and sputtering anger at the present, a distasteful amalgam of impotent nostalgia and impotent rage, is issued by the right's most committed shock troops; however, the leaders of the conservative movement and the elected officials who represent it were smart enough to craft a tale both more universal and more inspiring.[27]

Though George W. Bush comes from a long line of investment bankers and spent his youth among people for whom *summer* is a verb, it's no accident that in 1999 as he was preparing to run for the presidency, he bought himself a "ranch," the better to adopt the persona of that quintessential icon of American manhood, the cowboy. Bush vacations are organized around staged sessions of clearing brush (for some reason, the ranch has an inexhaustible supply of brush, always in need of clearing), in which Bush puts on his big hat, his big boots, and his big belt buckle and struts before the cameras, as genuine as the Marlboro Man.

The cowboy iconography needs no explanation to the American public. It speaks of all the things Republicans want people to believe they are: self-reliant, principled, manly, wielding mastery over the land, respectful of hearth and home, ready to brandish a righteous six-gun in the service of all that is pure and good.

The people for whom those images resonate with the greatest power are engaged in a permanent battle against history. It's vital to understand that the "culture war" is not a feature only of our day or of the last half-century but a permanent fact of American political and social life. After the 2004 election, the unsuccessful Oklahoma Democratic Senate candidate Brad Carson described a campaign stop in a church in which he had to explain his support for *Roe v. Wade* while standing under a projected photo of a fetus that measured twenty-by-twenty—that's feet, not inches. "The culture war is real," Carson wrote, "and it is a conflict not merely about some particular policy or legislative item, but about modernity itself."[28] As long as our nation has existed, this battle has been fought. On one side are those who believe things should stay as they are (or go back to how they were) for the simple reason that

that is how things were done before. On the other are those who see society as in a constant process of evolution and growth, as we reexamine our habits, our choices, and our values. The opponents of modernity feared the enlightenment views of the nation's founders, fought the elimination of slavery, and were appalled when women demanded the same legal rights as men. Today, they proclaim the necessity of sexual purity (for women mostly) and wax rhapsodic about the "sanctity of marriage." Yet the song is always the same, and the culture war will never end. Nothing will convince conservatives to lay down their arms; resolve one issue and they will find another with which to brand liberals as the "other" on whom all the problems besetting our nation may be blamed.

As David Leege and his colleagues observe in their book *The Politics of Cultural Differences*, for many conservatives the 1960s have come to represent a kind of original sin, a fall from grace of the previous paradisiacal era and the source of all the problems we experience today.[29] The fact that for some, Bill and Hillary Clinton have come to embody all they despise about the sixties may be the best explanation for the maniacal hatred these two moderate politicians inspire. In the conservative view, the sixties were not a moral and social awakening but a descent into decadence, with sexual libertinism, confused gender roles, and lack of proper respect for authority. This understanding of the 1960s forms the basis of the conservative master narrative, the story that undergirds the conservative philosophy, describes the past and the present, and provides the justification for future action. We can synopsize it this way:

After an era of decadence and weakness, strong and righteous Americans stood up for right against wrong. Despite the impediment of liberal apologists and appeasers, they defeated totalitarian communism, then turned their attention to releasing America from the shackles of big government and restoring respect for the family. Empowering entrepreneurs and liberating citizens, they cut onerous taxes and regulations, enabling Americans to live freer lives. But at every turn they are hindered by powerful liberal elitists who want to take Americans' money, waste it on programs for the lazy and the sinful, banish God from the nation and tell us all how to live our lives.

All of the Four Pillars of Conservatism—small government, low taxes, a strong defense, and traditional values—are expressed in this narrative. It has been repeated so often and become such a staple of conservative rhetoric that Republicans will reflexively use it even while doing quite the opposite of what it would seem to dictate.[30] And given their vise grip on governmental and economic power and their constituents' unquenchable thirst for anger and resentment, conservatives must maintain the perception that they remain outsiders and insurgents, bravely fighting their underdog battle against those who control Americans' lives, assault their children, and poison their culture.

Listen to talk radio, watch cable news, or observe a Republican campaign for virtually any office, and you find this story repeated over and over. It never runs dry or goes stale, for two main reasons: first, because it offers a coherent, easily understood explanation for why conservatives believe and advocate what they do, and second, because those telling the story feel it deep in their bones.

A New Progressive Master Narrative

"Whereas the right-wing has a good story that they believe," observed the writer Joshua Wolf Shenk, "liberals have a lame story—and they don't even believe it."[31] The time is long past for progressives to build their own master narrative, one that makes clear what progressives believe about the past and the present and can be repeated until progressives are blue in the face. Perhaps most crucially, the new progressive master narrative must be animated by an encompassing vision of the future, a description of America as progressives want it to be. As the writer Rick Perlstein has pointed out, conservatives have always had a clearer idea of where they want to go, whereas liberals focus more on the means of getting there. "Conservatives have always known what the world would look like after their revolution: hearth, home, church, a businessman's republic. The dominant strain of the American left, on the other hand, certainly since the decline of the socialist left, fetishizes fairness, openness, and diversity. . . . If the stakes for liberals are fair procedures, the stakes for conservatives are last things: either humanity trends toward Grace, or it hurtles toward Armageddon."[32]

An animating vision of the future is what creates a movement that is more than a collection of disparate grievances, and here we arrive at what may be the greatest stumbling block to the creation of a true progressive movement. While the conservative master narrative has for years provided a unifying vision around which a diverse collection of people can rally, the left has been a coalition of people with a vague affinity and a support for one another's goals but nothing resembling a common purpose. Activists on the left consider themselves to be advocates for the environment, women's rights, workers' rights, or a whole series of causes, but few see themselves as part of something we could call "the progressive movement." Few would claim that such a thing even exists.

The creation of that movement requires practical steps and careful planning and organizing, but it also requires an articulation of an overarching story that tells us who progressives are and what they believe. We can call this master narrative "A More Perfect Union":

Throughout our history, we have worked to make sure our society lives up to the ideals we all share: freedom, equality, opportunity. When we saw problems, we organized together for change, shining a light on injustice and unfairness and demanding that government do what is best for all of us and allow everyone to join in the blessings of our nation. Afraid of change and desperate to hold on to power, conservatives fought the changes with all their might. But the will of the people was too strong, and conservatives were defeated when they stood in the way of progress. Today we face many problems, and conservatives still fight against the people's will. But America will continue its advance toward a more perfect union, one where every person has the same rights, the same security, and the same opportunities, where communities and the nation come together to solve problems, where no one is excluded from our nation's prosperity, where the government works on behalf of all Americans.

The conservative master narrative tells a story that begins in the 1960s, but this progressive master narrative crosses the scope of American history, seeing it as a continuous progression to realize the noble ideas on which the country was founded. It posits government as a force that, when it works properly, creates justice, security, and opportunity. The abolishment of slavery, the enfranchisement of women, the G.I. Bill, the creation of Social Security and Medicare, and the civil rights and environmental movements are all events driven by progressives that fit within this narrative. The narrative also demonstrates progressive agency, with progressives and progressive government acting forcefully and creating positive change.

After the 2004 election, many Democrats began to wonder where their party should go. The perceptive ones understood that their problem isn't that Americans think Democrats are too liberal; their problem is that Americans think they don't stand for anything.[33] That opinion won't change until progressives and Democrats learn to tell stories—stories that not only make for effective arguments about policy but that tell Americans, in ways they will understand and assimilate, who progressives are and who conservatives are.

After I wrote this progressive master narrative and termed it "A More Perfect Union," I read a commencement address given by Barack Obama in 2005 at Knox College in Galesburg, Illinois, in which he told almost precisely the same story, including the reference to the preamble to the Constitution. Those who doubt that progressives are capable of speaking a language that is hopeful and patriotic while affirming their values should read Obama's words:

As a servant in Rome, you knew you'd spend your life forced to build somebody else's Empire. As a peasant in 11th Century China, you knew that no matter how hard you worked, the local warlord might come and take everything you had—and you also knew that famine might come knocking at the door. As a subject of King George, you knew that your freedom of worship and your freedom to speak and to build your own life would be ultimately limited by the throne.

And then America happened.

A place where destiny was not a destination, but a journey to be shared and shaped and remade by people who had the gall, the temerity to believe that, against all odds, they could form "a more perfect union" on this new frontier.

And as people around the world began to hear the tale of the lowly colonists who overthrew an empire for the sake of an idea, they started to come. Across oceans and the ages, they settled in Boston and Charleston, Chicago and St. Louis, Kalamazoo and Galesburg, to try and build their own American Dream. This collective dream moved forward imperfectly—it was scarred by our treatment of native peoples, betrayed by slavery, clouded by the subjugation of women, shaken by war and depression. And yet, brick by brick, rail by rail, calloused hand by calloused hand, people kept dreaming, and building, and working, and marching, and petitioning their government, until they made America a land where the question of our place in history is not answered for us. It's answered by us.

Have we failed at times? Absolutely. Will you occasionally fail when you embark on your own American journey? You surely will. But the test is not perfection.

The true test of the American ideal is whether we're able to recognize our failings and then rise together to meet the challenges of our time. Whether we allow ourselves to be shaped by events and history, or whether we act to shape them. Whether chance of birth or circumstance decides life's big winners and losers, or whether we build a community where, at the very least, everyone has a chance to work hard, get ahead, and reach their dreams.

We have faced this choice before.

At the end of the Civil War, when farmers and their families began moving into the cities to work in the big factories that were sprouting up all across America, we had to decide: Do we do nothing and allow captains of industry and robber barons to run roughshod over the economy and workers by competing to see who can pay the lowest wages at the worst working conditions? Or do we try to make the system work by setting up basic rules for the market, instituting the first public schools, busting up monopolies, letting workers organize into unions?

We chose to act, and we rose together.

When the irrational exuberance of the Roaring Twenties came crashing down with the stock market, we had to decide: do we follow the call of leaders who would do nothing, or the call of a leader who, perhaps because of his physical paralysis, refused to accept political paralysis?

We chose to act—regulating the market, putting people back to work, expanding bargaining rights to include health care and a secure retirement—and together we rose.

When World War II required the most massive homefront mobilization in history and we needed every single American to lend a hand, we had to decide: Do we listen to skeptics who told us it wasn't possible to produce that many tanks and planes? Or, did we build Roosevelt's Arsenal for Democracy and grow our economy even further by providing our returning heroes with a chance to go to college and own their own home?

Again, we chose to act, and again, we rose together.

Today, at the beginning of this young century, we have to decide again. But this time, it is your turn to choose.

7

MANIPULATING THE MEDIA FOR FUN AND PROFIT

Fighting the Right's Mighty Wurlitzer

In January 2005, a theretofore unknown University of Colorado professor of ethnic studies was invited to speak on a panel at tiny Hamilton College in upstate New York. Some Hamilton students objected to the invitation, citing an essay the professor had written after September 11 in which he said that the people who died in the attacks were not innocent because they were part of an oppressive capitalist system. Few people read the essay, and to that point few people had ever heard of the professor. Whether he would or would not speak on the panel would meaningfully affect the lives of precisely zero Americans (with the possible exception of the professor himself), and it represented the sort of campus mini-controversy about which students often become exercised, then promptly forget all about.

Yet within a few weeks, not only had the controversy not been forgotten, that professor of ethnic studies—one Ward Churchill—had become a national figure. His views were discussed and dissected in newspapers and magazines, on television and radio, and throughout the Internet. In the month following the appearance of a wire story about his potential talk at Hamilton, no fewer than

992 mentions of Churchill appeared in the news outlets covered by Lexis-Nexis, which does not include the hundreds of conservative talk radio shows on which Churchill was topic number one. With the exception of one day, every single episode of *The O'Reilly Factor* for a month featured some discussion of Ward Churchill. Do a Google search on his name nowadays, and you'll yield well over half a million hits.

The Churchill story is just one example of a script repeated again and again. Every few months, the right-wing media find a new whipping boy, usually a Hollywood actor or, even better, an obscure professor, who has committed a sin of political correctness or lack of patriotism. Leavened with the proper dose of indignation, the story is repeated, discussed, ruminated on, and raged about throughout the right-wing media, so that millions will understand that liberals are an "elite" with radical, anti-American views who hold regular people in contempt.

This, above all, is the distinguishing feature and political power of the right-wing media: their ability to latch on to a single story line and sing in a harmonious chorus of feigned outrage. In each of the major communication media, the right-wing noise machine[1] has a significant and powerful presence:

- *Radio*. This is the medium most wholly dominated by the right. By some estimates, more than 90 percent of the ideologically identifiable hours on American talk radio are conservative.[2] According to *Talkers* magazine, six talk radio hosts have audiences of more than 5 million listeners: Rush Limbaugh, Sean Hannity, Howard Stern, Michael Savage, Laura Schlesinger, and Laura Ingraham.[3] Although Stern vocally opposed George W. Bush during the 2004 election, he can hardly be described as a liberal in any meaningful way. The other five range from the extreme right of Limbaugh and Hannity to the maniacal racist right of Savage. Limbaugh is the gold standard; his formula of ridicule and resentment is duplicated by hundreds of talentless hacks across the country. Limbaugh's program is also beamed by the United States government to 177 countries over Armed Forces Radio; according to a 2005 analysis by the office of Senator Tom Harkin, AFR featured sixty-two hours and forty-five minutes of conservative talk radio per week, and not one single minute of progressive talk radio. In addition, there are over two thousand religious radio stations in America (nearly all of which are evangelical Christian), making it the country's third-most popular format after country music and news-talk.[4] One out of every seven radio stations in America is a religious station; there are almost twice as many as there were in 1998.[5]

- *Television*. The cable networks are dominated by conservative opinion-mongers. Consider these lineups:

  Fox News: Five weekday shows hosted by conservatives (Bill O'Reilly, John Gibson, Neil Cavuto, Shepard Smith, and Brit Hume); one show featuring a liberal and a conservative but dominated by the conservative (*Hannity & Colmes*); one panel show featuring only conservatives (*Fox & Friends*); and one show hosted by a liberal (Greta Van Susteren) but primarily devoted to sensational trials and missing white girls. Three weekend shows hosted by a single conservative (Oliver North, John Kasich, Cal Thomas), and one hosted by two conservatives (*The Beltway Boys*).

  MSNBC: One show hosted by a liberal (Keith Olbermann); one hosted by a personality (Chris Matthews) who once worked for the Democrats but who has become one of the most vicious critics of Democrats like Clinton, Gore, and Kerry, and one of George W. Bush's biggest fans ("He's a helluva president, everybody likes him");[6] one hosted by a radio personality who is difficult to pin down ideologically (Don Imus); one show hosted by a liberal and a conservative (*Connected Coast to Coast*); and two shows hosted by conservatives (Joe Scarborough and Tucker Carlson).

  CNN: A collection of shows led by people like Wolf Blitzer, Paula Zahn, and Anderson Cooper, none of whom has an identifiable ideology on the air.

- *Newspapers*. While there are many papers with editorial pages that lean slightly to the left, nothing comes close to the right-wing extremism of the editorial page of the *Wall Street Journal*, exceeded in circulation only by *USA Today*. Although the *Journal*'s news pages are relatively free of ideological bias, the same cannot be said of Rupert Murdoch's *New York Post* or Sun Myung Moon's *Washington Times*, which operate as little more than RNC propaganda sheets. The nation's op-ed pages are dominated by conservatives; the most widely syndicated political columnists in America are Cal Thomas (whose column appears in 550 newspapers; he also has a radio show on over 300 stations), Robert Novak (approximately 500 papers), and George Will (just under 500).[7] Although not strictly political, the column of Focus on the Family's James Dobson also appears in over 500 newspapers.

- *Internet.* A large number of well-coordinated blogs and news sites whose mission is to advance conservative story lines and vilify liberals and liberalism.

Of all these, only the last has a progressive presence in any way comparable to the conservative presence. What conservatives thus enjoy is a wide-ranging, multimedia apparatus that when tapped will vibrate like a gigantic tuning fork for weeks on end.

All this wouldn't matter much if the audience for the conservative media consisted only of conservatives, but the effects actually reach far wider. Consider how, during its first term at least, the Bush administration didn't seem beset by the scandals of venality and personal impropriety that seem to mark every administration. Is this because all of the thousands of people who work in Bush's executive branch are beyond reproach? Hardly. Rather, the remarkable contrast with the previous administration is the result of two factors. First, the Democrats control neither chamber of Congress, meaning they are not allowed to call hearings and thus have neither subpoena power nor the ability to create news events around administration misdeeds. Second, the lack of a meaningful left-wing media apparatus means there is no one to investigate, highlight, and express outrage at those misdeeds. The contrast with the parade of "scandals" that marked the Clinton years could hardly be clearer. If Bill Clinton cut himself shaving, four separate committees in Congress would immediately schedule hearings to investigate the sinister conspiracy revealed by the shaving incident, and talk radio would take up the cause with a campaign of wild speculation and slanderous accusations. Progressives simply have no comparable system to push such stories forward.

And it is here that the true power of the right-wing media becomes manifest. It's one thing when Rush Limbaugh tells his "dittoheads" (as his fans call themselves, proclaiming their voluntary abdication of independent thought) to get angry about something, but when that story is pushed onto the network news shows, it reaches millions who are not already committed conservatives. In 2002, Al Gore accurately described the way the system operates: "Something will start at the Republican National Committee . . . and it will explode the next day on the right-wing talk-show network and on Fox News. . . . And then they'll create a little echo chamber, and pretty soon they'll start baiting the mainstream media for allegedly ignoring the story they've pushed into the *zeitgeist*. And then pretty soon the mainstream media goes out and disingenuously takes a so-called objective sampling, and lo and behold, these RNC talking points are woven into the fabric of the *zeitgeist*."[8]

Gore knows whereof he speaks. During his presidential run, a series of stories about him—that he claimed he invented the Internet, or that he said he discovered the existence of toxic waste at Love Canal—circulated throughout the media despite being completely false.[9] As Mark Halperin, the political director of ABC News, described it, "The advantage the Republicans have is reaching a lot of people through Drudge and Fox News and Rush Limbaugh and well-organized surrogates who are willing to swarm the media with the same message over and over to drive the agenda, with what political professionals would call admirable shamelessness. Democrats do not have the same echo-chamber outlets for an as easy, or as unfiltered, crack at voters."[10] When it works, as it does so often, the din created by the right-wing machine gets louder and louder until reporters and editors at mainstream news outlets find it impossible to ignore.

Does this conservative pressure work? Listen to what the late ABC News anchor Peter Jennings said in 2004:

I think there is this anxiety in the newsroom and I think it comes in part from the corporate suite. I think that the rise, not merely of the presence of conservative opinion in the country, but the related noise being made in the media by conservative voices these days has had an effect in the corporate suites. And I think it worries people. And I might be dead wrong about you, but I hear more about conservative concern than I did in the past. On the plane yesterday on the way coming up here a guy walked by me, and I said, as I would under normal circumstances, good morning, and he looked at me, and I went by. And he was waiting for me when I got off the plane and he said: "America hater, leave the country immediately." And I was aghast. But it reminded me that not only is the differences in the country so strong at the moment, and we are perceived to be, I think infinitely more liberal by the way than the news media establishment is, that the general news, the word tsunami, this wave of resentment rushes at our advertisers, rushes at the corporate suites, and gets under the newsroom skin, if not completely into the decision making process to a greater degree than it has before.[11]

The most common response to this pressure is to adopt the "he said/she said" style that characterizes so much political news. Simply repeating what "both sides" are saying allows the reporter to sidestep any accusation of bias, but it also turns the journalist into little more than a conduit for spin, a mindless stenographer seemingly incapable of judgment. The more cynical political operative understands that the predominance of he said/she said news is, in fact, permission to lie, distort, and slander without consequence. So Republicans can say that George W. Bush stands eight feet tall and is able to bend metal using only the power of his mind, and when Democrats respond, "No, he can't," the reporter will refuse to adjudicate the dispute. A reasonable citizen is thus left to conclude, well, maybe he's only seven feet tall and his powers of telekinesis are substantial but not unlimited.

Of course, I'm exaggerating. Exaggerations equally egregious, however, go uncorrected in our news all the time. From assertions so laughable no sentient person could take them seriously to simple and outright lies, the he said/she said paradigm allows all manner of rhetorical sewage to pour into unsuspecting eyes and ears.

This takes place in a context in which the two sides of political debate are so unevenly matched in the skill with which they play the media game that it often resembles nothing so much as a contest between the Harlem Globetrotters and the Washington Generals. Consider what happens on the typical cable chat show when two people are invited on to discuss a controversial issue.* The progressive representative might be a professor who has written about the topic and who is knowledgeable and articulate. He doesn't have a lot of television experience, though, and his real problem is that he knows *too much* about the matter at hand. He gets halfway through a lengthy exegesis of the causes and effects of a controversy before getting cut off by the host (a conservative), having failed to make any discernable point, much less a persuasive one. The conservative representative, on the other hand, works at the Heritage Foundation. She, too, is very knowledgeable and articulate, but she has been on television dozens of times and has also gone through media training. She knows exactly the length of the answer she is supposed to give, and she is holding in her hand a set of simple, persuasive talking points she will be sure to hammer home multiple times before the five-minute segment is over.

On another cable channel, a similar discussion is taking place about the same issue. There you will find another hapless progressive making a completely different set of arguments, also being inter-

---

*Imagine this: You're sitting alone in a small room; behind you is a light box illuminating a large photograph of the skyline of the city you're in. You are facing a camera, through which a number of people can see you, although you cannot see them. Your only awareness comes from a bud in your ear that delivers extremely low-quality sound. For the next five minutes, an extremely agitated man who appears to dislike you intensely will yell at you through this earbud. He will be joined by another person who if anything is even more agitated and dislikes you even more. Before you arrived at the studio, you were "pre-interviewed" by a producer who asked your views on the subject to be discussed, so the host knows what you are likely to say. He will ask you questions designed to make you look foolish, then interrupt you when you attempt to answer. That is the experience of appearing on a cable talk show.

rupted before he can finish what he's saying. Opposite him is a representative of the American Enterprise Institute, holding in his lap the same set of talking points held by his colleague from Heritage, making exactly the same arguments, pressing home exactly the same message. Pick up the paper the next day and you'll find Republican members of Congress giving exactly the same message as well. Tune in to a conservative talk radio show and you'll hear the host reading off that same page of talking points, which were faxed to him the night before. As the Republicans understand, repetition is essential to persuasion. Once they have devised what they believe will be the most effective message, it is repeated again and again and again. People from all walks of life all over the country will, after a few days, be exposed to their simple message multiple times.

There are Democrats who understand this, too. Unfortunately, they simply don't have the same organization and hierarchy on their side to enforce something similar to the right's message discipline. So their message is fragmented, shooting off in a dozen different directions; listen to five different progressives or Democrats and you'll hear five different things.

POSTMODERN CONSERVATIVES

The right-wing media are more than just a highly integrated, stunningly effective system of news management. They also represent an assault on the foundations of journalism itself. The conservative canard of the "liberal media" is something I and others have debunked at length elsewhere.[12] It is enough to say here, however, that the endless braying about the alleged sins of the allegedly liberal press is a conservative strategy both to keep the media under pressure ("working the ref," as it is known) and to pose as plucky underdogs fighting against a powerful, hostile elite. This is particularly essential to the conservative project when conservatives' control over the country's political and economic life is so nearly complete.

The "liberal media" accusation is effective not only because of the work of well-funded groups like Accuracy in Media and the Media Research Center that exist for the sole purpose of harassing the press with absurd claims of bias. It is effective because conservatives at all levels have assimilated the "liberal bias" charge into their worldview and their talking points. Democrats are often displeased with news reporting, but Republicans can be counted on to cry "liberal bias" in virtually any debate about any issue, reinforcing the idea through constant repetition. Even the president of the United States has gotten into the act; in January 2002, George W. Bush walked to Marine One holding a copy of Bernard Goldberg's fact-free screed *Bias: A CBS Insider Exposes How the Media Distorts the News* with the cover carefully faced toward the assembled reporters, lest anyone fail to get the message.

The idea of "objective" news is a relatively recent development in the history of journalism. Up until the middle of the nineteenth century, American newspapers had explicitly partisan orientations, delivering reports to an audience whose members knew which side they were on and expected their news to be of and by that side. The 1830s saw the emergence of the "penny press"—inexpensive, often salacious newspapers that were precursors to many of today's tabloids. Because they sought to maximize their audience, the penny press avoided partisanship and often eschewed coverage of politics altogether. In 1848, eight years after the invention of the telegraph, a group of newspapers formed the Associated Press to lower the cost of reporting from far-flung locales; because its product had to be used by a variety of papers with different perspectives, the AP adopted an ideologically neutral who-what-where-when approach to news writing. Thus was born the notion of "objectivity," the idea that facts could be separated from value judgments.[13]

The idea that there was a single standard of the true and objective news held sway through the twentieth century. CBS News' Walter Cronkite, known as "the most trusted man in America," ended his nightly reports by telling his viewers, "That's the way it is"—and they believed him. Even when the right began to charge the press with harboring a liberal bias (beginning most notably with Vice President Spiro Agnew), they still advanced the idea that objectivity was possible; after all, the bias charge assumes that there is a standard the press is failing to live up to.

Yet today it seems as if the right-wing media are working to eradicate the very idea of objective news, even of journalism as a meaningful effort to arrive at a truth that can be commonly accepted. The stance of much of the right-wing media is that nothing anyone else says can be trusted, even when that individual is simply reporting facts. The Bush White House has made a number of moves—all but eliminating presidential press conferences, paying pundits to advocate its policies, spending hundreds of millions of dollars on PR firms whose activities include producing fake "news" segments given to local television stations,[14] giving White House press credentials to a phony "journalist" and sometime-male prostitute—that demonstrate a withering contempt for the very idea that journalism is something important to the functioning of a democracy. Journalists, White House chief of staff Andrew Card told the *New Yorker*, "don't represent the public any more than other people do. In our democracy, the people who represent the public stood for election. I don't believe you have a check-and-balance function."[15]

The Bush administration also focused its energy on courting the right-wing media, forums that not only feature relentless pro-Republican spin but also consistently attack the idea that facts that don't reflect well on the administration are facts at all. "It used to be we as the press would adjudicate the facts of the battle," said Scott Shepherd, a veteran political correspondent for the Cox newspaper chain. "We don't do that anymore. Now we present attacks. That's troublesome to me. We've gotten the idea if we say something is 'fact' then somehow we're biased. . . . The attacks have worked. People are intimidated."[16]

Though it has only been in existence since 1996, at the epicenter of the right-wing media universe lies Fox News, where conservatives are given little to challenge the idea that their conception of the world is the only reasonable one in existence. It's important to understand, however, that Fox News was not established simply to be a conservative propaganda organ. It avoided the failure of a predecessor begun in 1993, National Empowerment Television (which featured such attention-grabbing offerings as a program devoted to showcasing "America's abandonment of its traditional Judeo-Christian culture for the cultural Marxism of Political Correctness"[17]), by producing compelling television.

What owner Rupert Murdoch and network chief Roger Ailes understood was that they could build an audience and earn profits not simply by delivering news with an ideological bent but by offering a televised version of conservative talk radio: loud, fast, hyperkinetic, pumped full of testosterone and righteous anger, with every segment bracketed by a dramatic "whoosh" sound. To paraphrase *This Is Spinal Tap*, this news channel goes to 11.

Fox is distinguished from its competitors not just in its balance of voices but in its unapologetically opinionated style, where the line between reporting and editorializing is all but erased. Viewers are treated to a regular diet of stories dripping with contempt for Democrats, all built around Republican spin.[18] According to one study, seven in ten stories on Fox include reporters stating their own opinions, compared to less than one in twenty on CNN.[19] Fox's talk programs feature outsized personalities like Bill O'Reilly and Sean Hannity, whose specialty is pushing viewers' buttons of anger and resentment.

Hannity came to Fox from talk radio; O'Reilly added a radio show after becoming successful on television. As novelist David Foster Wallace observed about talk radio, "It is, of course, much less difficult to arouse genuine anger, indignation, and outrage in people than it is real joy, satisfaction, fellow feeling, etc. The latter are fragile and complex, and what excites them varies a great deal from person to person, whereas anger et al. are more primal, universal, and easy to stimulate (as implied by expressions like 'He really pushes my buttons')."[20]

This goes a long way toward explaining the dominance of conservatives on talk radio. It's not that conservatism as a whole is particularly well suited to the medium; rather, it's a particular kind of conservatism—the kind that lives on anger, on resentment, on fear of shadowy and sinister elites—that is so tailor-made for talk radio. And it just happens that this is the dominant feature of the contemporary conservative movement.

When conservative talk radio exploded in popularity in the early 1990s, Rush Limbaugh and others like him were pounding on the gates of power; at the time, Democrats controlled the White House, both houses of Congress, and a majority of state legislatures and governorships. Now the situation is reversed, but as any broadcaster worth his salt knows, paeans to the glory of the nation's elected officials make for dull radio and television. Triumphalism gets old pretty quickly, but the feeling of being oppressed is a scab that can be picked again and again, ready to bleed afresh every time. Given the relative power of conservatives and liberals today, this takes no small measure of creativity, but conservatives have shown that one can have the president's ear and still be at the mercy of unseen forces, with societal collapse mere moments away, forever on the simultaneous verge of total victory and utter annihilation.[21]

One primary agent of the coming catastrophe is, of course, the media themselves. The story conservatives tell over and over about the media—or rather, the "liberal media elite"—is that the news is created by a group of highly educated Northeasterners who look down their noses at regular Americans, as they twist the news to advance their sexually deviant, antireligious, anti-American agenda.

The canard of liberal news media bias has become a conservative shibboleth; endless complaints about the allegedly liberal media are the way they proclaim their identity, the poor oppressed right-wingers crushed under Dan Rather's foot, with only their control of all three branches of government to comfort them. Conservatives watch Fox and listen to Limbaugh precisely because those outlets reinforce their beliefs, showing a picture of the world in which their leaders are brave heroes and the opposition is a bunch of sniveling, deceitful traitors, where they can watch liberals get what they deserve on an endless loop of war cries and insults.

Progressives need their own media strategy, one that is more than just the mirror image of the conservative attacks on the press. Proclaiming that the media have a conservative bias, while true in some senses, will not do the job. Instead, progressives need to find their own stories to tell about both the mainstream media and the conservative media, stories that will work to discredit conservatives, minimize the right's impact on the national discourse, and provide a context in which progressive arguments can win the day.

FIGHTING BACK

When public health officials first attempted to reduce rates of teen smoking, they decided to reach kids directly through their favorite medium, television. All one had to do, they believed, was tell kids how hazardous smoking is to their health, and they could be persuaded not to take up the habit or to quit if they already were smokers. The ads were straightforward and informative, laying out the dangers with a clear message: smoking is bad for you, so don't do it.

As would surprise no one who had ever been a teenager, these ads were spectacularly unsuccessful. It wasn't until antismoking advocates shifted the target of the scorn portrayed in their ads from the effects of the product itself to the malevolence of its producers—the tobacco companies—that they began to get through to teens. Extensive experimental research revealed that

> Advertisements that directly attack the tobacco industry as the source of the tobacco problem; expose the way in which the industry manipulates, deceives, seduces, and addicts children and adolescents; and highlight the way the industry maintains adult smokers as life-long drug addicts to make profits are effective in challenging the legitimacy and credibility of the industry. . . . The theme of tobacco industry manipulation also demonstrates and reinforces the concept that smoking is a behavior that undermines adolescents' independence, reduces their control over life decisions, and makes them victims of the industry's deceit. Rather than mobilizing young persons to rebel against directives not to smoke, campaigns based on these themes empower them to rebel against an industry that is making its profits by deceiving them; seducing them; manipulating them; addicting them; and, ultimately, killing them.[22]

Since the right-wing media came into their own in the 1990s, liberal criticism has been like early efforts to convince teens not to smoke. Progressives have said that the right-wing media are dishonest, that they are little more than shills for the Republican Party, that they play to our worst instincts. All these criticisms are true, but none has stemmed either the growth or the influence of the right-wing media. So progressives need to begin talking about the right-wing media in a new way, one that follows the example of effective antismoking campaigns.

Progressives who want to counter the right-wing media are confronted with the problem of asymmetric warfare. No matter the success of some attempts to create a left-wing counterpart (for instance, the radio network Air America, which after some initial stumbles grew from nothing to fifty stations within about a year), the right-wing media will continue to exist and to spew forth a unified partisan message. The answer for progressives is to discredit right-wing media with a story that explains who they are and what they are doing.

The first part of this story is this: *The right-wing media are populated by radicals so extreme that they have no place in any civilized discussion of public issues.* There is certainly no shortage of examples. When Michael Savage says that immigration is "part of the grand plan, to push homosexuality to cut down on the white race," or when Bill O'Reilly advocates the terrorist murder of Americans by inviting Al Qaeda to attack San Francisco ("Every other place in America is off limits to you, except San Francisco. You want to blow up the Coit Tower? Go ahead."), progressives need to call it to the attention of both the wider public and the journalists who persist in believing that these hate-mongers are nothing more than energetic conservatives. This belief is possible because journalists generally don't listen to conservative talk radio, so they have no idea just what a vile stew it is.

Next, progressives need to force conservatives who consider themselves "mainstream" to either defend or repudiate the nutballs in their midst. Take G. Gordon Liddy, the convicted Watergate felon and popular radio host, who famously instructed his listeners to murder federal agents by telling the listeners that since those agents often wear bulletproof vests, head shots were more effective. As an article in the British publication *The Independent* revealed, "Liddy was made to salute the Stars and Stripes Nazi-style by the nuns at his school; even now, he admits, 'at assemblies where the national anthem is played, I must suppress the urge to snap out my right arm.' . . . When he listened to Hitler on the radio, it 'made me feel a strength inside I had never known before,' he explains."[23]

Liddy is more than a repellent creep; he and his ilk are tools for progressives to use. Just as African American leaders are always called upon to make their positions clear whenever a famous black person says something troubling, conservatives in positions of power should be confronted with the statements of conservative extremists and be forced to say where they stand. Whatever their response, progressives win: if conservatives defend people like Liddy, they can reasonably be tarred as extremists, and if they repudiate these types of people, they alienate at least some of their supporters. Either way, the issue puts conservatives on the defensive and demonstrates for the public the extremism that is such a fundamental part of the conservative coalition.

The goal is to discredit and isolate the right-wing media in order to convince the public that listening to the likes of Rush Limbaugh and watching Fox News are in and of themselves the mark of an unwillingness to tolerate opposing views, a taste for hateful outbursts, and a credulousness toward crackpot ideas. Right-wing media are overflowing not only with Republican spin but also with rhetoric that would be shocking to most reasonable people. Nearly every town in America big enough to have a radio station has its own low-rent Limbaugh, convinced that the path to success is a combination of histrionics, hyperbole, and hate.

So progressives need an apparatus to monitor and disseminate conservative excesses in the same way conservatives do to those of liberals. If a liberal professor somewhere says something stupidly anti-American, within hours it will appear on someone's Web site; that afternoon it will be reported on countless conservative radio shows; then in the evening it will be trumpeted on *Hannity & Colmes* and other Fox News shows. After a few days percolating through the conservative media, it may even reach the broadcast networks or mainstream newspapers, by which time tens of millions of Americans will have heard about this monumental crime against our nation. Conservative media outlets are constantly on the lookout for liberals against whom they can rage, with the obscurity and impotence of the perpetrator being no bar to national coverage. Progressives need to do something similar: find the outrageous statements that demonstrate the extremism of the right-wing media and disseminate them as widely as possible.[24]

The second and most important part of the story progressives need to tell about the right-wing media is this: *The right-wing media are a group of con artists selling snake-oil on behalf of the country's elite.* They lie, they distract, they hoodwink, in the service of getting regular people to do the bidding of the moneyed elites that pay for it all. They think you're stupid and easily manipulated, that all they have to do is give you a steady stream of inconsequential figures to be angry at, and you'll ignore the things that really affect your life. They do this because when you look at things clearly, you realize the problem isn't some Hollywood actor or professor of cultural studies. Those people may be silly at times, but none of them ever laid off your neighbor or made health insurance so expensive. The problem is the people who hold economic and political power in this country. And those people are conservatives—the last people in the world the right-wing media want you to think about.

This message has to be repeated over and over and over. Every time a progressive goes on a right-wing talk show, he or she has to turn the conversation to the subject of the show itself: why it talks about what it does and what (and who) it ignores.

This strategy won't convince your average dittohead to stop listening to Rush Limbaugh, but it will begin to peel away some of the moderates and liberals who do listen to these shows because they're entertaining and will prevent journalists from taking them seriously. On election night 2002, NBC brought Limbaugh on to give "analysis" (without an accompanying liberal, of course), bestowing on him a legitimacy he didn't deserve. If progressives are successful, that sort of thing won't happen again.

This story—that the right-wing media are a big scam—is pivotal to undercutting the power of the conservative argument against the "liberal media elite." Conservatives can tell their story about the media persuasively because they have effectively linked liberals with the idea of the "elite." By defining the elite by things like education and consumer taste, they disconnected the notion from any conception of the distribution of power and influence. So if progressives can reconnect the idea of the elite to the realities of power—who controls the government, who controls the economy, who has the power to affect your life—they can make the case that it is in fact conservative interests that are being served by the news media.

This critique of the right-wing media must be joined to a complementary critique of the mainstream media. In order to keep the press honest, progressives have to keep the mainstream news media under constant surveillance and, when necessary, criticism. This is something the right has been extraordinarily successful at over the last few decades. It funded groups to monitor the media and made the cry of "liberal media bias" a central tenet of its movement, to the point where the belief is embraced uncritically by nearly every conservative, up to and including the president of the United States. A 2004 Pew Research Center survey found that only 12 percent of Republicans said they believed what they heard on that forum of wild accusations and crazy conspiracy theories known as *The NewsHour with Jim Lehrer*. Only 23 percent said they trusted what they heard on C-SPAN.[25] As bizarre as the notion that C-SPAN is colored by liberal bias may be, conservatives have so integrated the notion of media bias into their worldview that many will immediately dismiss as irredeemably biased any presentation that does not laud Republicans as giants walking among mortals and hurl undisguised contempt at Democrats.

It will be nearly impossible to convince the most committed conservatives that their beliefs about the media are mistaken, but it's not necessary to do so. Instead, the goal should be to use their convictions against them, driving a wedge between the staunch conservatives and every other American who would like to think of himself or herself as a reasonable person.

The critics on the right are correct about one thing: reporters are more likely to be liberal than conservative, at least on some issues (particularly social issues like abortion or gay rights; on economic issues, reporters are more conservative[26]). The imbalance is hardly overwhelming, though; in the most recent version of a periodic survey of reporters, the Indiana University journalism professor David Weaver and his colleagues found in 2003 that 37 percent were Democrats, 19 percent were Republicans, and the rest were independents.[27] Because reporters know this, and because they are under unrelenting pressure from the right, they go out of their way to show how "objective" they are by beating the tar out of Democrats.

Republicans have even succeeded in convincing some in the press that if the *facts* don't reflect well on Republicans, then the facts must not be reported. In 2004, Michael Massing reported that the press was imposing a "balance" on reporting out of Iraq that distorted Americans' view of the war: "'At the moment, there's real sensitivity about the perceived political nature of every story coming out of Iraq,' a Baghdad correspondent for a large U.S. paper told me in mid-October. 'Every story from Iraq is by definition an assessment as to whether things are going well or badly.' In reality, he said, the situation in Iraq was a catastrophe, a view 'almost unanimously' shared by his colleagues. But, he added, 'Editors are hypersensitive about not wanting to appear to be coming down on one side or the other.'"[28] Before the war began, the *Columbia Journalism Review* reported that the *Nashville Tennessean*, despite the fact that 70 percent of the letters it received opposed the war, was printing as many pro-war letters as it could to avoid charges of bias.[29] Later, a small paper in Wisconsin printed a plea to its readers to send in more pro-Bush letters: "We've been getting more letters critical of President Bush than those that support him. We're not sure why, nor do we want to guess. But in today's increasingly polarized political environment, we would prefer our offering to put forward a better sense of balance."[30]

When journalists engage in this kind of phony "balance," they have to be attacked without mercy or sympathy, for they have betrayed the mission of their profession. To my journalist friends who resent this kind of pressure, my response is that, to quote Spider-Man, with great power comes great responsibility. Our very Constitution singles out the press for preferential treatment, and rightly so; democracy is quite simply impossible without an aggressive and fearless press corps. Thomas Jefferson, who was the target of relentless, scurrilous attacks from the newspapers of his day, said, "Were it left to me to decide whether we should have a government without newspapers, or newspapers without a government, I should not hesitate a moment to prefer the latter." When journalists buckle under accusations of bias, they have failed not only their readers but democracy itself, and they have to be called out for their cowardice.

Progressives, particularly those who work for candidates, need to rid themselves of the illusion that the press will treat them well because reporters may agree with them on this or that issue. Whether reporters as individuals are sympathetic to your agenda is *absolutely irrelevant* to whether you will be successful in obtaining the kind of coverage that will make your agenda more likely to be enacted. As it happened, many in the press found much of Ronald Reagan's agenda problematic; they also thought he was not particularly bright and was prone to an infuriating dishonesty. Nonetheless, Reagan received overwhelmingly positive coverage. "A lot of the Teflon came because the press was holding back. I don't think they wanted to go after him that toughly," former Reagan aide David Gergen told journalist Mark Hertsgaard. Ben Bradlee, the former executive editor of the *Washington Post*, said much the same thing: "We have been kinder to President Reagan than any President . . . since I've been at the *Post*."[31] One need only compare the presidencies of Bill Clinton and George W. Bush to see that whatever liberalism may lie in the hearts of reporters, it makes little difference in the coverage they give to presidents.

Yet reporters have to a large degree assimilated the conservative media critique. They have concluded that there must be something to the liberal bias charge, and the way to deal with it is by bending over backward to be tough on Democrats and treating Republicans with respect and deference. Almost daily, a broadcast or cable news program will feature a panel consisting of two opinionated conservatives "balanced" by two reporters. Sometimes even that "balance" is not enough; for instance, NPR reporter Mara Liasson plays patsy on Fox News discussions in which she is matched up with two conservative commentators, Fred Barnes and Mort Kondracke, in a discussion moderated by the conservative Brit Hume. Since Liasson is supposed to be an objective reporter, nothing resembling liberal opinion passes her lips, and thus no liberal voice is in evidence (although she reportedly assured Fox chief Roger Ailes that she was a Republican before he hired her[32]).

These kinds of propensities, combined with a performance during the Bush years that was nothing short of pathetic (particularly in the run-up to the Iraq war), provides the opening for progressives to tell a story about mainstream journalists: *Reporters are cowards.* They're afraid to have Republicans call them biased, they're afraid of losing access, they're afraid to challenge conventional wisdom, and their fear hurts the citizens they are supposed to be serving.

Progressives need to tell this story again and again, because charging reporters with cowardice may be the only thing that will embolden them to show a little more courage. When reporters pass on conservative talking points, they're being cowards. When they adopt conservative doublespeak, they're being cowards. When they refuse to report stories that might reflect badly on the president, they're being cowards.*

Like the liberal bias charge, this is an attack on reporters' professionalism. Reporters are told in journalism school that they are supposed to "comfort the afflicted and afflict the comfortable,"[33] yet in practice they all too often become handmaidens to power who lack the fortitude to stand up to the bogus charges of the right. They pass on talking points and spin, they allow misinformation to circulate through the atmosphere without bothering to correct it, they blindly accept the word of officials who have lied to them in the past, and they knuckle under to intimidation tactics. Point out the many cases in which they are not living up to the standards of their profession, and they may begin to respond.

The next thing progressives need is their own media apparatus. When conservatives decided that the mainstream media were

---

*After CBS admitted it had based a *60 Minutes* story about President Bush's National Guard service on documents that appeared to be phony, the network was so chastened that it spiked another story it had bumped in favor of the National Guard story. This one concerned President Bush's infamous false claim that Iraq had sought uranium from Africa—a claim, ironically enough, made on the basis of patently forged documents. "We now believe," said a CBS spokesperson, "it would be inappropriate to air the report so close to the presidential election." In other words, the Niger story was killed because it might reflect badly on President Bush not long before the election, an act of journalistic cowardice so mind-boggling it should make anyone who believes in an independent press shudder in fear.

biased against them, they worked not only to improve the coverage they got but also to build parallel sources that conservatives could turn to for information and inspiration. A network of magazines, newspapers, radio programs, and ultimately a cable news channel grew over time not only to serve conservatives but to pull the entire media universe to the right. Progressives need to find new and innovative ways of doing the same thing. They have already begun on the Internet, where progressive blogs serve hundreds of thousands, if not millions, of readers every day.[34]

Next, progressives—particularly, progressive politicians—must change the way they approach reporters and show a little courage of their own. Stop, stop, stop worrying about whether reporters like you. Stop worrying that David Broder might write a column tsk-tsking you for being too political. Stop trying to please the editorial page of the *Washington Post*. Free yourself from the shackles of the mainstream media. Not only will you feel liberated, you'll end up getting better news coverage.

Consider what happened in the aftermath of the 2000 election. While Al Gore was back in Washington, literally drafting op-eds to submit to the *New York Times*, George Bush was feasting on the corpse of Florida's election system. When Gore wanted someone to run his recount effort, he apparently asked, "Who's a respected, nonthreatening figure whose appointment will be greeted with nods of approval from the Washington establishment?" He came up with Warren Christopher. Bush, on the other hand, asked, "Who's the shrewdest, most ruthless son of a bitch I can find?" He came up with James Baker. Gore told his supporters not to stage public protests or seem too angry. Bush's people printed up "Sore Loserman" signs and intimidated election officials (after the brownshirt riot in Miami-Dade county organized by Republican congressional staffers shut down the counting there, the Bush campaign paid for a party to celebrate, complete with entertainment by Wayne Newton; Bush and Cheney called in with their congratulations). The Bush campaign spent four times as much money as the Gore campaign on the postelection wrangling. Did Bush and Cheney get criticized in the press for their behavior? Not for a minute.

The fact is that reporters like progressives, but they don't respect them because they think that progressives in general and Democrats in particular are weak, ineffectual losers (and much of the time, they're right). There is nothing for which reporters have greater admiration than skill—even when wielded unethically. The smoothly humming campaign machine, the mind-numbingly on-message operative, the victorious political strategist all can count on coverage ranging from the respectful to the worshipful. As cynical as they pretend to be, political reporters are like the nerdy kid who becomes the equipment manager of the high school football team, picking apart the quarterback's performance with a jaundiced eye while dreaming that he, too, could be throwing the winning touchdown.

One might ask why, if they are so obsessed with political skill, members of the Washington press corps had such a visceral reaction against Bill Clinton and have for so much of his presidency been so complimentary toward George W. Bush. The reasons are complex in both cases, but part of it has to do with the effort each seemed to expend. Clinton often looked like Babe Ruth—stays up until four in the morning drinking in a strip bar, then tumbles into the stadium and hits the winning home run, just because he's so good. Bush, on the other hand, is someone reporters completely understand. Though in many ways he has been just as politically successful as Clinton was, with Bush the artifice is obvious. Reporters can see every carefully constructed catch phrase, every practiced gesture, every quick glance down at the talking points aides have written for him. If politics is theater, Bush's presidency is one in which the stage crew is not hidden in the wings but standing next to the featured performer, visible for all to see. The response of the cynical reporter, who knows exactly what Bush is doing and how he does it, is to say, "Nice job, kid, you pulled it off."

Clinton notwithstanding, reporters have become so accustomed to Democratic failure and weakness that when a tough Democrat shows up, they are positively flabbergasted. So when Howard Dean—a budget-balancing moderate who had been endorsed numerous times by the NRA—became the chairman of the Democratic Party, reporters took it as an indication that the party was "moving to the left." They had a fixed image of what a Democrat is: weak, uncertain, accommodating, unwilling to stand up for his beliefs, afraid not only of Republicans but of his own shadow. When Dean undercut that image, their narrow imaginations could only conclude that he was an *ideological* extremist. If progressives show enough fortitude, though, over time those opinions may just begin to change.

There are a few things progressives must keep in mind about reporters as they craft their media strategies:

- *Reporters cannot be relied on to report the truth.* If your opponents lie, the lie will be dutifully passed along. The he said/she said style is ingrained not only as a time-saving device (and reporters are always pressed for time) but also as a means of remaining "objective." This means that the unscrupulous have permission to lie. The answer is that when your opponents lie, don't just dispute the facts, call them liars. If you repeat the word often enough, you can shift the discussion away from the he said/she said to whether or not they lied.

- *Reporters are endlessly cynical.* They will always be looking for hidden motives and will never believe a politician who says he believes something just because he believes it and not because it works to his political advantage. They assume that every politician is completely full of it on most issues. If you can establish certain areas in which your values are strong and unwavering, however, eventually reporters will accept your sincerity, at least in those limited areas. The key is choosing the issues well.

- *Reporters respect toughness and admire success.* Don't ever expect that the latest Republican dirty trick will be met with condemnation. Reporters love hardball campaign tactics, and the candidate who turns the other cheek will be scorned as a loser. If you win, you will be praised, and if you lose, you will be bludgeoned, no matter what happened along the way.

- *Reporters care about "substance" and "issues," but they don't care about substance and issues.* You can expect to be praised for *having* a ten-point plan, but you will be punished mercilessly if you force reporters to actually read it or listen to you talk about it. Political reporters don't want to know about the details of policy;

they're too busy speculating about politics to give the details much thought. Yet they still believe that policy is important, so if you can convince them you have substance, all the better.

- *Reporters say they hate spin, but they give the greatest respect to the most egregious spinners.* To take just one example, look at RNC chairman Ken Mehlman, who, if you asked him what time it was, would reply, "Americans are proud of George W. Bush's bold and strong leadership, and it's 2:30." You might think that a character like Mehlman, who offers the basest form of political rhetoric imaginable—an endless string of simplistic talking points and Bizarro World paeans to our smashing success in Iraq, the booming economy, and public excitement about Bush's Social Security plan—would be treated with withering contempt by the Fourth Estate. But you'd be wrong. Instead, Mehlman is offered praise precisely because of the unceasing tornado of spin he spits out. There are few things reporters respect more than a politician or an operative who stays fanatically on message.

The power of the conservative critique of the media lies in the fact that every conservative, from the most powerful politician to the most ordinary citizen, knows exactly what it is, believes it, and repeats it. Progressives need to disseminate their critique just as widely. What unites the critique of the right-wing media (that they are perpetrating a scam) and the critique of the mainstream media (that they are cowardly) is the idea of power. Both the right-wing media and the mainstream media are serving the powerful elite at the expense of the rest of us. The right-wing media do it because they are partners with the powerful, and the mainstream media do it because they fear and admire the powerful.

One benefit of this critique is that it covers a wide range of media issues that go beyond the content of journalism. Why do progressives support limits on media ownership, while conservatives oppose those limits? Because the powerful media companies whom conservatives serve want to control what you see, read, and hear. Why do progressives support a strong public broadcasting system, while conservatives don't? Because public broadcasting is there to serve all of us, not the interests of the powerful. Why do progressives favor community Internet, while conservatives oppose it? Because progressives want everyone to have affordable Internet access, while conservatives want it controlled by a few big corporations. Why is your cable bill so high? Because conservatives removed the regulations that controlled cable rates, allowing your cable company to give you the shaft.

Early in George W. Bush's presidency, *Washington Post* reporter John Harris wrote an unusually frank assessment of why the new president was getting so much better press coverage than his predecessor had. Harris outlined the essence of the problems faced by the progressive movement:

> Are the national news media soft on Bush? The instinctive response of any reporter is to deny it. But my rebuttals lately have been wobbly. The truth is, this new president has done things with relative impunity that would have been huge uproars if they had occurred under Clinton. Take it from someone who made a living writing about those uproars.
>
> The difference is not in journalists' attitudes toward Bush or their willingness to report aggressively on him. It is that nearly all the political and institutional forces that constitute Washington writ large have aligned to make Bush's life more pleasant than Clinton's ever was, even at the start of his presidency.
>
> There are many small reasons: Republicans and Democrats alike seem exhausted from the negativity and scandal of the Clinton era. The Bush team is mostly competent and well-focused, so it has given adversaries fewer handles to grab. And even his opponents seem to think the new president is a likable enough fellow.
>
> Above all, however, there is one big reason for Bush's easy ride: There is no well-coordinated corps of aggrieved and methodical people who start each day looking for ways to expose and undermine a new president.
>
> There was just such a gang ready for Clinton in 1993. Conservative interest groups, commentators and congressional investigators waged a remorseless campaign that they hoped would make life miserable for Clinton and vault themselves to

power. They succeeded in many ways. One of the most important was their ability to take all manner of presidential miscues, misjudgments or controversial decisions and exploit them for maximum effect. Stories like the travel office firings flamed for weeks instead of receding into yesterday's news. And they colored the prism through which many Americans, not just conservative ideologues, viewed Clinton.

It is Bush's good fortune that the liberal equivalent of this conservative coterie does not exist. Take the recent emergency landing of a U.S. surveillance plane in China. Imagine how conservatives would have reacted had Clinton insisted that detained military personnel were not actually hostages, and then cut a deal to get the people (but not the plane) home by offering two "very sorrys" to the Chinese, while also saying that he had not apologized. What is being hailed as Bush's shrewd diplomacy would have been savaged as "Slick Willie" contortions.

Try to recall this major news story during Clinton's first 100 days: Under pressure from Western senators, the president capitulated on a minor part of his 1993 budget deal, grazing fees on ranchers using federal lands. A barrage of coverage had an unmistakable subtext: Clinton was weak and excessively political and caved to special interests. Bush has made numerous similar concessions on items far more central to the agenda he campaigned on, such as deemphasizing vouchers in his education plan and conceding that his tax cut will be some $350 billion smaller than he proposed. For the most part these repositionings are being cast as shrewd rather than servile.

Do you suppose there would have been an uproar under Clinton if Democrats had been rewarding donors with special closed-door briefings by Cabinet secretaries? The *New York Times* reported the other day that GOP donors received just such a briefing with Health and Human Services Secretary Tommy Thompson as thanks for their efforts. Far from an uproar, the story has had only a faint echo. Clinton's "donor maintenance" coffees led to a year of congressional inquiries. . . .

What's going on here? It is not that reporters have been

charmed by Bush. It is not that Democrats are nicer, more decent people than Republicans. The difference is that the GOP conservatives' zeal to undermine Clinton—and the techniques they used to do it—flowed from special historical circumstances. For a generation before Clinton, conservatives believed they would never get a fair shake from the establishment news media—"an effete corps of impudent snobs," in Spiro Agnew's words.

One response of the conservatives was to create new voices of their own: think tanks, columnists, magazines, radio programs. These voices tended to be in concert. The sense of grievance and insurgency that fueled the modern conservative movement makes these activists more likely to network and promote a common message. . . .

For the most part, Clinton's foes and their contemptuous views of him were within the bounds of fair debate. But Democrats are not likely to give as good as they got. They simply aren't as well organized. And they are not shouting as loudly.[35]

When Bill Clinton came into office, the conservative movement had not an instant of doubt that it would fight him every day, with every ounce of its energy, as long as he held power (in fact, many of its members continued to fight him even after he left). Conservatives gave no quarter, thought no accusation was too ridiculous to make, and believed that too far was not far enough. Where they failed, it was mostly because they allowed their zeal to overcome their better political judgment.

Progressives need to approach the media wars with that same sense of purpose and with the understanding that the tug of war over media coverage of politics will never end. No matter how conservative or liberal the media become, the right will always complain about liberal bias, and its pressure will always need to be met with equal pressure in the opposite direction. As in politics more generally, total victory in the media war is not possible. The opponents can be struck down, demoralized, discredited, and marginalized, but they will always be there and they will always fight back. The answer for progressives is to start fighting back and never stop.

8

THINKING BIG

It's Not about the Next Election, Stupid

For about two hours, Clinton and a collection of his advisors listened as Marmor and Pollack squared off. Single payer, Marmor argued, could save billions by cutting out redundant insurance bureaucracies, would achieve universal coverage, better control costs, and guarantee doctor choice. Pollack, once an advocate of single payer himself, made the case that play-or-pay, not single payer, was politically feasible. . . .

After the two advocates finished, Clinton looked thoughtful, pointed to Marmor and said, "Ted, you win the argument." But gesturing to Pollack, Marmor recalls, the governor quickly added, "But we're going to do what he says." Even considering the Canadian system, everyone in the room agreed, would prompt GOP cries of "socialized medicine"—cries that the press would faithfully report.[1]

This conversation with Ted Marmor (an advocate of Canada's single-payer health-care system) and Ron Pollack (the head of FamiliesUSA that supported a "play-or-pay" plan) occurred in November 1991 before Bill Clinton had won a single primary, much less taken office and begun dealing with an unruly Congress and a recalcitrant opposition. Yet even then he was already compromising, turning away from what he knew the best solution was toward something that he believed—incorrectly, as it turned out—would inspire less opposition.

Fast forward fourteen years. As George W. Bush trooped around the country trying to convince Americans to embrace his Social Security privatization plan, Democrats were hounded by Washington pundits who demanded that they come up with a "plan" to address a shortfall in the program's finances that might come to pass, if economic growth is particularly anemic for the next forty or fifty years. With uncharacteristic unity, the Democrats stood firm, defended their values, and refused to compromise. For the first time in years, they achieved a major political victory, as support for Bush's plan dwindled steadily until it was shelved indefinitely.

The Democrats were aided in that fight by the fact that what President Bush was trying to do was simply unpalatable to the public. But the debate also showed that Democrats were committed immovably to Social Security as one of their basic values. Thus not only did they win, they came out looking better when it was all over. The task for progressives now is to assemble and promote a policy agenda that—win or lose in the short term—keeps the progressive movement moving forward.

In order to do so, they have to think big, to ask not what is achievable in the next session of Congress, but what they'd like to achieve in their fondest dreams. They have to ask what significant, dramatic changes they'd like to see and start advocating for them, no matter how long it might take. Thinking big defines you in the eyes of the electorate—not only for the content of what you're proposing, but for the very fact that you have ambitious ideas and firmly held beliefs.

Thinking big is also particularly important at a time when progressives are utterly without power in our nation's capital. When, for instance, the majority won't even allow votes on the amendments to legislation you'd like to offer, you are free to offer any pie-in-the-sky plan you want, no matter how unrealistic. Being out of power provides one with the opportunity to suggest ambitious solutions to the nation's problems without the need to actually translate them into the messy details of legislation. Those details can be added over time as the big ideas are debated and refined. If you don't start from the standpoint of the perfect world you'd like to see, however, you will find yourself, like Clinton on health care, compromising before you've even begun and failing to get anywhere.

A TWENTY-FIRST-CENTURY PROGRESSIVE AGENDA

Once progressives have defined and articulated their values, they need an agenda that flows from those values, policies they can advocate to show the American people what they're about. While there may be dozens of things progressives would like to see happen, they have to pick out a few big ideas to present to the American people in order to show who they are and where their priorities lie. Whatever else they contain, these big ideas must have three things in common. They must be consequential yet easy to understand; they must flow directly from progressive values; and they must tell a story about who progressives and conservatives are.

Although elaborating a progressive policy idea for every possible issue would require a book of its own (or two or three), we can examine how to present major policy ideas by discussing a few important areas where progressives have opportunities.

Let us begin with health care. In 1993, GOP strategist William Kristol warned his fellow Republicans not to compromise with Bill Clinton's push for health-care reform but rather to seek its total defeat. Meaningful health-care reform, Kristol wrote in an influential memo distributed throughout the right, "will revive the reputation of the party that spends and regulates, the Democrats, as the generous protector of middle-class interests. And it will at the same time strike a punishing blow against Republican claims to defend the middle class by restraining government."[2] Kristol was absolutely right—had the 1993 health-care reform effort succeeded, it would have enabled the Democratic Party to say for generations that Democrats were the ones who brought universal health care to the American public over the objections of Republicans.

The Republican strategy worked, and it was followed by an ideological capitulation by Democrats that the right probably hadn't even hoped for, as many on the left took exactly the wrong lesson from the debacle of the 1993 health-care reform effort. The lesson was not that dramatic health-care reform is impossible, or that the American people don't want it—on the contrary, dramatic health-care reform is overwhelmingly popular. The right lesson is that powerful interests will fight health-care reform, and if you put virtually no thought into how to fight those interests, you'll lose. Like so many other events of recent decades, the failure of health-care reform turned Democrats timid on the issue, convincing them that any legislative effort on health care that amounted to more than tinkering around the edges of the problem would bring substantive and political failure.

Well, it's time for them to get over it. The public wants and needs universal health coverage, and if the Democratic Party doesn't have the courage to stand up for that goal, then they don't stand for anything. Even if it takes years, the very fact that Democrats will be seen as willing to fight for universal coverage will enhance the party's image as the advocate for working people and will paint conservatives as opponents of health security.

All the conditions are in place for an issue that can bring Democrats tremendous political benefits. The problem is one the public cares deeply about, since it touches everyone's life. Democrats already enjoy a greater measure of trust on the issue than their opponents do. Those opponents are steadfastly opposed to doing anything about the problem. The issue is a logical extension of the fundamental values at the heart of progressivism. The progressive position is a clear and unambiguous contrast with the conservative position, and it can be stated in simple, easy-to-understand terms.

Yet Democrats steadfastly refuse to advocate for serious health-care reform. Scarred by the experience of 1993, they believe that it's better to play it safe, to come up with plans for tinkering with arcane details of health-care financing rather than planting a flag in the sand.

So if you ask Americans, what are Democrats advocating on health care, they wouldn't be able to tell you, because the answer is, not much of anything. Democrats have all but abandoned this issue, despite the fact that public sentiment could hardly be clearer. People don't just want better access to affordable insurance that will cover most of their costs minus a reasonable deductible and hopefully not-too-small lifetime limits providing premiums are paid on time and the provider is within your network. They want guaranteed health coverage for every American. Period.

Oh no, say Democrats, we can't advocate that—the Republicans will call it socialized medicine! Well, here's a hint: the Republicans will say *any* Democratic idea on health care is "socialized medicine," no matter what the content of that idea actually is. Given that, you might as well give the public something people can understand—not a complex, multilayered proposal, but a simple statement of principle: we want guaranteed coverage for every American.

Does this mean single-payer health care? It certainly could. It's important to note that there is not one single-payer system; each country that employs one does it in a slightly different way. We are perfectly free to devise a single-payer system that can correct some of the problems that have been experienced in other countries and that is suited to America's needs. Call it "Medicare for all," as some have, or come up with a new name like "Americare," but the advantages of single-payer health care are enormous. The savings in administrative costs alone from shifting from our current system to a single-payer system would be enough to pay for coverage for every one of the forty-five million uninsured Americans.[3]

Because it costs so much more than the single-payer systems that exist in most of the countries with which we compete, our bloated health insurance system puts American businesses at a tremendous disadvantage. Companies like General Motors are being absolutely crippled by health-care costs; in 2003, GM spent $4.5 billion on health care, or $1,200 for every car it produced.[4] In June 2005, Toyota announced that it was spurning the millions of dollars in tax incentives offered by Southern states and would instead build a new plant in Ontario. Toyota cited two reasons: first, that Canadian workers are easier to train (according to one Canadian business association leader, Nissan and Honda found they had to use "pictorials" to teach illiterate workers in Mississippi and Alabama how to use high-tech equipment[5]). Second, the fact that Canada has a single-payer health system means Toyota would not have to pick up the cost of its employees' health coverage.[6]

Yet like so many other corporations, car companies refuse to advocate for the one solution that would slash their costs, improve conditions for their workers, lower the price of their cars, and increase their profits. Why? The only answer anyone has been able to come up with is ideology: the ideology of the individuals who sit at the top of America's large corporations. These men (and a woman here and there) are overwhelmingly conservative Republicans who believe—despite the evidence screaming at them from their balance sheets—that market solutions are always superior to government solutions, and that to favor a single-payer system would be tantamount to embracing socialism.

To counter this resistance, progressives need to start a public campaign aimed specifically at getting businesses to embrace the principle of a national health-care plan, beginning with small and mid-size companies and moving through shareholders of large companies. As more and more companies sign on, executives will have to explain to their shareholders why they remain opposed to higher profits and a happier workforce.

Whatever the details of the plan they come up with, though, progressives need to repeat the simple contrast over and over: we want guaranteed health coverage for all Americans and conservatives don't. Guaranteed coverage for all is what author Rick Perlstein refers to as a "superjumbo project," a big idea that its advocates acknowledge may take years or even decades to enact. "The Democrats need to make commitments, or a network of commitments, that *do not waver* from election to election," he wrote. "If you are trying to build an institution that commands respect and power unto generations—that can reproduce itself—wise superjumbo projects have intrinsic value, whatever their precise content, whether they end up failing or succeeding."[7] The point is not whether single-payer health care could be enacted in the next session of Congress. The point is whether it's something progressives truly believe in—which it is—and what it says about them. If it's the right thing to do, progressives should be willing to commit to it with the understanding that it may take decades to achieve.

Single-payer health care is not a new idea, and Democrats are often criticized for not having enough new ideas. In truth, however, there are plenty of new progressive ideas around—Washington is practically brimming with them. Consider the Apollo Alliance, a project established by progressive, labor, and environmental leaders to push for a dramatic investment in new energy technologies as a way of reducing America's reliance on foreign oil and bringing our energy supply into the twenty-first century. The alliance's argument is that a new energy strategy can be presented not as a way to save wilderness areas or produce cleaner air but as a way to create millions of jobs and move our economy forward. One of the participants in the alliance gave this remarkable description of focus groups that the alliance sponsored:

> In 2003, in Erie, Penn. and Akron, Ohio, the Apollo Alliance did focus groups among undecided, working-class, swing voters—the very people who would determine the outcome of the 2004 election. I had the luck to observe the focus groups from the other side of a one-way mirror.
>
> Instead of starting the focus groups by asking people what they thought of global warming, our pollster Ted Nordhaus simply asked them how things were going. This open-ended question led, invariably, to focus group participants describing the collapse of the local economy. They would list, in depressing detail, the shutting of Hoover Vacuum and Timken Ball-bearing factories; gone to Mexico. They explained that the jobs that had been created in their wake—mostly service sector jobs in places like Wal-Mart—paid half as much and offered no health care or retirement benefits. Many said they were working two jobs to make ends meet.
>
> We then asked them what they thought of the idea of a major federal investment program to accelerate America's transition to the clean energy economy of the future: research and development, manufacturing of wind turbines and solar, energy efficiency. We didn't have to prove to them that such a program would pay for itself; they knew it would intuitively. Hadn't a similar program succeeded in the post-war period? Of course it had.
>
> What had been a roomful of tired and semi-depressed

working folks transformed itself into a roomful of excited, optimistic Americans in a period of just 20 minutes. The energy emanating from the room was palpable.

And then something extraordinary happened. Nearly every single person in the room started to sound like Sierra Club members. I could hardly believe what I was hearing. They waxed poetic about solar panels. They spoke of their children's future—their future—and the planet's future. They remembered episodes from the area's local history—like when thousands of jobs were created to retrofit smokestacks after the passage of the 1990 Clean Air Act Amendment—things that James Watt and Rush Limbaugh want them to forget. But more than that, Apollo tells a narrative about American greatness, our history of shared investment and prosperity, of our ingenuity, and how we build a better future.[8]

The Apollo Alliance argues that for an investment of $300 billion over ten years in new energy technologies, the country could see 3 million new jobs and a $1 trillion increase in GDP. It remains to be seen how successful the alliance will be in moving its program forward. For our purposes here, though, what's important about the Apollo Alliance is not just that it's a good idea, but that it tells a story about progressives: that they are thinking big, that they have new ideas, that they want to produce jobs, and that they are looking toward the future. The focus on job creation makes it impossible for conservatives to offer their usual caricature of environmental efforts as killing jobs to save spotted owls or endangered worms. Apollo's explicit goal is not only to appeal to traditional left constituencies like labor and environmentalists but to reach out to people concerned about their economic future whom Republicans have wooed successfully in recent years.

To many conservatives, the idea of enhancing renewable energy, or even investing in new technologies, sounds like fuzzy-headed enviro-wimpiness—real men get their energy by pulling it out of the ground with big, noisy machines. But a number of points work in progressives' favor. First, America simply doesn't have the oil reserves to satisfy our never-ending lust for black gold, and so as long as we depend on it, we will depend on Middle Eastern nations to sell it to us. This means that moving away from fossil fuels can be sold as pro-American and pro-independence—American energy for America. Second, the American people overwhelmingly support the use of alternative and renewable sources of energy. Third, use of these technologies is inherently hopeful, optimistic, and forward-looking—conservatives are stuck with the energy sources of the past, while progressives advocate the energy sources of the future.

Are the American people ready to hear and respond to this argument? A unique 2005 study by the University of Maryland showed just how progressive the American public's priorities are with regard to energy. Respondents were presented with figures on the latest federal budget and were told they could adjust the figures up or down as they would like to see tax money spent. Large majorities chose to cut the defense budget and increase spending on a variety of social programs, including education, job training, and medical research. The most popular program, however, was funding for conservation and renewable energy, which respondents chose to increase by an average of an astounding 1,090 percent.[9]

Let's take another good progressive idea, this one on taxes. In early 2005, the Center for American Progress released a comprehensive tax reform proposal based on a fundamental progressive principle: every kind of income should be treated the same. At the moment, our tax code is tilted in favor of the kind of income that wealthy people get when their money makes them more money. The CAP proposal taxes all income—wages, capital gains, dividends—according to the same rate schedule. It also eliminates the employee portion of the regressive payroll tax; moves to a simple, three-bracket structure; and eliminates the Alternative Minimum Tax. According to CAP documents, "Overall, the plan will reduce taxes for about 70 percent of tax filers earning under $200,000 a year, providing an average tax cut of over $600. Most of those making more that $200,000 a year will likely see an increase relative to current tax policy. The plan is fiscally responsible, reducing the deficit by nearly $500 billion over 10 years."

Were the CAP proposal to become the basis for legislation, it would no doubt be modified in one way or another. The point, however, is that it's a serious idea about tax reform that embodies progressive ideals and sets up a debate not between lower taxes and higher taxes but between fair taxes and unfair taxes.

These three issues—health care, energy, and taxes—are ones we have fought over before. But progressives also need to find not just new proposals on already controversial issues but entirely new issues that afford opportunities to tell stories about progressives and progressivism. Let's use community Internet as an example. This is an issue that most people have not thought about, but it could hardly be better positioned for progressives to tell a story about their hopeful, forward-looking agenda and to put conservatives on the defensive.

All over the country, towns and cities are realizing that in order to compete in the twenty-first century economy, their businesses and citizens need affordable broadband Internet access. Although America created the Internet, we are drastically behind the curve when it comes to both the speed and the scope of broadband availability. While the United States ranks fourth in total Internet penetration behind Sweden, Hong Kong, and Denmark, we don't crack the top ten in broadband penetration; two-thirds of American households have Internet access, but less than 30 percent have broadband (compare that to the 75 percent of South Koreans who have broadband).[10] Why has this happened? In no small part because a few huge telecommunication companies, insulated from real competition, have had no incentive to upgrade their technology or lower their prices. So Americans are saddled with Internet service that is incomplete, slower than it should be, and absurdly overpriced.

In response, cities and towns have begun exploring the installation of municipal broadband systems providing universal access at reasonable prices (some are wired systems and some are wireless ones that turn a city into one giant wireless hotspot). Not surprisingly, the telecom companies are appalled that their oligopolies would face competition from municipalities and have put tremendous lobbying muscle behind arresting the trend. They have already succeeded in passing laws in more than a dozen states limiting municipal broadband projects, in many cases offering companies like Verizon virtual veto power over a town's choice to provide a necessary service to its citizens.

This is not only inimical to economic growth, it strikes people as grossly unfair. Progressives believe that just as in the last century the government ensured that we all had access to electricity and roads, in this century we understand that we can't develop economically without broadband. If the telecom companies can't provide adequate service at affordable prices, then towns and cities have every right to set up their own systems.

For this issue to work to progressives' advantage, it has to be defined as a progressive/conservative split, with progressives on the side of community Internet and conservatives on the side of the telecom companies. When conservatives end up defending corporate oligopolies, we will quickly find that on this issue, one traditional line of demarcation—that conservatives are pro-business and liberals are anti-business—has been overturned. This conflict puts progressives on the side of small and mid-size businesses, economic growth, and new jobs, and puts conservatives on the side of a few greedy and unpopular corporations. It also shows how government can provide a needed service at a reasonable price, an idea that undercuts the entire conservative critique of government.

Progressives also need to rally behind a single electoral reform agenda that moves us toward fair and trustworthy elections. In addition to advocating voting equality for all Americans—including eliminating the Electoral College and providing full voting rights for residents of the District of Columbia—this agenda must include verifiable paper trails and adequate voting machines in every precinct in the country. We saw in Ohio in 2004 what kind of problems can result from too few voting machines, as people in Democratic districts found themselves waiting on line for hours in order to vote because there were not enough machines. So what if progressives advocated state laws mandating adequate voting machines based on a simple rule: each polling place must have at least one voting machine for every hundred registered voters. If there are five hundred registered voters in a precinct, you need five machines. Enactment of a 100-to-1 rule would ensure that everyone would be able to vote without having to wait for hours in the rain.

Some might object that this would cost a lot of money, but would it? The typical cost of an electronic voting machine is anywhere from $5,000 to $8,000. Yet optical scan voting—which has proven to be more reliable and easier to check—is much lower in cost. Even if you mandated an optical scanner at each polling place, you could increase the number of voting booths at very little cost, since each booth is basically a cheap plastic cube with a book guiding the voter where to mark the ballot.

The issue of electronic voting and the security and the access of the voting process are far too complex to address in detail here, but progressives should realize that the problems with voting are relatively easy to solve—if you're the one in charge of the voting process. Just as Katherine Harris, the Florida secretary of state and the state co-chair of the Bush campaign, made sure her candidate would come out ahead in the Florida counting in 2000, Kenneth Blackwell, the Ohio secretary of state and the co-chair of the state Bush campaign in 2004, worked overtime to make it as difficult as possible for Democrats to vote. Yet Democrats don't seem to have clued in to how important control of the secretary of state's office is. Right now, Republicans outnumber Democrats among the top state election officials, some in critical swing states. Democrats need to recruit their best candidates for these offices, invest heavily in the races, and implement a serious reform agenda to every state's voting process.

Progressives also need to take a stand against partisan gerrymandering—first, because it is simply undemocratic and, second, because it has put them at a disadvantage. The ultimate goal should be that every state's congressional districts are drawn by a nonpartisan panel; where state law allows, progressives should support voter initiatives to establish such panels. In the meantime, they should put a titanic effort into winning state legislative races in 2010, since the candidates elected in that year will choose each state's new district boundaries after the next census.

TIME FOR SOME BLUNT TALK

Finally, it's time for some blunt talk. First, Democrats need to stop nominating candidates for president who hate politics. As I mentioned in the introduction, too many of today's Democratic leaders are people who are good at policy and governing but don't seem to like, or be particularly gifted at, campaigning. For better or worse, the image of progressivism is going to be formed in part by nationally prominent Democrats, none more so than the candidates they nominate for president. The conservative attempt to define liberals as alien—to say, "He's not one of us"— will keep on succeeding if Democrats keep nominating people who don't love politics. Witness again the success of George W. Bush. You can practically count on one hand the number of Americans who had the kind of advantages he had in life, whose experiences were further from those of regular people, who were saved so often from their own weaknesses by the power and money wielded by their families and their associates. Yet Bush convinced people that he was just a regular guy. His success demonstrates that giving people the feeling that a politician is "one of us" is almost entirely a matter of style. Does it help if your policies are actually helping regular people? Sure, but it obviously isn't a requirement.

Finding candidates with what used to be called the "common touch" doesn't mean embracing the anti-intellectualism of the right. After all, Bill Clinton had degrees from Georgetown, Yale, and Oxford, but nobody thought he was an elitist. It was because he was possessed of a particular skill, the ability to talk to almost any kind of person in his or her language. This ability is crucial to national success and should be the first thing Democratic primary voters look for in coming years. If Democrats heed this advice, there will be many intelligent, capable politicians who won't have the opportunity to be their party's standard-bearer. Tough. They won't be winning the presidency anyway, so it's best they don't drag their party down with them.

Second, someone needs to sit down with liberal actors in Hollywood and give them a message they won't want to hear: Democrats want your money and your time and your effort and your input, but they need you to be quiet. It's not that you don't have interesting things to say, and it's not that your beliefs aren't strongly felt, because you do and they are. And it's not that you don't have good, all-American values, because you do. But when you get out in public pushing political goals, it *doesn't do a thing* to help those goals get accomplished, and it gives conservatives all the ammunition they could hope for.

So when you decide to get involved in the presidential campaign, you make a phone call and convince the campaign to allow you to get on stage and say a few words of support for the Democrat. Your thought is, "I'm a popular guy. People pay money to see me in movies. I'll bet I can convince them that this candidate is worth voting for."

I've got bad news for you: you can't. It just doesn't work that way. Your popularity may be transferable to some realms (say, convincing kids to buy a certain brand of gum), but politics is not one of them. What you do when you speak at that rally is give Rush Limbaugh a great big birthday present. The next day he'll be playing your speech on the air, using it to mock Hollywood celebrities who think they're better than regular folks, telling us how to vote. He'll come back to it for months to show how out of touch the Democrat is, with his fancy Hollywood friends.

This argument will probably make many Hollywood liberals angry. It isn't fair, and it's not how it should be. That doesn't matter, though. What they need to understand is that stoking resentment of people in the entertainment industry is a key part of the Republican strategy to paint Democrats as the "elite." It is the success of this strategy that keeps them winning election after election. When actors get involved in a public way, it only helps the right.

Actors may not like hearing this, but it's the truth. So perhaps what they could do is do what any citizen does: if they want to get involved, they should donate money, show up at a phone bank, make sure their neighbors get to the polls on election day—but don't get in front of the cameras. And don't bitch about your free speech rights. This isn't about your rights, it's about what's politically effective.

Let me make an analogy. Let's say someone walks into a campaign's headquarters wanting to volunteer. He's smart, committed, and could really be a big help, but he also happens to have a Mohawk hairdo colored green and moussed into two-foot-high spikes. If the people running the campaign are smart, they'll find a way to use his talents to serve the cause. What they won't do is give him ten minutes to speak at their next rally, because all anyone will be looking at is that hairdo, which will distract from the message of the campaign and ultimately do a disservice to the cause.

When it comes to appealing to the American people at large, the Hollywood celebrity is like that green-spiked Mohawk. When someone like Leonardo DiCaprio or Tim Robbins is directly involved in partisan politics, it's as if they come with a sign over their heads reading, "I'm a fancy-pants elitist and I think I'm better than you." And that doesn't help anybody—except Republicans.

Just like progressive celebrities, progressive activists need to spend less time thinking about what kind of activity will make them feel good and more time thinking about how to convince other people they're right. There is a long and honorable tradition of public protest in America, but in most political situations today, gathering a large number of people in a public place to walk together, hold signs, and listen to speeches is simply not an effective means of influencing policy. Liberals have a tendency to organize a protest about a given topic—say, the war in Iraq—then invite everyone with a cause to come along. So people turn on the news and see people marching with signs about Iraq, about racism, about abortion, about everything under the sun. Not only does it not persuade anyone, it actually turns people away from the cause. People who are perfectly willing to hear an antiwar message see a bunch of kids in Ché Guevara T-shirts and instinctively turn away, saying, "Those stupid hippies, what are they chanting about now?" The next time you're at a protest and some teenager shows up carrying a "Free Mumia" sign, grab him and toss him into the trunk of a car before he gets in front of the cameras.

Public displays like protests tell a story not only about the issue involved but about the participants. Cindy Sheehan, who became a national figure when she held a vigil outside President Bush's Texas ranch demanding that he meet with her so she could ask why her son was killed in Iraq, did more for the cause of opposition to the war than a hundred marches. As a grieving mother, she had symbolic power. The kid with the "Free Mumia" sign has symbolic power, too—but not in a way that does the progressive movement any favors.

CAPTURE THE FLAG

For too long, progressives have allowed conservatives to define them as unpatriotic. This happened largely because progressives accepted the conservative "love it or leave it" definition of patriotism, that loving one's country means not criticizing its government, that every military adventure is unquestionably right, that one must give oneself a repetitive stress injury so vigorous is the waving of one's flag.

But there is an equally compelling kind of patriotism that progressives advocate, the kind of patriotism that seeks to make America the best it can be. When parents encourage their children to study harder and get better grades, do we say that they don't love their children? When a wife tells a husband that he should exercise and eat right, do we accuse her of not loving her spouse? Of course not—we realize that family members often make demands of each other in one area or another, precisely because of their love and loyalty. A patriot understands that his country is a project in need of constant renewal; by always striving to improve our nation, we honor those who built it and those who fought and died to defend it. The homeowner who works to improve his house shows how much he loves his home; the one who looks at a hole in his roof and says, "What a great roof!" may love his home, but only in a weird way that will make the home weaker over time.

Most conservatives are tremendously patriotic, but their patriotism is largely symbolic. It isn't about making sacrifices for their country, and it isn't about making their country better. It's primarily about symbolism. Ask not what you can do for your country, they say, ask whether you can tape a flag to your car.

When people on the left criticize the actions of the American *government*—which, no matter which party is in charge, consists mostly of people we didn't elect making decisions we never voted on one way or the other—they are unfailingly accused of "hating America." Yet when some on the right condemn American *society*—which all of us comprise—nobody says any such thing. Despite some conservatives' constant cries that this country is a fetid cauldron of sin, that God is so disgusted with us that He brings terrorist attacks and hurricanes, that we are forever inches away from another Great Flood so complete is our depravity, no one ever questions their patriotism.

Maybe it's time someone did. Maybe it's time progressives started positing themselves as the true patriots, not just by implication but explicitly. Let's take the example of health care. It is a sort of patriotism—a mindless sort, but a sort nonetheless—to proclaim, "We have the best health-care system on earth," though we plainly don't. A substantive patriotism—the kind that seeks the best for America—demands that we work to make our health-care system the best. So why not accuse those who resist reform of being anti-American? Try this: "The insurance industry says America can't do any better than 45 million of us without coverage. The drug industry says Americans have to pay the highest prices in the world for medicine. And their Republican friends say we have to pay through the nose for it. I don't agree. Don't tell me America can't do better. Don't tell me America has to put up with this. Maybe Republicans don't believe America can do better, but I do. I ask my Republican friends: why do you have so little faith in America? Well, I'm a progressive, so I believe in what America can accomplish."

A little over the top? Perhaps, but has that ever stopped a conservative? There are lots of opportunities to frame issues in terms of progressive patriotism. Want to take issue with the administration's war on unions? Then point out that every one of the brave police officers and firefighters who gave their lives on September 11 to save their fellow Americans was a member of a union. Have problems with the administration's unprecedented secrecy? Say—don't imply, say—that the administration has contempt for the American people and democracy itself, and if you hate democracy, then you must hate America. Want to shame Republicans for their efforts to keep people from voting? Say that they are attacking the very essence of American democracy and thus America itself.

At first, progressives will no doubt be uncomfortable making this sort of argument. If they did it with regularity, though, they could begin to shift the commonly understood definition of patriotism away from the symbolic and toward the substantive. People on the left should also lose their squeamishness about using patriotic symbols, including the flag. The fact that the flag has been used by scoundrels doesn't mean you can't take it back and use it for good. Many on the left are wary of the flag because it is so often used in simplistic appeals to overwhelm reasoned argument. But by attaching the symbol to what they understand as patriotic values, they can begin to change its meaning.

There is a famous news clip from the 1960s of a Southern sheriff walking through a line of peaceful civil rights protesters. The protesters carry small American flags, and as the sheriff goes down the line, he angrily snatches the flags from as many hands as he can. The lesson is that the appropriation of patriotic symbols by the forces of justice makes the forces of intolerance panic, because they understand the threat it represents.

Progressives should also look for issues to push that invoke their substantive vision of patriotism. National service for all young people is an issue that frames the patriotism issue in a progressive way: it poses substantive, participatory patriotism against meaningless symbolic patriotism and allows you to argue that conservatives just don't want their kids to contribute anything to their country. In fact, national service is inherently progressive, since we'd be asking young people to actually *do* something to improve their country. A conservative national service, on the other hand, might consist of sending kids out to street corners to chant, "USA! USA!" all day long. One College Republican, when asked why he hadn't volunteered for duty in Iraq despite his conviction that other people should be fighting and dying there, responded, "I know that I'm going to be better staying here and working to convince people why we're there. I'm a fighter, but with words."[11]

MOVING THE DEBATE

On February 15, 2003, opponents of the soon-to-be-launched Iraq war staged what was, as far as anyone can tell, the single largest mass demonstration in human history. In coordinated protests in hundreds of cities in dozens of countries, somewhere between 10 million and 30 million people proclaimed their opposition to the war. The American media, which had given almost no coverage to the rapidly growing antiwar movement, were taken completely by surprise. In fact, their reporting on opposition to the war had assumed that it was a tiny, fringe phenomenon whose opinions were not shared by any but a small minority of the American public.

Why were American journalists so clueless about the scope and passion of opposition to the war? The answer can be found in who *wasn't* participating. Because they focus relentlessly on the actions, opinions, and intentions of the political elite, the national news media almost inevitably discount—or are simply oblivious to—anything in which the elite is not involved. Had Democratic members of Congress participated in protests against the war, the press would have taken the protests much more seriously. This is, for instance, what happened during the Vietnam War: while the antiwar movement had been active and growing for years, it was not until opposition to the war could be heard in Congress (particularly after the Tet Offensive in 1968) that the press began to report extensively on the antiwar movement and include more antiwar voices in the news.[12]

This occurs because of what the communication scholar W. Lance Bennett termed *indexing* (Bennett reports that in January 2003, a *Newsweek* reporter asked him, "We in the press have become aware of a substantial antiwar movement. Why do you think we are not reporting it?"[13]). The press indexes its coverage by assessing the positions of the major Washington players and constructing the debate around those relative positions. The "center" is therefore always defined as whatever falls midway between the positions taken by the two parties, who also define the "right" and the "left." Reporters and editors select the individuals who will be quoted and the voices that will appear on the op-ed pages based around the range of elite opinion. This is a process that occurs largely unconsciously, as the press merely goes through the same routines and returns to the same sources again and again.

The implication of media indexing is that if one side chooses, it can rather dramatically alter the debate. Although it oversimplifies to reduce any issue to a single left-right axis, if we were to array the two parties' positions on a line, it would look something like this:

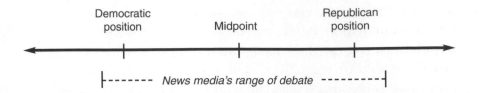

What would happen, though, if large portions of the Democratic Party, particularly its leadership, decided to move their position to the left? If the Republicans don't change their position, not only is the range of debate extended to the left, but the midpoint of debate around which news coverage will be built also moves to the left:

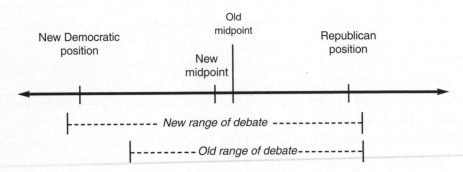

Let us return to the health-care debate of 1993. Despite its wide popularity in progressive circles, few prominent Democrats were willing to publicly advocate a single-payer health-care system. Since the news media did not hear elite voices advocating single-payer, it was dismissed as "politically impossible" and was not discussed as a potential solution to the nation's health-care problems. While a number of different plans were debated in the media, they all shared certain conservative assumptions: that markets in health care are efficient, that any reform must leave room for insurance company profits, and so on. Not only did the failure of the Clinton plan leave the nation without any reform, the debate did nothing to advance progressive principles.[14]

There are also plenty of examples in which the range of debate was expanded to include positions previously dismissed as the mark of fringe thinking. For instance, when Steve Forbes first began arguing for a flat tax, the idea was derided as loopy, hardly worthy of serious examination. But his persistence paid off, as more and more Republicans embraced the idea, and a flat tax has become part of any discussion of tax reform. The notion of tax progressivity—previously something so fundamental that it was accepted (at least in public) by all sides and thus not up for debate—has now become open to contestation.

This is not to say that shifting to a more progressive position is always and inevitably the most politically advantageous move. But narrowing one's advocacy in an attempt to move to the center can make the defeat of one's ultimate goals more likely by moving the range of possible outcomes to the right. Expanding the range of debate by advocating politically difficult positions and questioning seemingly fundamental assumptions can move the debate in the long term. Conservatives have always understood this; for instance, they have worked to move the debate on Social Security for decades. "It could be many years before the conditions are such that a radical reform of Social Security is possible," two Heritage Foundation analysts wrote in 1983. "But then, as Lenin well knew, to be a successful revolutionary, one must also be patient and consistently plan for real reform."[15]

If the progressive movement is going to think big, it cannot be constrained by the limits of the courage of Democratic politicians. It has to decide what it wants and advocate for it, even if that means going further than most Democrats are willing to go at a particular moment. There will always be those whose vision is constricted by the makeup of the current Congress or the outlook for the next election, but the progressive movement must have a vision that extends over decades. Without that vision, the vital changes progressives want to see will never come to pass.

9

TIME TO GET TOUGH

Don't Bring a Knife to a Gunfight

MALONE: You said you wanted to get Capone. Do you really wanna get him? You see what I'm saying is, what are you prepared to do?

NESS: Anything and everything in my power.

MALONE: And *then* what are you prepared to do? If you open the can on these worms you must be prepared to go all the way because they're not gonna give up the fight until one of you is dead.

NESS: How do you do it then?

MALONE: You wanna know how you do it? Here's how. They pull a knife, you pull a gun. He sends one of yours to the hospital, you send one of his to the morgue. That's the Chicago way, and that's how you get Capone! Now do you want to do that? Are you ready to do that?

—*THE UNTOUCHABLES* (1987)

In September 2004, Kerry campaign manager Mary Beth Cahill explained to an interviewer why the campaign wasn't hitting George W. Bush harder: "Win or lose, and my deep belief is he's going to win, you run a campaign you live with for the rest of your life."[1] Spoken like a true Democrat—six weeks before an election, and already thinking about how you'll feel once the campaign is over and you've lost.

Needless to say, the other side was hardly so squeamish. "By the time the White House finishes with Kerry," said one senior Republican early in the campaign, "no one will know what side of the [Vietnam] war he fought on."[2] While the Kerry campaign couldn't decide what its message was, the Bush campaign relentlessly attacked its opponent's character, following the same strategy Republicans do in almost every election. Try to imagine Karl Rove wondering about whether he ran a campaign he could "live with."

It would be nice, of course, if neither side felt the need to engage in character attacks. Ours would be a better country if politics consisted of nothing more than high-minded debates, if candidates came before an engaged and informed electorate and delivered detailed plans on policy and nuanced explorations of governing philosophy, and the citizenry carefully attended to and evaluated each one before making a choice.

But that's not the world we live in. Though Democrats sometimes act as if it is, Republicans surely do not. And when someone is coming at you with a knife, you don't reach for your ten-point plan, you reach for a weapon of your own.

Republicans understand this, which is why they not only exploit Democratic weakness but make strength itself the issue in election after election, so that each campaign becomes not only a referendum on strength but a case study demonstrating which side is stronger. In fact, each of the Four Pillars of Conservatism serves to advance the notion that conservatives are strong and liberals are weak. Why do conservatives believe in small government? Because they're independent and strong, making their own way without anyone's help. Why do they believe in low taxes? Because they made their money, and no pencil-necked bureaucrat is going to take it away from them. Why do they believe in traditional values? Because they have moral strength, resisting temptation and holding to traditional family roles. Why do they believe in a strong defense? Do you even have to ask?

This explains, among other things, the conservative obsession with France, land of cheese and wine, poets and philosophes. Conservatives are positively consumed by the evils of France, spilling out articles and books on the cowardice and perfidy of the "cheese-eating surrender monkeys" with their sissified berets and impressionist art. After France declined to join George W. Bush's Iraq adventure, the rage came to the fore with congressmen demanding that French fries be renamed "freedom fries" and activists pouring bottles of wine down the drain (though Germany was equally opposed to the war, no one suggested "freedom measles" or "freedom chocolate cake"). And what was the insult the Republicans aimed at John Kerry? Supposedly, he "looks French." Tom DeLay said to a group of Republicans, "Good afternoon, or as John Kerry would say, bonjour." The RNC circulated to reporters an item from Agence France-Presse revealing the shocking news that Kerry has a French cousin.[3] *Sacré bleu!*

Although very little is known about how the 2008 presidential race will play out, there is at least one thing of which we can be certain: the Republican candidate will portray the Democratic candidate, no matter who he or she is, as weak. Anyone who believes that nominating one candidate or another will scare the Republicans away from doing so should recall how so many Democrats were convinced that a president and a vice president who evaded service in Vietnam would never question the patriotism of a war hero.

The charge of weakness is not about military service, nor is it about defense policy. It is about character. Every attack from your opponent represents a test of strength. If you let yourself be attacked without response, or you decry his negativism or proclaim yourself "insulted," then you look weak. If you stand up and hit back twice as hard, you look strong.

This is one more thing John Kerry failed to grasp fully in 2004. Though he understood the problem, he had no idea what the solution might be. He thought that if he said, "I'm strong," often enough, people would believe it, and he wouldn't have to actually demonstrate any strength. In one speech, Kerry repeated the word "strength" twenty-one times and some variation of "strong" another sixteen times.[4] His eagerness to talk about his strength led to absurd passages like this one: "Strength means lifting up the middle class and giving them the bigger tax break, not just the wealthiest Americans. Strength means having a health care plan that lowers costs, not pretending that nothing's wrong. Strength means ensuring that our kids get a good education, not just in affluent neighborhoods but everywhere. Strength means balancing the budget, not passing on trillions of dollars in debt to our kids. And strength means leading in a way that brings opportunity to all and special privileges to none." And strength, apparently, meant saying the word *strength* over and over.

This isn't to say you can't convince people of something through endless repetition, but there are some things you need to demonstrate, not just assert, and strength is one of them. Just talking about your desire to kill people won't do it. Martin Luther King Jr. was a pacifist, and no one ever called him weak. So how can Democrats demonstrate their strength? First, by holding fast to their convictions. Second, by engineering controversies that afford opportunities for them to look strong. In other words, they need to pick some fights.

When they do, they'll have to overcome the fact that at first, reporters are going to react with shock and dismay. The press both expects and accepts a greater degree of viciousness and ruthlessness from Republicans than it does from Democrats. This is not only because Republicans are nasty more often than Democrats are, but because of the way they go about attacking the other side. When Democrats attack, all too often they do it reluctantly, with a measure of embarrassment. At the first sign of criticism, they back off and apologize, quickly turning the discussion from the content of their attack to the fact that they're attacking.

I've mentioned before how much fun George W. Bush had in 2004 poking fun at Massachusetts. What did Kerry say in response? Not a thing. But imagine if he had said in front of the cameras, "Mr. President, I've had just about enough of you insulting my home state and the fine Americans who live there. Why don't you try saying it to my face? Then we'll see how funny you think it is when I knock you on your phony Texas ass."

Would Kerry have gotten some criticism? Sure, but he would not have lost a single vote over it, and the ensuing controversy would have made him look tough and would have led to a discussion of the fact that Bush didn't seem to consider himself the president of all Americans.

Democrats have to learn when to pick fights—with their opponents and with the press. When George Bush was caught by a microphone calling the *New York Times* reporter Adam Clymer a "major league asshole," he was asked whether he was sorry. Bush said he was only sorry that the microphone picked up the comment. Did Bush lose any votes? No. He showed his contempt for the press (emphasizing the ridiculous story line that it was giving him less-than-adoring coverage) and showed himself to be a blunt, tough-talkin' guy. A number of reporters with whom I have spoken believe that the episode was a setup—that Bush knew the mike would pick up the exchange, and he initiated the "controversy" on purpose.

Let's take an example of how to do it wrong. In June 2005, party chairman Howard Dean gave a speech in which, talking about election reform, he said, "You think people can work all day and then pick up their kids at child care or wherever, and get home and then have a—still manage to sandwich in an eight-hour vote? Well, Republicans, I guess, can do that, because a lot of them have never made an honest living in their lives. But for ordinary working people, who have to work eight hours a day, they have kids, they got to get home to those kids, the idea of making them stand for eight hours to cast their ballot for democracy is wrong." What happened next was a perfect case study in how Democrats roll over and play dead. Republicans used a technique they often employ: respond to criticism by complaining that Democrats are actually criticizing not them but a larger, more sympathetic group.[5] As RNC chairman Ken Mehlman put it, "I'm not sure of the best way to win support in the red states is to insult the folks who live there." Members of the press, with their contempt for Dean and their eagerness to cast him as a loose cannon seldom far from the surface, went right along, pronouncing themselves shocked and scandalized. On CNN's "Inside Politics," Candy Crowley said, "This is one of those stories we will not let go easily."

When other Democrats were asked about Dean's comments, they should have said, "If the Republican leadership doesn't want us to call them elitist, they should consider doing something for working families for a change. But until they do, we're going to keep talking about how they're hurting regular Americans." This would have kept the focus on the critique. Instead, they played right into Republicans' hands by making Dean the issue. Joseph Biden said Dean "doesn't speak for me with that kind of rhetoric and I don't think he speaks for the majority of Democrats." John Edwards said much the same thing: "My own view is that the chairman of the DNC is not the spokesman for the Democratic Party. There are a group of people who speak for our party nationally and he's a voice in that chorus, but he's only a voice." House Minority Leader Nancy Pelosi said, "I don't think that the statement that the governor made was a helpful statement." What ensued was a days-long discussion in the press about whether Howard Dean was out of control.

A short time later, Karl Rove gave a speech at a meeting of the New York Conservative Party, in which he said, "Conservatives saw the savagery of 9/11 and the attacks and prepared for war; liberals saw the savagery of the 9/11 attacks and wanted to prepare indictments and offer therapy and understanding for our attackers." When Democrats proclaimed their outrage, not a single Republican attempted to distance him- or herself from Rove's remarks. Instead, they offered him their full-throated support.[6]

What the Republicans understood was that when a controversy like this arises, the question determining who wins the day is this: who is this controversy about? And they know that if you are the subject of the controversy, you lose. If your opponent is the subject of the controversy, you win. Democrats helped keep Howard Dean the subject of the controversy instead of turning it back on Republicans and their economic policies; Republicans worked to keep the focus not on Rove but on whether Democrats were strong enough in response to terrorism. When Democrats responded to Rove by talking about how they all supported the war in Afghanistan, they lost the day. Rove almost certainly devised his comments with the intention of stirring up a controversy. It wouldn't have been hard to predict that Democrats would react by saying, "We're not weak!" thereby reiterating the idea of Democratic weakness.

These kinds of controversies aren't about what was said, they're about who you are—they are about *ethos*. When Republicans go after someone like Dean, or like Dick Durbin, the Illinois senator who made an analogy between abuses at Guantanamo and those of despotic regimes, they aren't hoping that people will say, "Those Democrats have engaged in irresponsible rhetoric." They're hoping that people will say, "Goddamn, I hate those Democrat bastards."

In any contest of strength, Democrats start at a disadvantage, just as Republicans do when the question is not who is stronger but who cares more. The Republican candidates who win national elections are those who can temper their strength with caring and compassion, or at least a reasonable facsimile thereof. This was how George W. Bush got elected: he understood that he needed to file down the rough edges of the Republican image, so he came up with "compassionate conservatism," an idea that, though essentially meaningless in practice, could carry symbolic weight. He demonstrated this "compassion" not with policy proposals but with visuals. Unlike his predecessors, Bush would seize any opportunity he could to be photographed with African Americans and Hispanics, particularly children. Reporters swooned; according to one study, the predominant theme of coverage of Bush during the early period of the 2000 election was that he was a "different kind of Republican."[7] The strategy continued throughout his presidency; his 2004 campaign Web site featured a "Compassion Photo Album," consisting almost entirely of photos of Bush with black people.

Likewise, successful Democratic candidates are those who can go beyond their caring, compassionate image—what voters assume about Democrats as a starting point—and demonstrate their strength. Though Bob Shrum, the chief strategist for both Al Gore and John Kerry, was justifiably maligned, he at least understood this point. For that reason, he had Gore endlessly repeating that he would "fight" on this or that issue and had Kerry repeating the word *strength* ad nauseum, throwing in that he would "kill the terrorists" for good measure. Shrum's failure, and those of his candidates, was assuming that these words had a kind of magic power, that if you said the word *strong* enough times, people would believe that you were strong. But you have to find ways to *show* your strength, not just vouch for its presence.[8]

In recent years, we've seen an imbalance that makes it extremely difficult for liberals to gain ground: on one side, you have liberals who define their enemy as the things they want to change—poverty, poor health care, economic inequality, and so on. On the other, you have conservatives who define their enemy as liberalism. On one side, you have liberals who try at every turn to point out that they have some "conservative values" or that they're "fiscal conservatives." On the other side, you have conservatives who'd sock you in the mouth if you said anything about them was "liberal."

This contributes hugely to the general impression that conservatives know who they are, but liberals don't. If progressives are going to change this state of affairs, they must understand that conservatism is the enemy. But wait, they cry—I want to save the environment (or protect workers, or expand health care), not fight conservatives! Well, guess what: right now George Bush, Dick Cheney, Tom DeLay, and the rest of the gang have the environment tied to the rack, and they're turning the wheel. Good luck saving it with your little e-mail list while oil company lobbyists are writing legislation and regulations. It's time to win some elections.

If Democrats are serious about winning, they have to approach the next presidential election with this in mind: they must do to the Republican nominee, whoever he may be, what Republicans did to past Democratic nominees. In other words, he must be taken down. Not just out-argued or out-worked, but torn limb from limb, discredited to the point where no Republican will want to be seen with him in public. That can be done ethically and honestly—there's no need to make up stories or distort records or proposals—but it must be done without mercy. As the political analyst Charlie Cook said, "I think there is a naive view among Democrats that what you have to do is 'demonstrate a vision and tell the truth' and you win. Republicans know that you need to tear your opponent's heart out, chew it up and spit it out."[9]

Never again should a Democrat enter a campaign believing, "Oh, they'd never use *that* attack against us." Yes, they will—no matter what the subject, no matter how mean and dishonest, no matter how immune you think you are on a given topic. This attitude was the reason John Kerry's campaign waited a full month before responding to the lies being propagated by the Republican front group Swift Boat Veterans for Truth. Going into the campaign, Democrats believed that Republicans couldn't possibly attack Kerry's patriotism. After all, he was a war hero with a Bronze Star, a Silver Star, and three Purple Hearts, while his opponent got out of going to Vietnam with a cushy spot in the "Champagne Unit" of the Texas Air Guard, and that opponent's running mate got a series of deferments, later admitting to a congressional committee that he had "other priorities than military service."

Of course, they did attack Kerry's patriotism, just as they had with innumerable Democratic candidates before. Something else also happened in 2004. For decades, Republicans had conceded that Democrats had a better ground game: when it came to organizing voters and getting them to the polls, Democrats and their allies in the labor movement just did it better. But after the 2000 election, Republicans looked at how Al Gore had accumulated more votes than George W. Bush and saw some compelling research emerging in political science demonstrating that person-to-person contact is the most cost-effective means of enhancing voter turnout. So they decided to change things. In the 2002 election, they implemented as a pilot program the "72-hour project," a new voter turnout effort in key congressional districts. Then in 2004, for the first time in memory, their comprehensive voter mobilization effort actually outperformed the one put on by the Democrats—despite the fact that the latter was unprecedented in size and expense.

That left Democrats facing an extraordinary realization: there is now not a single area of campaigning—not organizing, not message development, not candidate recruitment and training, not fund-raising, and certainly not ruthlessness—at which Republicans are not demonstrably better than Democrats. Of course, the one thing the Republicans are terrible at is the one thing Democrats do well: governing.

First Thing We Do, Let's Kill
All the Consultants

Howard Philips, one of the key figures of the "New Right" that emerged after Goldwater's defeat in 1964, described the establishment figures they displaced by saying, "there are an awful lot of [Old Right] conservatives in America who think their role is to lose as slowly as possible."[10] The same could be said of many Democrats in Washington today.

Not all Washington Democrats, of course. But there is a permanent Washington establishment on both sides of the ideological divide for whom victory and defeat are almost beside the point. Those on the Democratic side circulate between Capitol Hill, the Democratic Party, and the hundreds of interest groups and think tanks. They came to Washington for a variety of reasons, some more idealistic than others, but the longer they stay, the more entrenched and comfortable they get. As the years pass, they begin to realize that even when their side loses, they do nearly as well as they would have if they had won; they keep their jobs or find new ones and keep on doing almost exactly what they were doing before. Eventually, some may even come to expect defeat.

No group embodies this culture more than Democratic political consultants, to whom winning and losing are virtually irrelevant. Of course, they'd rather win than lose, but they get paid either way, and there is always another election coming down the pike with a new crop of candidates who need help and advice.

This is not to say that all political consultants are immoral people. I worked for a time in political consulting, and what I found in that industry reminded me of something an attorney friend of mine once said about law school. In law school, you'll find many intelligent, creative people who are committed to working for a better world. You'll also find some of the biggest assholes you'll ever meet in your life.

The point, however, is not that political consultants are bad people—some are, some aren't. The point is that what they do is by its nature inimical to building a long-term progressive movement—but not because they're cynical manipulators. The reason progressives need to work around political consultants is that consultants approach politics with a 50 plus 1 mentality. All they need to do is to get their clients to 50 percent plus one vote. Once they've done that, they've been as successful as they need to be.

My brief career in the consulting field ended during the 1994 primary season. Crime was the number-one issue that year, and for client after client, the firm for which I worked was crafting attacks on crime. We tarred our clients' opponents (all Democrats, since we were a Democratic firm and this was the primaries) as "soft on crime" by finding an obscure vote they had made years before to say they were letting criminals out of jail to roam our neighborhoods. In one case, we even sent hundreds of thousands of letters, each containing a spent shell casing, to unsuspecting voters to dramatize the crime wave enveloping our streets (this tactic, creative though it may have been, was too clever by half and caused a backlash).

Upon reading the text of one direct mail piece attacking one opponent, I finally had had enough and complained to my boss, the head of the firm. Not only was this unfair, I told him, but it was exactly the kind of thing that turns people off from politics. His reply stuck with me: "Our job is not to elevate the discourse. Our job is to help our clients win. That's what they hired us for, that's what they pay us for, and that's what we have to do." Later I participated in a conference call with a candidate and a group of consultants as she raised questions about the plan they had laid out for her. She complained that the plan contained nothing but talk of crime, while she said she had many other issues she wanted to campaign on. My boss said this: "You hired us because you want us to help you win. Based on our analysis of the survey data, I can tell you that *every second* you spend talking about anything but crime contributes to your defeat." She gave in.[11]

Of course, he was absolutely right, and that's just the problem. Political consultants have no interest in creating a lasting progressive movement. They don't even have much of an interest in who controls Congress, beyond the fact that incumbents are the best clients (lots of money to spend, too busy to micromanage,[12] and all but guaranteed to win). Their focus is necessarily narrowed to getting their own clients to 50 percent plus one, and if doing so means undermining the image of progressivism or belittling their own party, that's what they will recommend. They are masters of tactics but have no need for strategy; they think only in the short term.

In 2005, some prominent bloggers got in a public spat with the Democratic Congressional Campaign Committee, the arm of the Democratic Party that funds congressional races. The bloggers were pushing the DCCC to put money into more races than the couple of dozen it ordinarily funds in order to contest seemingly safe Republican seats. The DCCC's reply was that it has a limited amount of money, and every dollar it spends in a lost cause is a dollar it could have spent in a race in which a Democrat has a real shot at winning.

This is a perfectly reasonable position to take, if your vision is constricted to the short term. After all, the DCCC, both the members of Congress who lead it and the professionals who staff it, gets a stark report card every other November, showing how many races were won and how many were lost. It gets little credit for spending effort and money in a district where the Democrat ends up winning 45 percent, even if the last Democrat to run there got substantially less.

The argument on the other side is that if you look at the long term, you can win by losing. A race in which your party doesn't bother to field a candidate helps keep the district solidly Republican. One in which you mount a serious effort, though, even a losing effort, does a number of things for you. It identifies activists on whom you can call in the future. It expands the debate that people in the district hear about the issues of the day. Even if 50 percent is a ways off, it does begin to convert some people to your cause. All of these factors come to matter in future races, both in the district and statewide. In short, it strengthens your party. But if your only concern is whether it's possible to reach 50 percent in the present election, those things won't much matter.

There are other areas in which progressives have been unable to expand their vision enough to see the possibilities of winning by losing. When President Bush nominated John Roberts to the

Supreme Court, progressives who had been gearing up for a dramatic fight were flummoxed. Roberts had little paper trail and a moderate countenance, making it difficult to make the case that his ascension to the court would bring disaster. As a result, the opposition they mounted to him was haphazard and formless. Some wanted to talk about abortion, some wanted to talk about privacy, some wanted to talk about the scope of executive power, some wanted to talk about legislative power and the Commerce Clause. Despite all the practical preparation that had taken place—building e-mail lists, assembling biographies of potential nominees, organizing supporters—the campaign against Roberts had no unifying theme that told Americans what the Supreme Court means to progressives and to the country.

Roberts's nomination took the wind out of progressives' sails because they had prepared to defeat a nominee with very little thought to what the battle itself could do for them over the long term. As a result, not only did Roberts get confirmed, but the debate over that confirmation did nothing to advance the progressive cause. If your focus is only on whether a Supreme Court nominee is confirmed or a piece of legislation is passed or a candidate wins, without much consideration to whether you can advance your long-term goals even if you don't prevail, then your movement never takes the steps forward it needs to grow.

Many in the Washington Democratic establishment will see a growing, pugnacious progressive movement as a threat. Many of them genuinely believe that fighting too hard is a path to defeat. As Rick Perlstein pointed out, this view comes in part from a generational difference:

> The trauma of the generation of people who are running the Democratic Party was being blindsided by the political failures of left-of-center boldness. If you look at a lot of the most resonant and stalwart centrists and Democratic Leadership Council (DLC) Democrats, for a lot of them, their political coming-of-age was being blindsided by conservatism. For Bill Clinton, it was losing the governorship in 1980. For Joe Lieberman, it was losing a congressional race in 1980. For

Evan Bayh, the chair of the DLC, it was seeing his dad lose his Senate seat to Dan Quayle in 1980. But the formative traumas of my generation of Democrats—and I'm 35—have been the failures of left-of-center timidity. So there really is a structural generational battle among Democrats.[13]

Particularly in the Democratic Party's centrist wing, many have accepted the Republican myth that America is a fundamentally conservative country. One article in the DLC's magazine *Blueprint* in 2005 was subtitled, "Bill Clinton's greatest achievement was advancing progressivism in a conservative nation."[14] As we saw earlier, this notion is just false, but the idea that Democrats would be spreading it is particularly shocking. And despite the over-whelming evidence that America is a progressive country, would you ever catch a Republican admitting it?

IT'S NOT ABOUT THE DEMOCRATS

Politicians are naturally risk-averse. They know that everything that they say in public gets noted, and an intemperate or foolish remark—the kind ordinary humans make each and every day—can come back to haunt them. They are always worried about offending individuals or groups. In order to keep their jobs, they have to go out and plead with thousands of people, many of whom are indifferent, ignorant, or incoherent, to look kindly upon them. A single misstep could be the end of their careers.

Though the right politicians can provide a movement with strength and leadership, politicians can't be counted on to give a movement what it needs. When the conservatives who backed Barry Goldwater in 1964 crawled from the wreckage of his defeat, they didn't look for another presidential candidate on whom they could pin their hopes (Richard Nixon, as far as they were concerned, was not a real conservative). Instead, they built their movement from the ground up, understanding that if they were successful, in time Republicans would come to them. And they did; sixteen years after Goldwater, a figure who was nurtured in their movement won the presidency, and every Republican with national ambitions since then has tried to portray himself as Ronald Reagan's heir. The conservative movement started as a rebellion against the Republican establishment and eventually *became* the Republican establishment. The descendents of the Rockefeller Republicans against whom Goldwater's supporters were rebelling are now the outsiders, dwindling in number with each passing year.

When they started, though, the architects of the conservative movement decided that what the Republican Party wanted or was capable of doing was almost irrelevant; they would take the initiative and work to build support for their agenda all by themselves. Richard Viguerie, one of the key figures in that movement, described it this way:

> Throughout this period, the leaders of the New Right consciously thought of *themselves*—not the Republican Party—as the alternative to the Left and the Democrats. And thanks to the independence provided by direct mail fundraising, none of their organizations depended on the Republican Party or a handful of big business donors for their existence. The great majority of these leaders were people who did not hold public office, and had never held public office. Conservatives did not look to elected officials for their leadership. The politicians were necessary to organize votes for or against something, of course, but generally they did not provide the leadership on key issues. That came from the New Right leaders, who utilized alternative media.[15]

Progressives should look to this history and understand that their goal is not to find the right Democrat but to build their movement until it produces its own leaders and no Democrat is able to ignore it. Waiting for a politician to come along and lead you out of Egypt is a prescription for failure; progressives need to stand up and start walking. If they are successful, they can transform the Democratic Party, making it stronger, more financially stable, and less governed by fear.

Building a movement that is not defined by candidates also makes progressive citizens feel like they are part of something larger than themselves into which they have real, tangible input.

We can see this in microcosm in the greater success that progressive blogs have had over conservative blogs. This is not to say that conservative blogs haven't also been successful, but both in total and at the very top, the progressive blogs have garnered more readers. Why? As Chris Bowers of MyDD.com has argued persuasively, the answer is community. While nearly all of the top-ranking progressive blogs allow readers to post comments, only a few of the top-ranking conservative blogs do. The ability to post comments allows readers to participate and cultivates a sense of community, as they interact not only with the creators of the original content but with one another as well. The most successful political blog, Daily Kos, was one of the first to allow "diaries," giving readers the ability not only to comment on existing stories but to create entire mini-blogs of their own within the Kos site. After the 2004 election, when most political blogs saw dramatic declines in readership, the Daily Kos audience actually grew.

Howard Dean's 2004 presidential campaign did something similar, not only featuring the most supporter-driven Web site of any campaign to date but encouraging "Deaniacs" to devise their own events, materials, and even Web video. Campaigns have always been terrified of giving volunteers any leeway to take this kind of creative initiative out of fear that something a supporter creates will cause controversy or dilute the campaign's message. Despite that risk, this kind of "open-source campaign" not only energizes volunteers, it creates activists: people who will continue to provide their time and financial support to the cause for years to come.[16]

The creation and nurturing of activists is particularly critical to the future of the progressive movement, since so much of progressive politics is now carried out by professionals, particularly in Washington. Out of the 1960s, a generation of activists made careers out of political action, coming to the capital to lobby government directly. The number of progressive interest groups grew exponentially, and many of these groups had little substantive contact with the people whose interests they represented. Their "membership" consisted of a list of contributors with whom they communicated through newsletters and fund-raising appeals but who had little input and were given little to *do* to advance their preferred cause.[17]

But something is changing. There is a growing hunger among progressives to do more than write a check. The Internet has allowed people with similar views to find one another, exchange ideas, and plan action. These people—and there are a few million of them—are ready to turn themselves into a real movement. That would mean more than money and more than bodies getting other bodies to the polls on election day. Real movements also encourage in their members the desire and willingness to proselytize, to try to convince their families, their friends, their coworkers, and even strangers to sign on to the movement's goals. Christopher Hayes made a comparison between this kind of organizing and missionary work:

> Once upon a time, organizing meant more than coordinating e-mail petitions or hosting house parties to raise money and awareness. It meant something much closer to what we now think of as missionary work. A union would send an organizer into, say, a small mining town in Pennsylvania. He would reach out to the miners, get to know them and their families, and tell them what a union was and how it could help them. He would try to convince them to risk their livelihoods by banding together and demanding a safer workplace and better wages. This was difficult, often bloody work. But when it worked—and often it didn't—it effected a transformation of the miners who joined the union. They now had a new identity. Even if they had joined solely for higher wages or a mine less likely to kill them, after suffering lockouts, harassment and possibly beatings, they would have an entirely new perspective on bosses and power. They would be more progressive.
>
> This is what social movements at their best do. They pull back the curtain on power and expose its workings. They politicize those without political engagements by transforming personal grievances in the workplace, at home and in society into political issues. Before the labor movement, a dangerous workplace, low wages and arduously long workdays were just crappy things about a person's life. Before feminism, stifling

your personal ambitions in favor of doting on your husband was just a drawback to being a woman.[18]

Passive citizens don't proselytize; members of a movement do. And in recent years, all the proselytizing has come from the right. Conservatives have worked hard not just to motivate their own supporters but to turn opponents into supporters. In the process, they remade the Republican Party in their image.

Progressives building their movement—and those in the Democratic establishment who are willing to join that movement by taking chances and working for long-term success—need to refocus their energy with a new mentality, one that sees politics not as a contest or a game but as an unending war, one in which the enemy must be utterly vanquished. This doesn't mean being overcome by rage and hatred—quite the contrary. It does, however, mean never underestimating the viciousness of your foes and being willing to fight until the end.

10

THE PROGRESSIVE
MOMENT

We began this book by looking back at the aftermath of the 1964 election, the nadir of conservatism in America. Defeated and discredited, conservatives decided to build a movement, with the understanding that their mission would be long and difficult. Whatever one thinks about their values and goals, one cannot deny that they were strong, principled, smart, and determined. Their labor bore substantial fruit—the election of presidents and legislators, the slashing of taxes on the wealthy, the enhancement of corporate power, and the partial rollback of the Great Society, to name a few of their achievements.

Progressives in 2006 are in much better shape than conservatives were in 1964. Unlike conservatives, they actually have public opinion on their side. They have numerous wealthy donors looking for ways to advance their cause. They have millions of potential activists with a desire to get involved. And they have the lesson of the last forty years of history.

Of all the things progressives can learn from conservatives, none may be more important than changing the way they look at the political world in order to create a single entity known as the

234

progressive movement. For too long the left has been a collection of identity-based and single-issue groups, each of which held its focus so narrowly that acting together was difficult if not impossible. Progressives need to stop thinking of themselves as environmentalists or pro-choicers or civil rights advocates and start thinking of themselves as members of the Progressive Movement.

That movement will not coalesce until progressives define, simply and clearly, who they are and what they believe. Time and again, they have responded to conservative attacks by becoming timid and fearful. Unsurprisingly, many Americans concluded that if progressives don't seem to have the courage of their convictions, they must have neither courage nor convictions. Bill Clinton said that Americans would prefer someone who is strong and wrong to someone who is weak and right. It's time for progressives to show Americans what they haven't seen in a long time: someone who is both strong and right.

And to paraphrase the old bumper sticker, progressives need to think nationally and act locally. Conservatives built their movement from the ground up by running candidates in local elections and organizing local groups. If you're a progressive and you think your local Democratic Party organization is moribund or ineffectual, why not get a few like-minded friends together and take it over? Run for school board or town council. Write letters to your local paper and call in to your local radio shows, letting your neighbors know that there is a strong progressive voice in your community. Don't wait for the next presidential election to get involved—start building your movement now.

As I write, the nation is suffering through the full realization of conservative government. The war in Iraq, an adventure brought to us by soulless men with delusions of grandeur and a ghoulish indifference to the spilling of the blood of others' children, grows more miserable by the week. America's image in the world has never been worse, and each day more angry young men decide to give their lives to kill Americans. A hurricane reveals the pervasive incompetence and cronyism of the executive branch. Corporate profits skyrocket, yet the corporate share of federal taxes falls to near-record lows, while poverty levels rise during a period of economic growth.

More Americans join the ranks of the uninsured every day, while the Republican Congress directs ever more tax dollars to pork projects and corporate welfare. The government's finances, in surplus just a few short years ago, have sunk to a deficit so vast that climbing out of it begins to seem impossible.

The catastrophe of the Bush presidency presents progressives with an opportunity the likes of which they have not seen in years. There is virtually no issue on which they cannot point to the failure not only of conservative government but of conservative ideology. The American people are disgusted with those in charge and are looking for change. The conservative model of limited government—which in practice turned out to be government just as big but more characterized by cronyism and disastrous neglect—has been thoroughly discredited. The Republicans who took over Congress in 1994 posing as reformers made the sins of their predecessors look laughably amateurish as they turned Capitol Hill into a monument to corporate gluttony and the corruption of one-party power.

So when the conservatives who have brought us to this point come before the American people with their power on the line, they will be asked how and why they made such a mess of things. Their answer will be the same as it always has been: forget about the promises we made to you and ignore our failures. Just look at those weak, elitist liberals. They have nothing but contempt for you and everything you value. And if we elect those liberals, it'll all *really* go down the tubes. Ridicule them, fear them, hate them with all your might.

If progressives love their country, they must refuse to take one more such beating. They must get off their knees, stiffen their spines, look their foes in the eye, and give as good as they get. Politics is too important to be treated like a game. Conservatives fight like their lives depend on it; it's time for progressives to do the same. If progressives don't have the will to fight, then they don't deserve to govern.

So when those Democrats who would be president come before the electorate with the hopes of winning the support of the millions of progressives looking for someone to lift our nation out of the hole in which it finds itself, they must answer a few questions if they hope to win and hope to lead:

- Can you state in one sentence exactly why it is that you are a progressive?
- Are you willing to stand unapologetically for progressive values in the knowledge that they are in fact the values most Americans share?
- Do you know how to argue using not just *logos* but *pathos* and *ethos* as well, and do you understand that the latter is the most important of the three?
- Do you appreciate that strength does not flow from a ten-point plan? And just how do you intend to demonstrate your strength to voters?
- Can you stop worrying about what the editorial pages of the *New York Times* and the *Washington Post* say about you? In other words, do you understand that playing to what the establishment media say they want is not a winning media strategy?
- Are you committed to goals that may take years or even decades to achieve?
- Do you understand that no matter what is on your résumé, Republicans will attack your character? And are you willing to hit back just as hard, if not harder?

No candidate who cannot answer these questions to the satisfaction of progressives deserves their votes, in any election for any office. But these are not only questions that politicians must answer; they are questions all progressives must ask themselves. The future of their movement depends on it.

Just as we have been so many times before, progressives will be proven right by history in the battles we wage today and tomorrow. But being right does not guarantee success, and none of our goals will be achieved overnight. It will be a process that stretches over decades, as we slowly but inexorably move our country toward the fullest realization of the vision on which it was founded. Without question, there will be missteps and defeats along the way. But if we succeed, we will leave to our children and grandchildren a country that is more fair, more just, more prosperous, and more free than the one we found.

In the preamble to the Constitution, the Framers wrote that the document, and thus the government that it established, had as its purpose "to form a more perfect Union, establish Justice, insure domestic Tranquility, provide for the common defence, promote the general Welfare, and secure the Blessings of Liberty to ourselves and our Posterity." Two centuries into the great democratic experiment, we know that justice, domestic tranquility, the common defense, the general welfare, and the blessings of liberty are never completely secure. Their advancement depends on people of good will thrusting themselves wholeheartedly into politics, the ongoing battles that determine who we are as a nation and what we will become. The quest for that more perfect union requires all we can give—our vigilance, our energy, our faith, our strength, and our commitment. This is our country, and if we believe in its future, it demands nothing less.

ACKNOWLEDGMENTS

I began work on this book during the 2004 presidential campaign. In the weeks and months that followed the election, I participated in hundreds of conversations about the future of progressivism and the Democratic Party with friends, colleagues, and even some strangers, each one of whom had an impact on the development of the book. Although at certain points in these pages I have said some uncomplimentary things about certain portions of the Washington Democratic establishment, I doubt that I would have been able to write this book without listening to and participating in the lively debate that continues on the left concerning that future.

My thinking on these topics was heavily influenced by discussions with my talented colleagues from the *Gadflyer*, especially Tom Schaller, Sean Aday, Jeff Stanger, Joshua Holland, and Sarah Posner. Throughout the process, Tom in particular offered invaluable critique and insight. His analysis of the Democrats' future prospects, particularly in the South and the Southwest, are the subject of his upcoming book, *Whistling Past Dixie*, which I am confident will shape the debate on where and how Democrats ought to be spending their money and energy in upcoming elections.

I also received helpful comments on early drafts from Darrin Bodner, James Devitt, Ayelet Waldman, and Ricki Waldman. My editor, Eric Nelson, displayed both wisdom and commitment in shepherding the book. I am deeply indebted to my agent, Amy Rennert, for her work and advocacy on my behalf. Finally, like most of what I do, this book would have been impossible without the superhuman support of my wife.

NOTES

Chapter 1. Returning Fire

1. According to the Annenberg Public Policy Center's National Annenberg Election Survey, more than one in five Kerry voters made such a donation.
2. Tom Baxter, "Speech Hints at Agenda," *Atlanta Journal and Constitution*, January 21, 2001, p. 2B.
3. For a history of the 1964 campaign and how it planted the seeds of the conservative movement, see Rick Perlstein, *Before the Storm: Barry Goldwater and the Unmaking of the American Consensus* (New York: Hill & Wang, 2001).
4. Speech at Boston Garden, Boston, Massachusetts, November 3, 1952.
5. Not only that, Nixon was speaking to a union, the International Association of Machinists (St. Louis, Missouri, September 15, 1960).
6. Speech in San Diego, California, September 5, 1988.
7. Convention speech, Atlanta, Georgia, July 21, 1988.
8. Speech at Cerritos College, Norwalk, California, October 31, 1988.
9. Speech in Springfield, Ohio, October 30, 1992.
10. Henry Brady and Paul Sniderman, "Attitude Attribution: A Group Basis for Political Reasoning." *American Political Science Review* 79 (1985): 1061–78.
11. The trend exists among liberals growing to dislike conservatives more, but the decline is not nearly as steep. David King identified this trend using NES data between 1964 and 1994 ("The Polarization of American Parties and Mistrust of Government," in Joseph Nye et al., *Why People Don't Trust Government* [Cambridge, Mass.: Harvard University Press, 1997]); the last decade's worth of NES data show that the trend is continuing.
12. *Hannity & Colmes*, July 15, 2002.
13. David Plotz, "The Natural," Slate.com, August 18, 2000.
14. For Democrats, the question asked about the Democratic Party's "traditional positions on such things as protecting the interests of minorities, helping the poor and needy, and representing working people."
15. Mark Schmitt has argued that despite the attention progressives have recently paid to the Powell memo, there is little evidence that it was actually used as much of a continuing plan for conservatives (Mark Schmitt, "The Legend of the Powell Memo," *American Prospect Online*, April 27, 2005).
16. This is the estimate of the *Washington Post*, in current dollars as of 1999: Robert Kaiser and Ira Chinoy, "How Scaife's Money Powered a Movement," May 2, 1999, p. A1.
17. Karen Paget, "Lessons of Right-Wing Philanthropy," *American Prospect*, September 1/October 1, 1998.
18. Michael Dolny, "Special Report: Think-Tank Coverage," *Extra!* June 2004.
19. Michael Schuman, "Why Do Progressive Foundations Give Too Little to Too Many?" *The Nation* (January 12, 1998).

20. Efforts in this area are starting, albeit slowly, from groups like the Center for American Progress and People for the American Way.

21. John McCaslin, "Inside the Beltway," *Washington Times*, December 23, 2003, p. A7.

22. E. J. Dionne, *Stand Up, Fight Back: Republican Toughs, Democratic Wimps, and the Politics of Revenge* (New York: Simon & Schuster, 2004), pp. 87–88.

23. John McCain may be the only moderate who has a real shot to win the nomination, although he is, of course, a unique case. McCain's work on behalf of Bush's reelection, despite his lingering resentment over the atrocious slanders Bush's allies threw at him during the 2000 primaries, seemed to many to be a way for McCain to show party stalwarts that he was still a loyal Republican in preparation for a 2008 run.

24. The flustered reporter replied, "I'm sorry, I didn't think I was going to talk about 'man on dog' with a United States senator, it's sort of freaking me out." Associated Press, April 22, 2003.

25. Speech on Senate floor, July 12, 2004.

26. Nicholas Lemann, "William Jennings Bush," *New Yorker* (September 10, 2001): 44.

27. Newt Gingrich, "Building the Conservative Movement after Ronald Reagan," Heritage Foundation Reports, April 21, 1988.

28. Jacob Hacker and Paul Pierson, *Off Center: The Republican Revolution and the Erosion of American Democracy* (New Haven, Conn.: Yale University Press, 2005).

29. Of the ten states with the lowest rates of union membership, nine are in the South: North Carolina (2.7%), South Carolina (3%), Arkansas (4.8%), Mississippi (4.8%), Texas (5%), Virginia (5.3%), Utah (5.8%), Oklahoma (6.1%), Georgia (6.4%), and Tennessee (6.7%). Of the ten states with the highest union membership, nine are Democratic states, the only exception being Alaska: New York (25.3%), Hawaii (23.7%), Michigan (21.6%), Alaska (20.1%), New Jersey (19.8%), Washington (19.3%), Minnesota (17.5%), Illinois (16.8%), California (16.5%), and Rhode Island (16.3%). The median yearly income for a unionized worker is $40,352. For a worker not represented by a union, the median income is $31,824. Data for 2004 from the Bureau of Labor Statistics.

30. Michael Lind, *Made in Texas: George W. Bush and the Southern Takeover of American Politics* (New York: Basic Books, 2003), p. 183.

31. Kimberly Conger and John Green, "Spreading Out and Digging In: Christian Conservatives and State Republican Parties," *Campaigns and Elections* (February 2002).

CHAPTER 2. BEYOND RED AND BLUE

1. To take just one example, just before the 2004 election the *New York Times* published a pair of articles speculating on what defeat would mean for both parties. The article about Republicans, titled "A Confident Opposition," described how they would remain true to their beliefs. The one about Democrats predicted "another bout of recrimination, self-examination and transformation." Elisabeth Bumiller, "A Confident Opposition"; Adam Nagourney, "What If They Lose?" *New York Times*, October 24, 2004.

2. This is not to say they won't do so if asked by a pollster, but their actual positions on issues will have only a slight relationship to the spot they pick.

3. The following dossier was collected by the *American Prospect*: "In red states in 2001, there were 572,000 divorces. . . . Blue states recorded 340,000. . . . In the same year, 11 red states had higher rates of divorce than any blue state. . . . In each

of the red states of Louisiana, Mississippi, and New Mexico, 46.3 percent of all births were to unwed mothers. . . . In blue states, on average, that percentage was 31.7. . . . Delaware has the highest rate of births to teenage mothers among all blue states, yet 17 red states have a higher rate. . . . Of those red states, 15 have at least twice the rate as that of Massachusetts. . . . There were more than 100 teen pregnancies per 1,000 women aged 15 to 19 in 5 red states in 2002. . . . None of the blue states had rates that high. . . . The rate of teen births declined in 46 states from 1988 to 2000. . . . It climbed in 3 red states and saw no change in another. . . . The per capita rate of violent crime in red states is 421 per 100,000. . . . In blue states, it's 372 per 100,000. . . . The per capita rate of murder and non-negligent manslaughter in Louisiana is 13 per 100,000. . . . In Maine, it's 1.2 per 100,000. . . . As of 2000, 37 states had statewide policies or procedures to address domestic violence. . . . All 13 that didn't were red states. . . . The 5 states with the highest rates of alcohol dependence or abuse are red states. . . . The 5 states with the highest rates of alcohol dependence or abuse among 12- to 17-year-olds are also red states. . . . The per capita rate of methamphetamine-lab seizures in California is 2 per 100,000 . . . . In Arkansas, it's 20 per 100,000. . . . The number of meth-lab seizures in red states increased by 38 percent from 1999 to 2003. . . . In the same time frame, it decreased by 38 percent in blue states. . . . Residents of the all-red Mountain States are the most likely to have had 3 or more sexual partners in the previous year. . . . Residents of all-blue New England are the least likely to have had more than 1 partner in that span. . . . Residents of the mid-Atlantic region of New York, Pennsylvania, and New Jersey were the most likely to be sexually abstinent. . . . Residents of the all-red West South Central region (Texas, Oklahoma, Arkansas, Louisiana) were the least likely. . . . Five red states reported more than 400 cases of chlamydia per 100,000 residents in 2002. . . . No blue state had a rate that high. . . . The per capita rate of gonorrhea in red states was 140 per 100,000. . . . In blue states, it was 99 per 100,000." "Dossier: Red State Values," *American Prospect* (January 4, 2005).

4. According to the Census Bureau, the states with the highest income are New Jersey, Maryland, New Hampshire, Alaska, Connecticut, Minnesota, Virginia, Massachusetts, Delaware, and Colorado. The poorest states are West Virginia, Mississippi, Arkansas, Louisiana, Montana, New Mexico, Oklahoma, Alabama, Tennessee, and Maine.

5. According to a report by the conservative Tax Foundation, as of 2002 the top ten "taker" states—those that took in more in federal spending than they paid in federal taxes—were North Dakota ($2.03 in spending for every dollar paid), New Mexico ($1.89), Mississippi ($1.84), Alaska ($1.82), West Virginia ($1.74), Montana ($1.64), Alabama ($1.61), South Dakota ($1.59), Arkansas ($1.53), and Hawaii ($1.52). Only Hawaii was won by Kerry, and of the others, only New Mexico was even close. The top ten "giver" states are as follows: New Jersey ($.62), Connecticut ($.64), New Hampshire ($.68), Nevada ($.73), Minnesota ($.77), Illinois, ($.77), Massachusetts ($.79), Colorado ($.79), New York ($.81), and California ($.81). All except Nevada and Colorado were won by Kerry. Further information can be found at www.taxfoundation.org.

6. And this was a news story, not an editorial (there's the liberal media for you). Todd Purdum, "An Electoral Affirmation of Shared Values," *New York Times*, November 4, 2004, p. A1.

7. *All Things Considered*, National Public Radio, December 21, 2004.

8. Admittedly, this is a somewhat crude way to measure whether the House is representative or not. And this is not to say that nonpartisan redistricting would necessarily result in a perfectly representative House. It does show, however, at least in

rough terms, how the Republicans have benefited from partisan redistricting.

9. Ronald Brownstein, "GOP Has Lock on South, and Democrats Can't Find Key," *Los Angeles Times*, December 15, 2004. Of course, some counties have a few thousand people in them and some have a few million, and Republicans tend to do better in the former. Nonetheless, these figures are striking.

10. A hat tip to Matthew Yglesias for pointing out these extraordinary figures.

11. Alaska and Hawaii were not included in this survey. In smaller states such as Montana or North Dakota, the number of respondents is fairly small, so results for those states may be less than perfectly precise.

12. Actual figures are 50.3 percent and 19.4 percent. Data are from 1998, the last year the GSS asked this question.

13. David Sears and Nicholas Valentino, "Race, Religion, and Sectional Conflict in Contemporary Partisanship," paper delivered at the annual meeting of the American Political Science Association, September 2001. As Susan Jacoby wrote, "The Christian right would like today's public to forget exactly where religious conservatives stood on civil rights forty years ago. One of the more repellent ironies of modern religious correctness has been the attempt by fundamentalists to wrap themselves in the mantle of those men and women of faith who risked their lives to fight racism. In the sixties, right-wing fundamentalists were, almost without exception, hard-core segregationists." *Freethinkers: A History of American Secularism* (New York: Henry Holt, 2004), p. 326.

14. This quote can be found here: www.pbs.org/wgbh/amex/wallace/filmmore/transcript/.

15. Speech accepting the Peace Prize of the German Book Trade, Frankfurt, October 12, 2003.

16. John C. Green, "The American Religious Landscape and Political Attitudes: A Baseline for 2004," Pew Forum on Religion and Public Life, September 2004.

17. John Green, Corwin Smidt, James Guth, and Lyman Kellstedt, "The American Religious Landscape and the 2004 Presidential Vote: Increased Polarization," Pew Forum on Religion and Public Life, February 2004.

18. Their Twelve Tribes are the Religious Right (12.6% of the electorate), Heartland Culture Warriors (11.4%), Moderate Evangelicals (10.8%), White Bread Protestants (7%), Convertible Catholics (8.1%), the Religious Left (12.6%), Spiritual but Not Religious (5.3%), Seculars (10.7%), Latinos (7.3%), Jews (1.9%), Muslims and Other Faiths (2.7%), and Black Protestants (9.6%). Details of their analysis can be found at Beliefnet.com.

19. David Kirkpatrick, "Evangelical Leader Threatens to Use His Political Muscle against Some Democrats," *New York Times*, January 1, 2005, p. A10.

20. C. Kirk Hadaway, Penny Long Marler, and Mark Chaves, "Overreporting Church Attendance in America: Evidence That Demands the Same Verdict," *American Sociological Review* 63 (February 1998): 122–30.

21. In the General Social Survey, the number of people saying they attended church a few times a year or less increased from 43 percent in 1972 to 53 percent in 2002, while the number saying they attended once a week or more decreased from 35 percent to 24 percent. For more on this topic, see Stanley Presser and Linda Stinson, "Data Collection Mode and Social Desirability Bias in Self-Reported Religious Attendance," *American Sociological Review* 63 (February 1998): 137–45.

22. Ronald Inglehart and Wayne Baker, "Modernization, Cultural Change, and the Persistence of Traditional Values," *American Sociological Review* 65 (2000): 22.

23. A number of the researchers associated with the World Values Survey use factor analysis to locate two axes of opinion, what they call *traditional vs. secular-*

rational values and *survival vs. self-expression values.* While based on the data these are undeniably two distinct factors, the survey items that make up the two factors contain thematic overlap that makes interpretation difficult and makes me hesitant to use these broad groupings as a basis for discussing American opinion. For instance, agreement with "abortion is never justifiable" is a "traditional" value, while agreement with "homosexuality is never justifiable" is classified as a "survival" variable. In fact, given the number of opinions about traditional family relations that load on the "survival" dimension, it might be better understood as a *nonreligious traditional vs. modern* factor. For more on this see Wayne Baker, *America's Crisis of Values* (Princeton, N.J.: Princeton University Press, 2005).

24. Hanna Rosin, "Beyond Belief," *Atlantic Monthly* (January/February 2004): 118.

25. Alan Wolfe, *One Nation, After All* (New York: Penguin, 1998), p. 55.

26. I use the term *fundamentalism* here as "the belief that there is one set of religious teachings that clearly contains the fundamental, basic, intrinsic, essential, inerrant truth about humanity and deity; that this essential truth is fundamentally opposed by forces of evil which must be vigorously fought; that this truth must be followed today according to the fundamental, unchangeable practices of the past; and that those who believe and follow these fundamental teachings have a special relationship with the deity." (Bob Altemeyer and Bruce Hunsberger, "Authoritarianism, Religious Fundamentalism, Quest, and Prejudice," *International Journal for the Psychology of Religion* 2 (1992): 113–33.

27. The Barna Group describes its mission this way: "The ultimate aim of the firm is to partner with Christian ministries and individuals to be a catalyst in moral and spiritual transformation in the United States."

28. "Most Adults Feel Accepted by God, but Lack a Biblical Worldview," Barna Group, August 9, 2005. This study and others may be found at www.barna.org.

29. Osteen was quoted in the *New York Times* saying, "I don't get deep and theological." John Leland, "A Church That Packs Them in, 16,000 at a Time," July 18, 2005.

30. Alan Wolfe, *The Transformation of American Religion: How We Actually Live Our Faith* (Chicago: University of Chicago Press, 2003), p. 3.

31. As one example, eleven states currently have laws legalizing medical marijuana: the "blue" states of California, Hawaii, Maine, Maryland, Oregon, Vermont, and Washington, and the Western "red" states of Alaska, Colorado, Montana, and Nevada.

32. Ana Maria Arumi, a polling specialist working for NBC at the time of the election, offered an explanation of the 44 percent result, as described here in a report by the Pew Hispanic Center: "The selection of sample precincts in the NEP produced an overrepresentation of Cuban respondents in Miami-Dade County, a population that is typically the most pro-Republican segment of the Hispanic electorate. A better assessment of the Hispanic vote, she said, could be developed by aggregating exit polls conducted individually in the fifty states and the District of Columbia. That analysis showed that Bush had drawn 40 percent of the Hispanic votes, she said." Roberto Suro et al., "Hispanics and the 2004 Election: Population, Electorate, and Voters," Pew Hispanic Center, June 27, 2005.

33. Figures from the 2000 National Annenberg Election Survey. The complete 2004 data were not publicly available at press time.

34. According to the 2004 National Annenberg Election Survey, 44 percent of Hispanics said they were Democrats, compared to 23 percent who said they were Republicans (based on interviews in both English and Spanish with 3,592 Hispanic respondents).

35. Robert Dallek, *Flawed Giant* (New York: Oxford University Press, 1998).
36. This hardly means that the GOP no longer serves its corporate constituency. Quite the contrary—when bills are being written and influence is being exercised, America's economic masters get more from today's Republicans than they could possibly wish for.
37. The lines in this figure are smoothed for clarity using a three-unit moving average.
38. These National Election Study data are collapsed from a question giving voters seven options, from "extremely liberal" to "extremely conservative." The Harris poll, which gives only the options conservative, liberal, and moderate, has for thirty years shown conservatives numbering around 40 percent, liberals around 20 percent, and moderates around 35 percent. Much of the difference can be attributed to the fact that, unlike the Harris poll, the NES includes in the text of the question, "or haven't you thought much about this," prompting those without firm opinions to answer that they don't know.
39. These two graphs show data from the NES postelection surveys only.
40. E. J. Dionne, "Democrats in Disarray," *Washington Post*, September 27, 2005, p. A23.
41. Portions of this section were published in October 2005 in *American Prospect Online*.

CHAPTER 3. A PROGRESSIVE COUNTRY

1. For instance, Republicans derailed the 1994 crime bill by ridiculing a small provision providing support for "midnight basketball" programs meant to keep young people in urban areas off the street. The image of government paying for black kids to play basketball was enough to build opposition to the bill as laden with pork.
2. James Kuklinski et al., "Misinformation and the Currency of Democratic Citizenship," *Journal of Politics* 62(3) (August 2000): 790–816.
3. Carol Vinzant, "The Democratic Dividend," Slate.com, October 4, 2002.
4. Michael Kinsley, "Do the Math," *Washington Post*, August 1, 2004, p. B7.
5. See, for instance, John Evans, "Have Americans' Attitudes Become More Polarized?—An Update," *Social Science Quarterly* 84 (March 2003): 71–89.
6. *Loving v. Virginia*, 388 US 1 (1967).
7. Data from the General Social Survey.
8. Ibid.
9. An October 2002 Time/CNN poll found 47 percent of adults admitting to having tried marijuana, and 80 percent supported medical marijuana.
10. Numerous polls peg support for legalization at 33 or 34 percent. In an August 2000 Gallup poll, 47 percent said possession of small amounts of marijuana should not be a criminal offense.
11. See, for instance, "Private Sexual Behavior, Public Opinion, and Public Health Policy Related to Sexually Transmitted Diseases: A US-British Comparison," *American Journal of Public Health* 88(5) (1998): 749–54.
12. The General Social Survey has asked about premarital sex consistently since 1972; see David Harding and Christopher Jencks, "Changing Attitudes toward Premarital Sex: Cohort, Period, and Aging Effects," *Public Opinion Quarterly* 61 (2003): 211–26.
13. This is true with regard to schools as well: a map of where corporal punishment by teachers in public schools is legal looks almost identical to the red/blue electoral map: it is legal in most of the red areas, particularly the South, but illegal in most of the blue areas.
14. William F. Buckley, "Publisher's Statement," *National Review* (November 19, 1955).

15. Leonard Steinhorn, "Scrooge's Nightmare," Salon.com, November 25, 2004.
16. Ibid.
17. Remarkably, Bush got healthy support even from those who support civil unions. While Kerry won the votes of gay marriage supporters by 77 to 22 percent and Bush won among those who opposed any legal recognition by 70 to 29 percent, Bush actually narrowly outpaced Kerry, 52 to 47 percent, among supporters of civil unions.
18. A February 2004 *Newsweek* poll showed that Americans favored allowing gays in the military by 60 to 29 percent; a Fox News poll six months earlier put the number at 64 to 25 percent.
19. See Judith Treas, "How Cohorts, Education, and Ideology Shaped a New Sexual Revolution on American Attitudes toward Nonmarital Sex, 1972–1998," *Sociological Perspectives* 45: (2002) 267–83.
20. "Hamilton College Gay Issues Poll," August 27, 2001, performed by Zogby International for Hamilton College and MTV.
21. Of course, even people who consider themselves biblical absolutists will probably change their beliefs eventually. The Bible is full of mandates—for instance, that the punishment for working on the Sabbath is death—that no one advocates today.
22. Thomas Frank, *What's the Matter with Kansas?* (New York: Metropolitan Books, 2004).
23. *Stenberg v. Carhart*, 530 US 914 (2000).
24. And yes, I realize I am using the pro-life side's preferred appellation for themselves.
25. Sarah Blustain, "Choice Language," *American Prospect* (December 2004).
26. The Centers for Disease Control calculates the abortion rate—the number of abortions per 1,000 women aged 15–44. In 1990, the rate was 24; by 2000, when Clinton left office, it had declined to 16.
27. Among the Republican hawks so willing to send other people's children to die but who managed to avoid serving in Vietnam themselves are George W. Bush, Dick Cheney, Paul Wolfowitz, Richard Perle, Dennis Hastert, Tom DeLay, Newt Gingrich, Bill Frist, Rudy Giuliani, Rush Limbaugh, Bill O'Reilly, and Bill Kristol, to name but a few.
28. A June 2005 Gallup poll found only 44 percent of Americans saying the Iraq war had made us safer from terrorism; a July 2005 Pew poll put the number at 39 percent.
29. Michael Tomasky, "The Pathetic Truth," *American Prospect Online* (September 13, 2004).

CHAPTER 4. KNOWING WHO YOU ARE

1. In the seminal work in this area, a 1964 article titled "The Nature of Belief Systems in Mass Publics," Philip Converse argued that most Americans knew shockingly little about public affairs. Copious subsequent research has upheld the fundamental truth of Converse's findings, though scholars studying voter heuristics argue that people are able to make good decisions with little information.
2. The National Election Studies asks respondents this question. In recent years, the percentage answering correctly has ranged from a high of 66 percent in 1998 (just after the Clinton impeachment) down to a low of 28 percent in 2002.
3. In fact, this is one of the many myths surrounding Bush's religiosity. Despite popular belief, Bush did not have a single "born again" experience, nor is he an evangelical by the common definition of the term. For more on this, see Ayelish McGarvey, "As God Is His Witness," *American Prospect Online* (October 19, 2004).
4. Ryan Lizza, "Bad Message," *New Republic* (November 22, 2004): 18.

5. Mark Schmitt, "It's Not What You Say about the Issues . . . ," The Decembrist (http://markschmitt.typepad.com/decembrist), September 14, 2004.

6. In one of the field's classic works, Angus Campbell and his colleagues wrote that public opinion "is best understood if we discard our notions of ideology and think rather in terms of primitive self interest" (Campbell et al., *The American Voter* [New York: Wiley, 1960]). In 1981, however, Donald Kinder and Ronald Kiewet published an article in the *British Journal of Political Science* titled "Sociotropic Politics: The American Case," in which they demonstrated quantitatively the ten-uousness of the connection between self-interest and voting decisions. Kinder and Kiewet's results were duplicated in a variety of situations and elections in subse-quent years. The one situation where self-interest is consistently found to be a fac-tor in public opinion is tax policy, most particularly where the effects of a proposal to cut or raise taxes are clear and substantial.

7. In a 1998 survey of California voters I conducted with other researchers at the Annenberg Public Policy Center, we asked, "When it comes to political issues, would you say most people form their opinions by thinking about what is best for themselves or by thinking about what is best for the country as a whole?" Three-quarters of the respondents (76 percent) answered that most people think about what's best for themselves.

8. Nina Eliasoph, *Avoiding Politics: How Americans Produce Apathy in Everyday Life* (Cambridge, U.K.: Cambridge University Press, 1998).

9. As the political scientist Philip Klinkner pointed out, "Four years ago, those attend-ing church once a week or more were 42 percent of the electorate and gave Bush 59 percent of their vote—for a performance of 25 percent (that is, 42 percent mul-tiplied by 59 percent). In 2004, these voters were 41 percent of the electorate and gave Bush 61 percent of their votes, for a performance of 25 percent—no change from 2004." "Money Matters," *New Republic Online* (November 10, 2004).

10. Focus on the Family is an enormous empire, with an annual budget well over $100 million and 1,400 employees. Dobson's column appears in more than 500 newspa-pers, surpassing every other columnist save Ann Landers and Dear Abby. His radio program is heard on 3,000 stations across the country, and his daily television pro-gram appears on 80 stations. The Focus on the Family headquarters is so vast, it has its own zip code. Trained as a child psychologist, Dobson first came to promi-nence as the author of best-selling books on child rearing, including *Dare to Dis-cipline*, which advocated unremittingly harsh parenting methods.

11. See my previous book, *Fraud: The Strategy Behind the Bush Lies and Why the Media Didn't Tell You* (Naperville, Ill.: Sourcebooks, 2004).

12. Michael Kinsley, "When Ideology Is a Value," *Washington Post*, November 28, 2004, p. B7.

13. As an example, a July 2004 article in the *Washington Post* stated that an argument between the Kerry and the Bush campaigns "shows how values and cultural issues will play a prominent role in each party's strategy for victory, especially in the South and in rural communities." The assumption is that voters in the South and in rural communities have and care about values, while the rest of America doesn't. Jim VandeHei and Mike Allen, "Rhetoric on Values Turns Personal," *Washington Post*, July 10, 2004, p. A1.

14. Carol Eisenberg, "Morally Speaking, Iraq Was Bigger Issue," *Newsday*, November 10, 2004, p. A27.

15. For instance, an experiment by David Domke, Dhavan Shah, and Daniel Wackman found that voters faced with value-based appeals use "noncompensatory" decision strategies in deciding their votes: instead of weighing a candidate's position on all

issues to arrive at a decision, the one issue on which they were presented with a value-based appeal tended to trump the other issues. "'Moral Referendums': Values, News Media, and the Process of Candidate Choice," *Political Communication* 15 (1998): 301–21.

16. The boat in question was the presidential yacht *Sequoia*, which was built in 1925 and first used by President Hoover. It was most famously employed by Richard Nixon, who used it to sail around the Potomac as he brooded during the Watergate crisis. Jimmy Carter sold the yacht, and in 2004 the Republicans inserted a provision into an appropriations bill to buy it back.

17. Jefferson Cowie, "Nixon's Class Struggle: Romancing the New Right Worker, 1969–1973," *Labor History* (August 2002): 257; Arlie Hochschild discussed Cowie's article in "Let Them Eat War," *Mother Jones* (October 8, 2003).

18. Stuart Rothenberg, "Democrats Face Cultural Conundrum in 2006 and 2008," *Roll Call*, November 22, 2004.

19. Terry Mattingly, "Missing the Moral-Values Story," Scripps-Howard News Service, November 17, 2004.

20. Media Matters for America discovered and documented Crowley's error.

21. The quotes are from Brooks's book *On Paradise Drive*. For a critique of Brooks's sociology of stereotypes, see Nicholas Confessore, "Paradise Glossed: The Problem with David Brooks," *Washington Monthly* (June 2004).

22. Figures as of September 2005.

23. George Will, "The Left, at a Loss in Kansas," *Washington Post*, July 8, 2004, p. A17.

24. George Gurley, "Coultergeist," *New York Observer*, August 26, 2002.

25. Sasha Issenberg went to Franklin County, Pennsylvania, which Brooks had held up as a model of red-state authenticity, to see whether Brooks was painting an accurate picture. It turned out that Brooks didn't bother letting the truth get in the way of a good story. The distortions Issenberg documented are too numerous to detail here, but it is enough to say that the true Franklin County is virtually the opposite of the one Brooks described. Issenberg called Brooks for comment: "I went through some of the other instances where he made declarations that appeared insupportable. He accused me of being 'too pedantic, of taking all of this too literally,' of 'taking a joke and distorting it.' 'That's totally unethical,' he said." "Boo-Boos In Paradise," *Philadelphia Magazine* (April 2004).

26. Lamenting that her former boss was not president during the Elian affair, Noonan wrote, "Mr. Reagan would not have dismissed the story of the dolphins as Christian kitsch, but seen it as possible evidence of the reasonable assumption that God's creatures had been commanded to protect one of God's children." "Why Did They Do It?" *Wall Street Journal*, April 24, 2000.

27. "President Backbone," *Wall Street Journal*, April 7, 2003.

28. Herman Cain, *They Think You're Stupid: Why Democrats Lost Your Vote and What Republicans Must Do to Keep It* (Macon, Ga.: Stroud & Hall, 2005).

CHAPTER 5. SAY IT LIKE YOU MEAN IT

1. *ABC World News Tonight*, February 3, 2005.

2. See Kathleen Hall Jamieson and Paul Waldman, eds., *Electing the President: The Insiders' View* (Philadelphia: University of Pennsylvania Press, 2001).

3. Lloyd Free and Hadley Cantril, *The Political Beliefs of Americans* (New Brunswick, N.J.: Rutgers University Press, 1964).

4. Even Fox News, which in its polls asks people whether they want to pay higher taxes in order to have more government or lower taxes with less government, has

of late been showing only half of the population supporting smaller government. This question's wording can be seen as an admirable attempt to get respondents to consider tradeoffs, or an attempt to find the lowest possible support for a strong government.

5. This particular reframing has been suggested before, but it bears repeating. See Jeff Faux, *The Party's Not Over: A New Vision for Democrats* (New York: Basic Books, 1996); E. J. Dionne, *Stand Up, Fight Back: Republican Toughs, Democratic Wimps, and the Politics of Revenge* (New York: Simon & Schuster, 2004).

6. Jacob Hacker, "Insurance Policy," *New Republic* (July 4, 2005).

7. "Religious Lawmaker Wants to Ban Sports on Sundays," Associated Press, September 23, 2005.

8. The majority of Americans pay more in payroll taxes, those that go toward Social Security and Medicare, than they do in income taxes.

9. The Houston company was Bush's number-one lifetime contributor; its chairman was an old Bush family friend; Bush spent the 2000 campaign flying around on the Enron corporate jet; and Enron had a hand in determining both Bush's energy policy and the makeup of the Federal Energy Regulatory Commission, the very agency that let it get away with creating an energy crisis in California. Yet somehow the Democrats let Bush get away with distancing himself from it.

10. This is not to say that Costco is always a perfect corporate citizen. It has, for example, pressured some municipalities into using their controversial "eminent domain" powers to force out other private property owners in order to clear space for a Costco.

11. James Dao, "Bush, Wooing Pennsylvania, Attacks Gore's Character," *New York Times*, October 27, 2000, p. A26. Needless to say, this is a credo conservatives only occasionally live by. When Dick Cheney was unable to get through a meaningless photo session with members of the Senate in 2004 without snarling "Fuck yourself" to Senator Pat Leahy, Cheney offered that he "felt better" afterward.

12. Under current federal standards, any sex education program receiving federal funds must be "abstinence only," mentioning contraception only to discuss its failures and teaching, among other things, that "sexual activity outside of the context of marriage is likely to have harmful psychological and physical effects." Yet when a 2003 Kaiser/NPR/Harvard survey asked people whether they thought "The federal government should fund sex education programs that have 'abstaining from sexual activity' as their only purpose," or "The money should be used to fund more comprehensive sex education programs that include information on how to obtain and use condoms and other contraceptives," 67 percent chose the latter. Only 12 percent said that "How to use and where to get contraceptives" was not an appropriate topic for sex education, though the federal standards prohibit such discussion. An evaluation of ten state abstinence-only programs concluded, "Abstinence-only programs show little evidence of sustained (long-term) impact on attitudes and intentions. Worse, they show some negative impacts on youth's willingness to use contraception, including condoms, to prevent negative sexual health outcomes related to sexual intercourse. Importantly, only in one state did any program demonstrate short-term success in delaying the initiation of sex; none of these programs demonstrates evidence of long-term success in delaying sexual initiation among youth exposed to the programs or any evidence of success in reducing other sexual risk-taking behaviors among participants." Debra Hauser, *Five Years of Abstinence-Only-Until-Marriage Education: Assessing the Impact* (Washington, D.C.: Advocates for Youth, 2004).

13. Marshall Wittman, "Moose on the Loose," *Blueprint* (October 4, 2004).

14. John Micklethwait and Adrian Wooldridge, *The Right Nation: Conservative Power in America* (New York: Penguin, 2004), p. 12.
15. Christopher Hayes, "Decision Makers: Lessons Learned about Undecided Voters," *New Republic Online* (November 17, 2004).
16. Over the course of his presidency, Bush has displayed an oddly effective combination of bloodlust and bonding. When he talks about war and killing, his eyes flicker with a gleeful fire, yet he lets barely a month go by without a public statement about whom he has hugged. In September 2004, I documented no fewer than twenty-six statements in which Bush spoke proudly of hugging, from "They've seen me make decisions, they've seen me under trying times, they've seen me weep, they've seen me laugh, they've seen me hug" (August 24, 2004) to "There's only one person who hugs the mothers and the widows, the wives and the kids upon the death of their loved one. Others hug, but having committed the troops, I've got an additional responsibility to hug and that's me and I know what it's like." (December 13, 2003). See "Hugger in Chief," The Gadflyer (www.gadflyer.com), September 3, 2004.
17. My thanks to Dennis Yedwab for relating the story of Wellstone's 1996 campaign.

CHAPTER 6. TELLING THE STORY
1. Neal Gabler, "Liberalism's Lost Script," *American Prospect* (April 2004): 49–50.
2. This is a point made by Donald Kinder and Lynn Sanders, *Divided by Color: Racial Politics and Democratic Ideals* (Chicago: University of Chicago Press, 1996). For a discussion of the implications for public opinion polling, see John Zaller and Stanley Feldman, "A Simple Theory of the Survey Response: Answering Questions versus Revealing Preferences," *American Journal of Political Science* 36 (1992): 579–616.
3. For more on the topic of stories and memory, see Roger Schank and Robert Abelson, "Knowledge and Memory: The Real Story," in Robert Wyer, ed., *Knowledge and Memory: The Real Story* (Hillsdale, N.J.: Lawrence Erlbaum, 1995), pp. 1–85.
4. See Melanie Green and Timothy Brock, "In the Mind's Eye: Transportation-Imagery Model of Narrative Persuasion," in *Narrative Impact: Social and Cognitive Foundations* (Mahwah, N.J.: Lawrence Erlbaum, 2002).
5. This is from a memo titled "The Environment: A Cleaner, Safer, Healthier America" that Luntz wrote to instruct Republicans on how to talk about the environment.
6. Much of the critical research in this area was conducted by Nancy Pennington and Reid Hastie; see "Explaining the Evidence: Tests of the Story Model for Juror Decision-Making," *Journal of Personality and Social Psychology* 62 (1992): 189–206.
7. Kathleen Hall Jamieson, *Eloquence in an Electronic Age* (New York: Oxford University Press, 1988), chapter 6.
8. Bush's own life story—at least, in its mythologized version—closely parallels the classic quest narrative described by Joseph Campbell in *The Hero with a Thousand Faces*. Although some of the elements are out of order, most are there: the call to adventure (the minister who implied in a sermon that Bush should run for president), the hero's reluctance, the meeting with the magical figure who gives guidance (Billy Graham), the enduring of suffering, culminating in the hero being born again (alcoholism), and the ultimate redemption.
9. William Gamson, *Talking Politics* (Cambridge, U.K.: Cambridge University Press, 1992), p. 32.

10. See George Marcus, W. Russell Neuman, and Michael MacKuen, *Affective Intelligence and Political Judgment* (Chicago: University of Chicago Press, 2000).

11. Leonie Huddy and Anna H. Gunnthorsdottir, "The Persuasive Effects of Emotive Visual Imagery: Superficial Manipulation or the Product of Passionate Reason?" *Political Psychology* 21 (2000): 745–78.

12. Michael Cobb and James Kuklinski, "Changing Minds: Political Arguments and Political Persuasion," *American Journal of Political Science* 41(1) (1997): 88–121.

13. In 2004, Joshua Green reported in the *Atlantic Monthly* about a race run by Karl Rove opposing the Alabama judge Mark Kennedy: "Some of Kennedy's campaign commercials touted his volunteer work, including one that showed him holding hands with children. 'We were trying to counter the positives from that ad,' a former Rove staffer told me, explaining that some within the See camp initiated a whisper campaign that Kennedy was a pedophile. 'It was our standard practice to use the University of Alabama Law School to disseminate whisper-campaign information,' the staffer went on. 'That was a major device we used for the transmission of this stuff. The students at the law school are from all over the state, and that's one of the ways that Karl got the information out—he knew the law students would take it back to their home towns and it would get out.' This would create the impression that the lie was in fact common knowledge across the state. 'What Rove does,' says Joe Perkins, 'is try to make something so bad for a family that the candidate will not subject the family to the hardship. Mark is not your typical Alabama macho, beer-drinkin', tobacco-chewin', pickup-drivin' kind of guy. He is a small, well-groomed, well-educated family man, and what they tried to do was make him look like a homosexual pedophile. That was really, really hard to take.'" From Joshua Green, "Karl Rove in a Corner," *Atlantic Monthly* (November 2004).

14. The concept of framing was introduced by Erving Goffman in his 1974 book *Frame Analysis: An Essay on the Organization of Experience*. Scholars soon began to apply the concept to news stories and the way they select and categorize reality, most notably Gaye Tuchman's *Making News: A Study in the Construction of Reality* (New York: Free Press, 1978) and Todd Gitlin's *The Whole World Is Watching: Mass Media in the Making and Unmaking of the New Left* (Berkeley: University of California Press, 1980). As Gitlin defined them, "Media frames are persistent patterns of cognition, interpretation, and presentation, of selection, emphasis, and exclusion, by which symbol-handlers routinely organize discourse, whether visual or verbal" (p. 7).

15. For an exploration of the effects on citizens of these frames, see Joseph Cappella and Kathleen Hall Jamieson, *Spiral of Cynicism: The Press and the Public Good* (New York: Oxford University Press, 1997).

16. See, for instance, Amos Tversky and Daniel Kahneman, "The Framing of Decisions and the Psychology of Choice," *Science* 211 (1981): 453–58.

17. This quote appeared in an article written by Lars-Erik Nelson, December 16, 1983.

18. Omaha, Nebraska, February 5, 2005.

19. For more on this propensity, see Kathleen Hall Jamieson and Paul Waldman, *The Press Effect: Politicians, Journalists, and the Stories That Shape the Political World* (New York: Oxford University Press, 2003).

20. Jonathan Chait, "Fictional Character," *New Republic* (November 22, 2004).

21. See chapter 2 of Kathleen Hall Jamieson and Paul Waldman, *The Press Effect: Politicians, Journalists, and the Stories That Shape the Political World* (New York: Oxford University Press, 2003).

22. Or, as Matt Taibbi put it, "To be full of shit in American politics is a signal to our political press that you are serious." *Spanking the Donkey: Dispatches from the Dumb Season* (New York: New Press, 2005), p. 64.
23. The "projection" effect has been well-documented; see, for instance, Milton Lodge et al., "An Impression-Driven Model of Candidate Evaluation," *American Political Science Review* 83 (1989): 399–419.
24. Thomas Edsall and Mary Edsall, *Chain Reaction: The Impact of Race, Rights, and Taxes on American Politics* (New York: W. W. Norton, 1991), p. 178.
25. Bush said this on September 14, 2001, in a speech at the National Cathedral.
26. Portions of this section were published on TomPaine.com (Paul Waldman, "The Right's Siege Mentality," April 25, 2005).
27. As Thomas Frank points out, "Conservatives often speak of their first bout of indignation as a sort of conversion experience, a quasi-religious revelation." *What's the Matter with Kansas: How Conservatives Won the Heart of America* (New York: Metropolitan Books, 2004), p. 122.
28. Brad Carson, "Vote Righteously!" *New Republic* (November 22, 2004).
29. David Leege et al., *The Politics of Cultural Differences* (Princeton, N.J.: Princeton University Press, 2002).
30. For instance, in 2002, George W. Bush signed the most pork-laden farm bill in history, full of $180 billion of agricultural welfare, yet proclaimed, "It will allow farmers and ranchers to plan and operate based on market realities, not government dictates." "Cringe for Mr. Bush," *Washington Post*, May 14, 2002, p. A20.
31. Joshua Wolf Shenk, "Get Me Rewrite!" *Mother Jones* (May/June 2004).
32. Rick Perlstein, "Eyes Right," *Columbia Journalism Review* (March/April 2003): 52.
33. A January 2005 Democracy Corps poll asked people whether they associated a series of ideas more with the Democrats or the Republicans. On many of them— "shares your values," "future oriented," "for families"—the two parties were within a few points of each other, but 55 percent said they associated "know what they stand for" more with the Republicans, while only half as many (28 percent) said the Democrats.

CHAPTER 7. MANIPULATING THE MEDIA FOR FUN AND PROFIT

1. I borrow this term from David Brock, *The Republican Noise Machine* (New York: Crown, 2004).
2. In 2004, Democracy Radio conducted a survey of 691 radio stations in the top 120 markets in the country, then inventoried nationally syndicated radio shows. They found 2,349 hours of locally produced conservative talk radio on the air per week, compared to 555 hours of locally produced progressive talk radio; and 39,382 hours of nationally syndicated conservative talk radio, compared to 2,487 hours of syndicated progressive talk radio. In total, this adds to 41,731 hours of conservative talk (93 percent of the total) versus 3,042 hours of progressive talk (7 percent).
3. The one name missing from this list is Tom Joyner, who is a progressive and who, according to ABC Radio, has 8 million listeners, which would give him a larger audience than any host except Limbaugh, Hannity, Savage, and Stern. Interestingly, *Talkers* does not consider Joyner to fall into the "talk radio" category because the stations on which his show runs are not talk stations but "urban" stations, and Joyner does play music.
4. Mariah Blake, "Stations of the Cross," *Columbia Journalism Review* (May/June 2005).
5. According to the radio ratings service Arbitron, 2,014 of America's 13,838 radio stations are religious stations; in 1998 there were 1,089 religious stations among

12,840. Paul Nussbaum, "Broadcasting to the Choir," *Philadelphia Inquirer*, September 19, 2005.

6. David Brock, *The Republican Noise Machine: Right-Wing Media and How It Corrupts Democracy* (New York: Crown, 2004), p. 241.

7. The figures for Thomas are from his Web site; those for Novak and Will come from a 1999 survey in *Editor & Publisher*.

8. Josh Benson, "Gore's TV War: He Lobs Salvo at Fox News," *New York Observer*, December 2, 2002, p. 1.

9. For more on how the press eviscerated Gore in 2000, see Paul Waldman, "Gored by the Media Bull," *American Prospect* (January 13, 2003).

10. Eric Boehlert, "They Knew How to Win. Does John Kerry?" Salon.com, September 1, 2004.

11. Forum at the Joan Shorenstein Center, Kennedy School for Government, Harvard University, July 25, 2004.

12. See Paul Waldman, *Fraud: The Strategy behind the Bush Lies and Why the Media Didn't Tell You* (Naperville, Ill.: Sourcebooks, 2004), chapters 4 and 5; Kathleen Hall Jamieson and Paul Waldman, *The Press Effect: Politicians, Journalists, and the Stories That Shape the Political World* (New York: Oxford University Press, 2003); Eric Alterman, *What Liberal Media? The Truth about Bias and the News* (New York: Basic Books, 2003).

13. For a history of the idea of objectivity, see Michael Schudson, *Discovering the News: A Social History of American Newspapers* (New York: Basic Books, 1980).

14. These "video news releases," or VNRs, are a common technique of PR professionals working for corporate clients. Local television news programs air corporate VNRs each and every day in virtually every city in the country; they are almost never identified by their true source. According to a study by congressional Democrats, the Bush administration spent more than $250 million in taxpayer money on PR services, including the production of VNRs, during its first term. When the Government Accountability Office issued a ruling in 2005 that government use of VNRs constituted illegal propaganda, the White House Counsel responded that the GAO had no enforcement authority, and federal agencies could continue to use them if they wished.

15. Ken Auletta, "Fortress Bush," *New Yorker* (January 19, 2004).

16. Eric Boehlert, "They Knew How to Win. Does John Kerry?" Salon.com, September 1, 2004.

17. David Grann, "Robespierre of the Right," *New Republic* (October 27, 1997): 20.

18. The Fox reporter Carl Cameron once began a story about John Kerry with, "Criticized as aloof and out of touch with the common man, the millionaire Massachusetts senator met with low-income African-American kids . . ." On another occasion, he offered, "The problem for Kerry may be who he is: an Ivy League millionaire, who has rubbed elbows with the world's wealthiest sophisticates, while most of rural America is considered Bush country." Bush, of course, is an Ivy League millionaire who has . . . well, never mind.

19. "The State of the News Media 2005," a study by the Project for Excellence in Journalism, reported, "In the degree to which journalists are allowed to offer their own opinions, Fox stands out. Across the programs studied, nearly seven out of ten stories (68%) included personal opinions from Fox's reporters—the highest of any outlet studied by far. Just 4% of CNN segments included journalistic opinion, and 27% on MSNBC. Fox journalists were even more prone to offer their own opinions in the channel's coverage of the war in Iraq. There, 73% of the stories included

such personal judgments. On CNN the figure was 2%, and on MSNBC, 29%. The same was true in coverage of the Presidential election, where 82% of Fox stories included journalist opinions, compared to 7% on CNN and 27% on MSNBC."

20. David Foster Wallace, "Host," *Atlantic Monthly* (April 2005): 58.

21. Portions of this section were previously printed on TomPaine.com ("The Right's Siege Mentality," April 25, 2005).

22. Michael Siegel, "Mass Media Antismoking Campaigns: A Powerful Tool for Health Promotion," *Annals of Internal Medicine* 129(2) (July 15, 1998): 128–32.

23. "G. Gordon Liddy: Voice of Unreason," *The Independent* (November 22, 2004).

24. The organization for which I work, Media Matters for America, has been doing this with some success since mid-2004.

25. "News Audiences Increasingly Polarized," Pew Research Center, June 8, 2004.

26. David Croteau, "Examining the 'Liberal Media' Claim: Journalists' Views on Politics, Economic Policy and Media Coverage," Fairness & Accuracy in Reporting.

27. David Weaver et al., "The Face and Mind of the American Journalist," 2003. Results of this study may be viewed at www.poynter.org.

28. Michael Massing, "Iraq, the Press, and the Election," *New York Review of Books*, December 16, 2004.

29. Brent Cunningham, "Rethinking Objectivity," *Columbia Journalism Review* (July/August 2003).

30. "Wisconsin Daily Asks Readers to Send Pro-Bush Letters," *Editor & Publisher* (May 11, 2004).

31. Mark Hertsgaard, "Beloved by the Media," *The Nation* (June 28, 2004).

32. David Brock, *The Republican Noise Machine: Right-Wing Media and How It Corrupts Democracy* (New York: Crown, 2004), p. 325.

33. This quote comes from something written by the journalist and humorist Finley Peter Dunne around the turn of the twentieth century.

34. The best-read progressive blog, Daily Kos, at this writing averages well over half a million visits per day and at times has exceeded 1 million.

35. John Harris, "Mr. Bush Catches a Washington Break," *Washington Post*, May 6, 2001, p. B1.

CHAPTER 8. THINKING BIG

1. Tom Hamburger, Ted Marmor, and Jon Meacham, "What the Death of Health Reform Teaches Us about the Press," *Washington Monthly* (November 1994). This article was cited by Jeff Faux, *The Party's Not Over: A New Vision for Democrats* (New York: Basic Books, 1996).

2. "GOP Group: Clinton Health Plan Should Be 'Erased,'" *Congress Daily*, December 3, 1993.

3. The authors of one study of the costs of health-care bureaucracy concluded, "In 2003 the United States will spend $399.4 billion ($1,389 per capita) on health bureaucracy, of a total health expenditure of $1,660.5 billion ($5,775 per capita). The states could save $286.0 billion in 2003 if they streamlined administration to Canadian levels by adopting a single-payer national health insurance system. The potential savings are equivalent to at least $6,940 for each of the 41.6 million Americans uninsured in 2001. These potential administrative savings are far higher than recent estimates of the cost of covering the uninsured in the United States. For instance, researchers from the Urban Institute estimate that covering all the uninsured with an 'average' private insurance policy would cost $69 billion annually. Thus the $286.0 billion in administrative savings could cover every uninsured per-

son, with $217 billion left over to upgrade coverage for those who are currently underinsured—for example, to offer first-dollar drug coverage to seniors." David Himmelstein, Steffie Woolhandler, and Sidney Wolfe, "Administrative Waste in the U.S. Heath Care System in 2003: The Cost to the Nation, the States, and the District of Columbia, with State-Specific Estimates of Potential Savings," *International Journal of Health Sciences* 34(1) (2004): 79–86.

4. Kirstin Downey, "A Heftier Dose to Swallow; Rising Cost of Health Care in U.S. Gives Other Developed Countries an Edge in Keeping Jobs," *Washington Post*, March 6, 2004, p. E1. It should be noted that Chrysler has been unique among the Big 3 in advocating real health-care reform.

5. Steve Erwin, "Toyota to Build 100,000 Vehicles Per Year in Woodstock, Ont., starting 2008," *Canadian Press*, June 30, 2005.

6. Keith Naughton, "A Collision Course for GM and the UAW," *Newsweek* (June 20, 2005): 47.

7. Rick Perlstein, "How Can the Democrats Win?" *Boston Review* (Summer 2004).

8. Adam Werbach, "Is Environmentalism Dead?" Speech delivered to the Commonwealth Club, San Francisco, 2004.

9. Steven Kull, "The Federal Budget: The Public's Priorities," Program on International Policy Attitudes, University of Maryland, College Park, March 7, 2005.

10. Internet penetration figures from Nielsen Net Ratings as of June 2005; broadband penetration percentage is from Forrester Research as of August 2005. On international broadband rankings, the International Telecommunications Union ranked the United States 16th in January 2005, while the Organization for Economic Cooperation and Development ranked the United States 12th in December 2004.

11. Max Blumenthal, "Generation Chickenhawk," *The Nation* (June 18, 2005).

12. For more on this, see John Zaller, *The Nature and Origins of Mass Opinion* (New York: Cambridge University Press, 1992), and Daniel Hallin, *The Uncensored War: The Media and Vietnam* (New York: Oxford University Press, 1986).

13. W. Lance Bennett, "Operation Perfect Storm: The Press and the Iraq War," *Political Communication Report* (Fall 2003).

14. It should be noted that while Republicans like to think the Clinton plan was some form of "socialized medicine," part of the reason it was so convoluted was precisely because it wasn't socialized enough, working so hard to graft reform onto a system whose market features make it inefficient and costly. The plan's main cost-containment feature was an enhancement of the role of HMOs, something that ended up happening anyway—to most Americans' chagrin.

15. The paper was written by Stuart Butler and Peter Germanis; cited in Janet Hook, "They Invested Years in Private Accounts," *Los Angeles Times*, January 30, 2005.

CHAPTER 9. TIME TO GET TOUGH

1. Ellen Goodman, "Calm Eye in Kerry's Storm," *Boston Globe*, September 16, 2004, p. A19.

2. Deborah McGregor, "Dean's Sprint Threatens to Rob Democrat Race of Drama," *Financial Times*, December 9, 2003, p. 13.

3. Dana Milbank, "GOP Exposé: Kerry, Closet Frenchman," *Washington Post*, March 23, 2004, p. A17.

4. The speech was delivered to a gathering of the Democratic Leadership Council in Phoenix on May 7, 2004.

5. For instance, when Tim Russert asked President Bush to explain his absence from the National Guard, Bush narrowed his eyes and said, "I would be careful to not

denigrate the Guard. It's fine to go after me, which I expect the other side will do. I wouldn't denigrate service to the Guard, though, and the reason I wouldn't, is because there are a lot of really fine people who have served in the National Guard and who are serving in the National Guard today in Iraq." Of course, no one had "denigrated the Guard."

6. The *American Prospect* magazine called the offices of all fifty-five Republican senators to see if any wanted to distance himself or herself from Rove's remarks. One office, that of Rick Santorum, returned with a statement saying Rove did not speak for him. However, Santorum himself did not make a public statement on the issue.

7. "A Question of Character," Project for Excellence in Journalism, 2000. The predominant theme of Gore's coverage during this period was that he was "scandal-tainted."

8. This was not Shrum's only failure; despite his reputation as a strategist, both those campaigns were utterly without form and coherence.

9. Elizabeth Wilner, "Hey Pal, What Happened to Your Gloves?" *Washington Post*, September 19, 2004, p. B3.

10. Richard Viguerie and David Franke, *America's Right Turn: How Conservatives Used New and Alternative Media to Take Power* (Chicago: Bonus Books, 2004), p. 130.

11. In these kinds of situations, most candidates do what their consultants tell them—after all, they're the ones with the experience. While a candidate may be running in his or her first, second, fifth, or tenth race, an experienced consultant has been involved in one way or another in dozens or even hundreds of campaigns. The candidate who turns down a consultant's advice is rare.

12. As a general rule, the more important the office a candidate is running for and the more seasoned the candidate is, the less he or she is involved in the mechanics of the campaign and the more the candidate leaves to the consultants. A candidate making his or her first run for city council will be consumed with the details of the campaign and will insist on approving every minute detail, while a senator running for reelection may not speak with some of his or her consultants for months at a time.

13. Christopher Hayes, "The Case for a Democratic Marker," *In These Times* (July 21, 2005).

14. Marshall Wittman, "Seize the Legacy," *Blueprint* (July 23, 2005).

15. Richard Viguerie and David Franke, *America's Right Turn*, p. 128.

16. Of course, Howard Dean lost, but his failure was in spite of the innovative aspects of his campaign.

17. For a history of the institutionalization of political advocacy, see Theda Skocpol, *Diminished Democracy: From Membership to Management in American Life* (Norman: University of Oklahoma Press, 2003).

18. Christopher Hayes, "How to Turn Your Red State Blue," *In These Times* (March 22, 2005).

INDEX

257